TENDULKAR IN WISDEN

AN ANTHOLOGY

Edited by
Anjali Doshi

With a foreword by
Ricky Ponting

B L O O M S B U R Y
LONDON · NEW DELHI · NEW YORK · SYDNEY

John Wisden & Co Ltd
An imprint of Bloomsbury Publishing Plc

50 Bedford Square
London
WC1B 3DP
UK

1385 Broadway
New York
NY 10018
USA

www.bloomsbury.com

WISDEN and the wood-engraving device are trademarks of John Wisden & Company Ltd,
a subsidiary of Bloomsbury Publishing Plc

First published 2016

© John Wisden & Co 2016

Anjali Doshi has asserted her right under the Copyright, Designs and Patents Act, 1988,
to be identified as Editor of this work.

Every reasonable effort has been made to trace copyright holders of material reproduced in this
book, but if any have been inadvertently overlooked the publishers would be glad to hear
from them. For legal purposes the Acknowledgments on p. 242 constitute an
extension of this copyright page.

www.wisden.com
www.wisdenrecords.com
Follow Wisden on Twitter @WisdenAlmanack
and on Facebook at Wisden Sports

British Library Cataloguing-in-Publication Data
A catalogue record for this book is available from the British Library.

Library of Congress Cataloguing-in-Publication data has been applied for.

ISBN: HB: 978-1-4729-2735-4
ePub: 978-1-4729-2736-1

2 4 6 8 10 9 7 5 3 1

Typeset in Minion by Deanta Global Publishing Services, Chennai, India
Printed and bound in Great Britain by CPI Group (UK) Ltd, Croydon CR0 4YY

To find out more about our authors and books visit www.wisden.com. Here you will find extracts,
author interviews, details of forthcoming events and the option to sign up for our newsletters.

For Ma, Pa and Babu

Contents

A Note on Editing

Tendulkar in Wisden is not a comprehensive compendium of all his innings: few publishers could afford that much paper. But it is a selection of his best, which in turn highlight themes that were central to his career.

Reports have been edited with two aims in mind: to keep the focus on Tendulkar, and to retain the basic narrative and context of each game. *Wisden* match reports rarely feature players' first names, so they have been introduced at first mention in every chapter. To make clear the distinction between the narrative voice and previously published material, the editor's input is italicised.

The brief scores for Test matches highlight significant individual performances, including all hundreds and five-fors; for one-day internationals, the qualification is hundreds and four-fors.

Tendulkar's scores are highlighted in a separate line, while his bowling figures are recorded only if he took a wicket or more (the exception is his one-over spell in the Hero Cup semi-final against South Africa in 1993-94, when he didn't take a wicket, but bowled a tight final over to win the game). In Tests, his batting and bowling contributions are listed chronologically.

Foreword

S achin is the greatest batsman I ever played with or against, because he made batting look so simple. His technique was always rock solid, but he still managed to take the game away from you really quickly. He was also the most rounded batsman I have known. If I had to describe him in five words, I would say: competitive, passionate, driven, composed, complete.

Australia played so much cricket against India in my time that we spent hours and hours coming up with plans for Sachin in our team meetings – how we were going to bowl to him and, if we were lucky, get him out. And yet he would continually find a way to combat our plans. He was not just a gifted batsman, but had the mental side of his game sorted out too. At Sydney in 2003-04, when he was going through a rough time, he didn't play a single cover-drive: I had immense appreciation for that level of discipline and determination. It's one thing to have a plan, but to go out there and execute it over the course of an innings that lasted ten hours and 13 minutes, 436 balls and 241 runs was just incredible. And he was still not out at the end of it.

All of us – the batsmen of his generation, including Rahul Dravid, V. V. S. Laxman and Jacques Kallis – were constantly chasing the benchmarks he set. Even though he's a couple of years older than I am, it seemed he would outlast me – and he did. A few years before I retired, it got to the stage where I had a really good sequence, even though he was always a lot of runs and hundreds ahead of me. But the moment I got a bit closer, he'd do something and kick away again. We were always trying to play catch-up, and he always managed to stay ahead. It was an indication of his class.

One of the downsides of international cricket is that you don't really get to know an opponent away from the field and the changing-rooms. And that was the great thing about playing in the IPL with Sachin. Over the last couple of years – during my association with the Mumbai Indians – I've got to know him better. You learn a lot more about someone when you're not competing against them. His love for the game is infectious and remarkable. He could sit all day talking about cricket, he doesn't really like the spotlight and he's a quiet guy. And it was a delight to get to know him away from publicity's glare and over a glass of wine – Sachin and I have done a lot of that over the last couple of years, and I think we've both been able to appreciate each other a lot more as a result.

Different parts of your personality come out in the heat of the moment. We always had great respect for each other, even though we may not always have seen eye to eye on certain things. But that's what sport is about at the highest level. Once you have a chance to step back from its intense environment, you get a feel for the other person. Sachin is not that different as a team-mate from what he was as an opponent. He was always a mild-mannered guy who never let his emotions get the better of him on the field. And that's what he's like off the field too – calm and relaxed. But you can see he gets nervous around the changing-room. I enjoyed sitting back and observing him – he has his tics and superstitions.

One of my most cherished memories is getting to open the batting with Sachin, even if it didn't last too long thanks to my poor form! It was good to talk to him about his batting philosophy, to get an insight into his mindset and fundamentals. I was also fortunate to get a real sense of his approach to batting – the intricate attention paid to every detail about equipment, preparation and technique – and it was unlike anything I had ever seen in the Australian dressing-room.

I've always had a good understanding of the pressure he played under for a long time, especially as it's so vastly different from the lives we lead back home. I remember a Test in Mumbai in 2001 – Sachin walked out to bat and was facing up to Damien Fleming. He had to pull away because the crowd was going crazy. I saw this adulation at even closer quarters during the IPL. We returned to the hotel after our first win during the 2013 season and there were 2,000 people in the hotel foyer at 1 a.m., all yelling and cheering "Sachin, Sachin".

For me, he's the greatest batsman after Don Bradman. While I hold Brian Lara in high regard because of his match-winning ability, I don't think any batsman can achieve more out of the game than Sachin has. The word "great" is often bandied about, but great is something that's achieved over a long period of time. Sachin played 200 Tests and 463 ODIs (and one Twenty20 international), scored 34,357 runs and 100 international hundreds – *that* is great. Younger players may reach No. 1 over a period of 12 or 18 months – that's not great. That's having a good year. If you can do it as long as Sachin did, only then can you be considered great.

His abiding love for the game and pursuit of goals were astonishing – just to keep motivating yourself every day for 24 years to stay hungry and fit is what I admire so much. He had dreams of winning a World Cup, and he finally got to do it in his sixth tournament, in 2011. I don't know if he ever dreamt of playing 200 Test matches, because that's not something that occurs even in a cricketer's wildest dreams. And I don't believe anyone will ever play 200 Tests again, or score 100 hundreds.

Those who know Sachin will tell you how much he absolutely hates losing, even if it's just a friendly game of table tennis. He's now really getting into golf. And I'm hoping to get on the golf course with him in Mumbai soon and – maybe, just maybe – beat him in a round or two…

Ricky Ponting

Ricky Ponting played for Australia in 168 Tests and 375 one-day internationals between 1995 and 2013 – captaining the team in 77 Tests and 247 limited-overs games and scoring 41 Test and 30 one-day centuries. Ponting and Tendulkar opposed each other in 29 Tests and 55 one-day internationals, and shared the dressing-room during their time at the IPL franchise Mumbai Indians.

Introduction

That Sachin Tendulkar had his nose bloodied by a Waqar Younis bouncer in the Fourth Test of his debut series is a cherished part of his legend – the ball deflecting from the peak of his helmet, the blood all over his shirt, the gaggle of Pakistani fielders advising the 16-year-old he would be better off in an emergency ward, the Indian team doctor asking him if he would rather return to the dressing-room, and a squeaky voice replying, "No, I will play." Every detail of this display of courage will continue to be passed on when Indians speak of their greatest cricketer.

Wisden's report of that Test, at Sialkot in December 1989, says: "India were rescued by Sidhu and Tendulkar, who stood firm in a century stand, even though the youngster was bounced repeatedly by the Pakistani pacemen. At one stage umpire Holder had to warn Wasim Akram for intimidatory bowling. Tendulkar batted three and a quarter hours for his second fifty of the series…" There is no mention of Tendulkar's nose; even cricket's book of record does not record everything.

It's one of the few items of Tendulkarana that has escaped the Almanack's attention down the years. We are told, for example, that the percentage increase in Indian satellites launched between 1989 and 2013, the span of his Test career, was 414.28, and that the total number of Test runs scored and wickets taken was 999,645 and 30,052. There were moments when it felt as if he scored most of those himself.

Fifty years from now, it is likely he will still top the tables for the most Test and limited-overs centuries (51 and 49), the most Test runs (15,921), the most one-day international runs (18,426), the most Test appearances (200) and the most one-day caps (463).

It comes as something of a shock to learn he played only a single Twenty20 international (bowled Langeveldt 10, at Johannesburg in December 2006). But it is safe to predict that many of these records will continue to feature in the book's 226th edition in 2089, a century on from his debut.

It is hard to think of a better fit for a publication that is built on numbers and records. A few more: Tendulkar made 664 international appearances at 61 venues in 15 countries (Don Bradman made 52 at ten in two). He scored 34,357 runs for India, including 69 centuries on the subcontinent and 31 outside, held 255 catches, took 200 wickets, won 76 Man of the Match awards, and faced an estimated 50,000 balls, for each of which he had one-fifth of a second to get into position, and one-tenth of a second to connect bat with ball. India's population when Tendulkar made his Test debut was 851 million. When he retired, it had reached 1.23 billion. And so – perhaps the most mind-boggling statistic of all – 400 million Indians alive in 2013 had never known cricket, or life, without Tendulkar.

But numbers never tell the full story. *Tendulkar in Wisden* aims to reflect on how and why the Tendulkar story – from innocent boy wonder to what cricket writer Rahul Bhattacharya called a "man-child superstar" – resonated with cricket-lovers around the world, and became the voice of post-liberalisation India. At a time when Indians regarded all things Western as symbols of progress, wealth and success, they finally had their own champion. The voice of a 42-year-old country was fuelled by Tendulkar's achievements, as he united the many Indias – rich and poor, urban and rural, educated and illiterate, workaholic and jobless, male and female – in a way no sports star had before him. Not the eight Olympic gold-medal-winning hockey teams, nor the two-time Wimbledon semi-finalist Ramanathan Krishnan, nor even the cricket World Cup-winning heroes of 1983.

A confluence of factors explains the connection with Tendulkar: a newly open economy, post-Emergency disillusionment, the aftermath of the 1984 anti-Sikh riots, and the 1992–93 riots in Mumbai (Tendulkar's own city), toppled governments, rising prices, corrupt politicians, the introduction of colour television, a burgeoning middle class, a booming media, and a young nation's search for new heroes. There was a need for good news, and a growing sense that India deserved it.

Then there's the question of expectation. There is no sportsman in the world who has had to bear a greater burden than Tendulkar, not even Michael Jordan or Muhammad Ali, despite the significance their achievements hold for African-Americans. "Wilton St Hill and Learie Constantine were more than makers of runs and takers of wickets to the people of Trinidad and Tobago," wrote C. L. R. James in *Beyond a Boundary*. "Who will write a biography of Sir Donald Bradman must be able to write a history of Australia in the same period."

This is as true of Tendulkar. There is perhaps no cricketer who lends himself better to an anthology: a player who has inspired some of the sport's best literature of the contemporary era, provoked endless debate over his best innings, provided delight to a distressed nation, and made cricket-lovers around the world marvel at his balance and brilliance.

To make the intricate art of batsmanship look as easy as Tendulkar did, while struggling with himself, the conditions and opposition bowlers; to will his mind to focus on every ball, switching on and off those 50,000 times; to forget the bad shots and the balls that whizzed past that nose at 95mph; to be aware of the dangers, yet to stop them clouding his mind; and, amid all this, to attain the stillness to transcend doubts and distractions... to do this every year for 24 years, at the highest level, without losing his hunger, was perhaps his greatest achievement of all.

Tendulkar in Wisden, then, is a partnership of the world's greatest modern cricketer and the world's most enduring cricket publication. The anthology gives us a chance to step back and reflect, without the urgency and immediateness of daily reports or even yearly round-ups. The intention here is to create something timeless rather than breathless – breathtaking though Tendulkar's batting may have been.

This is also an opportunity to keep the conversation going, and *Wisden* has selected Tendulkar's ten best innings. The process of choosing the highlights' highlights was not an easy one. There will be those who disagree with the list, and question whether he played enough match-winning innings to be counted among the greatest. One may agree with the criticism that Tendulkar did not finish as many matches as he should have: his 136 against Pakistan at Chennai in 1998-99, a match India lost by 12 runs, was the most infamous example. But to say he did not play enough match-winning hands is to discount the number of wins he set up in the first innings, and to overlook their modest bowling resources during the first half of his career, when India were obliged to play a more defensive game.

While his is a great career to contemplate, and there is joy to be had in its consideration, the anthology does not gloss over the unhappy phases – the two captaincy stints, the career-threatening injuries, the run-ins with coaches and selectors. It was important, as well, to reflect the controversies, not least the accusations of ball-tampering in South Africa in November 2001, which led Indians back home on to the streets in protest. There is also the more minor criticism made by several writers about Tendulkar's evolution from a batsman who terrorised bowlers to an accumulator who did not. Yet even this is another matter for debate, for which of those states means more than the other?

At times, the act of editing Tendulkar's career down to a 248-page book felt as challenging as bowling to him must have been. It is not possible to carry match reports of all the significant innings he played (and there were plenty more besides the 100 hundreds). Some matches had to be left out altogether, such as the quarter-final of the Wills International Trophy against Australia at Dhaka in October 1998, when Tendulkar made 141 and took four for 38, and the Independence Cup final against Pakistan, in the same city earlier that year, when he made 95 and took three for 45. Some match reports, such as the account of his 134 in the final of the Coca-Cola Trophy against Australia at Sharjah, also in 1998, are referred to, but have not been included at length.

I was struck by how little *Wisden* tells us about Tendulkar the person until 1997, when Mike Selvey profiled him as one of the Five Cricketers of the Year. "When he married Anjali, a doctor and friend from his childhood, he rejected massive sums from satellite TV for live coverage, keeping the ceremony a family affair," wrote Selvey. "He knows his worth, and is wealthy beyond the dreams of almost a billion Indians, but he is not a grabber. His father, a university professor, imparted a sense of perspective and a work ethic."

Writing on Tendulkar has often lured sportswriters into hyperbole; the temptation is understandable, though *Wisden* has always preferred understatement, and readers of this book may be thankful for that. Even so, when you read the match reports – no matter their length – the focus is often on Tendulkar, whether he succeeded or failed.

To provide a vast breadth of writing and opinion, I dipped into other Wisden publications as well: *The Wisden Cricketer*, *Wisden Asia Cricket*, *Wisden Cricket Monthly*, *Wisden India Almanack*, WisdenIndia. com and *The Nightwatchman*. Magazines and websites allow a different perspective: without them, it would have been harder to convey the warp and weft of Tendulkar's career in a cohesive tapestry.

It remains to be seen how history will view Tendulkar's achievements, especially his 100 international hundreds. While some pundits believe it is artificial to combine hundreds from different formats, my own sense is that the statistic will come to be regarded as being as elusive and unattainable as Bradman's average of 99.94. Still, there is no substitute for actually having been there while he was in his pomp. As the sports journalist Rohit Brijnath once said: "I will read everything on Muhammad Ali. But I wish I lived in his time, through Vietnam and his ban, I wish I had experienced him… it's the same with Tendulkar. He was an experience. You were either there or you were not."

We hope that *Tendulkar in Wisden* is the next-best thing.

Anjali Doshi

Chapter 1

Tendulkar: Five Perspectives

"Tendulkar belongs with the Jordans, the Woodses and the Beckhams as a high-value icon of personal success in a globalised economy," wrote Mike Marqusee in Wisden Asia Cricket *magazine in 2002.* "But his specific historical significance resides in his relationship to India and in India's relationship to the world."

Tendulkar first made an appearance in Wisden Cricketers' Almanack *in 1989, as a 15-year-old schoolboy cavorting to a world-record 664-run partnership with Vinod Kambli in the Harris Shield. He followed it with a century on first-class debut, for Bombay. The 1990* Wisden *recorded:* "Technically sound, and alert to the loose ball, Tendulkar showed an astounding maturity for one so young and looked to be a Test cricketer in the making."

Year after year, the Almanack documented Tendulkar's feats, mainly through match reports (he was a Cricketer of the Year in 1997). But it wasn't until 2003 that it explored his role as an Indian icon – the people's hero, to whom a diffident nation looked for solace, inspiration and distraction.

There were a couple of reasons for the delay. The early 1990s belonged to Brian Lara's record-breaking performances, both in England and against them: for an English publication, he was hard to ignore. Around the same time, the Indian board – drunk on the financial success of co-hosting the 1996 World Cup – were busy shipping off their team to meaningless limited-overs tournaments. In the 1990s, Lara played 162 one-day internationals to Tendulkar's 228.

Most significantly, perhaps, cricket writers and fans needed the perspective of time and distance to comprehend and articulate Tendulkar's relationship with India: the unanimous gasp of dismay each time he got out, the collective switching-off of the telly, the identification with his achievements and appropriation of them, and their callous abandonment of him when he flopped. "For most of a billion people, unmoved by any other sport, he is escape as much as he is hope, standing like some solitary national advertisement of success," wrote Rohit Brijnath, the Indian sportswriter, in Wisden 2003. *"Tendulkar is not allowed to fail."*

This chapter is an attempt to understand Tendulkar from five perspectives, all post-millennial, that examine his place in the cricketing firmament and in social history. Not surprisingly, some themes recur: comparisons with Bradman, the burden of a billion expectations, a life under the spotlight's glare, India's relationship with success and failure, and its desperate search for heroes in the age of celebrity.

As Brijnath explains elsewhere: "Politicians and generals, artists and thinkers do not breach India's cultural and social divide. Mostly it is cinema and cricket that link a disparate nation; as if opinions on these subjects are an essential ingredient of Indian-ness. Shahrukh and Tendulkar everyone knows. The actor leaps tall buildings, which is about where the batsman sends Shane Warne occasionally. But there is a difference. The actor is, in fact, a fake, a teller of tall stories; Tendulkar's art is no lie."

Some opinions, especially in the pieces written in the early 2000s, may seem outdated. Marqusee, for instance, placed Tendulkar on the pedestal of global sport alongside Tiger Woods and Michael Jordan, long before controversy blighted the golfer's career. For the most part, though, these essays stand the test of time – in their predictions and deliberations. As Peter Roebuck wrote in Wisden Asia Cricket *in 2002: "There are great innings to be played and the afternoon and evening of his time in cricket may prove to be his best."*

The Populist

BATTING FOR A BILLION   Rohit Brijnath, *Wisden 2003*

Sachin Ramesh Tendulkar is now 30, he has a wife and two children, his face is wreathed in a goatee and faintly lined by time and travel, but to the world, and to India in particular, he is still a boy wonder. Thirteen years and 105 Tests have passed since he first took guard at Karachi in November 1989, but the poet's son with the almost-falsetto voice and the supremely dignified manner continues to write an elegant, belligerent and unprecedented history. When he walks to the crease – one eye occasionally turning to the sun, one hand hitching up his box – it is cricket's equivalent of Michelangelo ascending a ladder towards the ceiling of the Sistine Chapel. He is short, 5ft 4in, and his stance is a study in stillness, his body finely balanced, his muscles relaxed. His mind has already mapped the geography of the field: as the ball is bowled, rarely does tension or indecision impede the instructions from brain to body. Only sometimes, so it seems, will he silently struggle within, caught between the responsibility he carries for his team and the force of his natural attacking instincts.

Then he plays. He is both tyrant and technician, batting with a thug's ferocity and a sculptor's finesse, though sometimes he fails to strike the necessary balance between the two. In his room, he occasionally takes one last look at his technique in front of the mirror; on the field, most days, we see that genius reflected.

He will uppercut the ball gleefully for six with muscle, and next ball, in a perfect marriage of feet and bat and judgment of length, slide it softly past the bowler for four. He will generously shoulder arms and allow the ball to pass him as if it is not worthy of being struck, then explode into a flurry of shotmaking that has the scoreboard ticking over like a slot machine. In full cry, his bat looks wider than the Laws allow, though he hardly needs its full extent: as Greg Chappell once put it, he would do well batting with a single stump, like Bradman in the backyard.

The crowd is a blur, the roar a hum, for he is too busy, as he said years ago, "reading the bowler's mind", or, better still, manufacturing shots that "compel the bowlers" to bowl where he wants them to. It is not so much that there are shots he does not have; it is merely that he has chosen not to play them.

Many things are unique to Tendulkar, and most of all the fact that the man has stayed faithful to the gifts he was given as a boy. Once, according to a possibly apocryphal story, a junior Indian team on tour was awakened by a thumping on the roof. On investigation, it was Tendulkar lost in some midnight practice.

Later, too, he took little for granted. When Shane Warne toured India, Tendulkar went into the nets, scuffed the pitch on the leg side and had a spinner pitch it there; before India toured Australia, Tendulkar had the seamers deliver the ball from closer to his end, artificially manufacturing the pace and bounce he expected to face. The net has remained his temple. Asked about this once, he was gently annoyed that people felt it all came so naturally to him, thus discounting how disciplined his journey had been: his gifts, he explained, were oiled with sweat.

He will never be the greatest batsman in history: that seat is taken. But as much as Donald Bradman's Test average (99.94) outstrips Tendulkar's (57.58), the gap diminishes substantially when other factors are taken into account. Tendulkar travels more in a year than Bradman did in a decade; he has had to manage the varying conditions of 49 Test grounds, to Bradman's ten; he has already played twice as many Tests as Bradman, and over 300 one-day games, nearly all of them under the unrelenting scrutiny of television. And whereas Bradman had to cope with the expectations of a small populace, not given to idolatry, in an age of restraint, Tendulkar must play god to one billion expectant worshippers.

Steve Waugh has said, "You take Bradman away and he is next up, I reckon," though those who swear by Vivian Richards are not completely convinced. Still, his peers – Brian Lara in particular – have been pushed aside by sheer weight of consistent numbers. Tendulkar has 32 Test centuries to Lara's 18; by the end of the World Cup, he had 34 one-day centuries, with his nearest rival his captain, Sourav Ganguly, on 22. But one statistic will please more than most. Starting when he was 20, in 1993, his Test averages for each calendar year read like this: 91.42 (8 Tests), 70 (7), 29 (3), 41.53 (8), 62.50 (12), 80.87 (5), 68 (10), 63.88 (6), 62.69 (10), 55.68 (16). The year when he averaged 29, he had only two completed innings. Otherwise, in the worst of years, his average is 41 – the usual benchmark of a very good player. This, better than anything, reflects the unwavering purity of his purpose.

He has not really known bad years, has never woken to a slump, though in the West Indies in 2002 he had successive Test scores of 0, 0, 8, 0, which – as if to prove the point – was enough to make eyebrows rise in astonishment. So true has his form been that it is easy to overlook the distinctive burdens he has carried. Wasim Akram once suggested that when Tendulkar is out, heads droop in the Indian dressing-room. Rarely has Tendulkar had the comfort of knowing that the men who follow him are as certain in rising to a challenge.

More demanding is his nation, for when Tendulkar plays, India stills, it quietens, till it is almost possible to hear a collective exhalation with every shot. In a land where governments stutter, the economy stagnates and life itself is an enduring struggle against failure, he is deliverance. For most of a billion people, unmoved by any other sport, he is escape as much as he is hope, standing like some solitary national advertisement of success. Tendulkar is not allowed to fail.

His genius has caged him, for he cannot walk any street without sparking a riot, nor sit unmolested in any restaurant. That he must indulge his passion for cars by driving through Mumbai's deserted streets in the hours before dawn points to the absurdity of his existence. It is easier written than lived. But he finds no refuge in rages or sulks; his serenity is startling for a man surrounded by an audience prostrated in hysterical worship. It points to a gift of temperament but also to his balance as a man. When a spectator invaded the field and escorted him off the ground at Lord's in 2002, he did not flinch or fuss, brandish his bat or bellow, but coolly walked on, the very picture of a warrior monk. Later, he said the fellow meant no harm.

It may well be that the sight of Glenn McGrath at the other end does not offer so much a threat as relief. If Tendulkar is India's escape, it may well be that the crease is his escape, the place where he finds his full expression. Only once, under persistent interrogation, did he admit: "People expect too much of me, a hundred every innings. They call and say, 'You scored a hundred in Kanpur, so why not in Delhi?' They must accept my failures."

And there have been a few. His career has been marked by two curious blemishes. In 105 Tests, he has won only nine match awards, and although there are mitigating factors – India have mostly been abysmal abroad, as tradition dictates, and their spinners have claimed most of the honours at home – it is still an incongruously low number. It is linked to a more damning charge, that his batting, in contrast to Lara's, has wrought too few victories. It suggests that his beauty is often ineffectual, painting masterpieces in isolation, and that he is apt to leave more of a memory than an impact. Two matches are repeatedly cited as evidence: Barbados, March 1997, when he made four on a dicey wicket as India failed to chase 120 for a historic win; and Chennai, January 1999, when he made a stirring 136 against Pakistan, chasing 271, but then played a shot of poor discipline and fell with just 17 needed [the last three wickets then fell for four runs and India lost by 12].

He has said, "I have been disappointed with myself... I have to learn to finish Tests," and it must eat at his stomach like an acid. This is the boy who, on his first tour of Pakistan, lost a set of tennis to Sanjay Manjrekar and then pleaded with him to play on to salvage his honour. He is a proud man, but too graceful also to state the obvious. Many of his 31 Test centuries have either set up wins or fended off defeat.

In March 1998, in Chennai, Australia were 71 ahead of India on first innings, and as Tendulkar explained then: "They had a lead and I said this will be the innings of a player's life. Because 75-plus by any player would be a big score in the second innings and would help us win the game."

In a quiet moment, the Indian coach, Anshuman Gaekwad, corralled Tendulkar and told him, "I want you to score." Tendulkar, who was still only 24, replied: "I will get it for you, don't worry." He made 155 and India won the Test.

Still, if we are intent on nailing Tendulkar, then we must crucify his team as well. If he has failed us, they have failed him, specifically in their willingness to turn an ensemble piece into a one-man show. Perhaps we should acknowledge too that our own expectations distort the picture. To indict him for getting out for 136 against Pakistan is to disregard the fact that the rest of the team contributed 86 runs between them, and 52 of those came from [the wicketkeeper] Nayan Mongia. Similarly, if we are quick to remember Tendulkar's cheap dismissal in Barbados in the second innings, we are quicker to forget that, in a low-scoring match, he had already made a valiant 92.

He stands now, closer to the end of his career than the beginning, with 8,811 Test runs, sixth on the all-time list. The only current player ahead of him is Steve Waugh, who is nearing retirement. Barring catastrophe, Tendulkar will surpass Allan Border's 11,174 with some ease; Sunil Gavaskar's record 34 centuries will be outstripped as well. In the one-day game, Tendulkar already stands alone and untouchable at the summit – Border and Gavaskar rolled into one, with more than 12,000 runs, while nobody else has 10,000, and 34 centuries. He even has a hundred wickets.

In the Test arena, Bradman will never be equalled. In Tests and one-dayers together, the reality of international cricket today, Sachin Ramesh Tendulkar will take some catching, too.

The Persona

A PURITY OF GREATNESS   Peter Roebuck, *Wisden Asia Cricket*, September 2002

Sachin Tendulkar has almost all the ingredients required by those seeking greatness in their sportsmen. He is a master of his chosen game, has a formidable record, is a fierce competitor, and has been around for a long time. Clearly, he is not a flash in the pan, nor yet a lightweight capable of performing only in his own backyard. Indeed, his greatest innings have been constructed in places as far-flung and demanding as Perth and Birmingham. Nor does his standing rely upon a few memorable innings played under blue skies and against a tiring attack. On the contrary, Tendulkar rises when his game is subjected to the most critical scrutiny, for he knows then that errors will be punished and puts his mind to their eradication.

Tendulkar's contemporaries do not doubt his position in the game, and their testimony is compelling. Steve Waugh, no slouch himself, and not a man inclined to throw compliments around, regards Tendulkar as *the* batsman of the post-war era, outstripping Everton Weekes, Peter May and Vivian Richards, not to mention various South Africans denied the opportunity to confirm their abilities. Tendulkar is greater than any of these. We tend to remember these fellows at the height of their powers and to forget about those bad patches and human failings that arise in every sporting life – for the performer is made of flesh and blood, besides which luck also has a part to play.

Such is Tendulkar's standing that foreign coaches use him as a model for aspiring batsmen and crowds gather behind the nets when he is at work. At his best, his game is perfect because he attends to the details and understands his craft. Then his bat seems as wide as Park Lane and his head as still as Lord Nelson's in Trafalgar Square. Tendulkar's body seems to move in unison with the game, as if it flows through him, informing every muscle of its duties.

Of course, it is not always like this, for Tendulkar is human, a point he constantly makes lest anyone imagine he was Merlin armed with a wand or that anything was easy or inevitable. We do sportsmen a disservice when we put them beyond the vulnerabilities of daily discourse and into another world where a button can be pressed and, lo, the deed is done. Sometimes Tendulkar loses the precision upon which his game depends. Bad habits creep in and then the flow of runs slows, and it is not until the mistake has been detected and corrected that the mastery returns. Tendulkar needs to work at his game or else it will slide. This does not make him less of a genius, for it is a romantic illusion to suppose that anyone can play as if in a dream. Tiger Woods practises every stroke and trains harder than his rivals. Indeed, he has challenged and changed the idea that fitness does not matter in golf. He is stronger in mind and body and then starts to play. A lot of sweat and some tears lie behind his greatness.

Inevitably we ask more of Tendulkar than has so far been delivered. For a start we expect him to score a hundred every time and forget that he is in so many ways just another fellow about town. Tendulkar has been the child prodigy from Shivaji Park and has survived to score centuries against the Australians. Not every brilliant youngster outlasts his acclaim.

Tendulkar has been the measured master in the middle-age, taking his time, concentrating upon putting runs on the board, a player aware of his responsibilities and somehow managing to make his way. But there is a step, still, to take, a move towards authority, the missing ingredient, the characteristic seen in Frank Worrell when he led the West Indians, and in Wally Hammond as he surveyed the scene and made his scores. Tendulkar is an energetic, and often inspiring, competitor but he has rarely been inclined to impose himself except by his deeds. We have seen the power of his strokes and the honesty and strength of his mind but not yet the force of his will.

Tendulkar lacks the arrogance that often accompanies greatness, the gleam in the Don's eye or the swagger in Richards's step. This makes it harder for him, for his breeding demands respect and his humility requires that he conduct himself quietly when others might rage. There is no anger in Sachin's cricket. He is a competitor rather than dominator. Perhaps this is his weak point, for there have been so many wonderful innings and so few memorable events. Sachin does not take things by the scruff of the neck. Nor, though, does he lose his head – his life and career move along without the dramas that followers almost demand.

In some respects it is easier for Woods because he is the master of his own fate. There is just him and that little ball. Obviously luck does play a part in the short run, but Tiger can choose when he plays, how he practises and who carries his bag. The ball is still and no one is trying to knock off his head or putting mint on the ball to make it swing. Nor are there umpires upon whose sight and hearing the whole thing depends. Sachin must follow an agenda set by officials more concerned about their coffers than his state of mind or practice arrangements. He must rely on team-mates to give support, for batsmen play in pairs and a match is 11 against 11. And he could still fall foul of a dozing white-coat. In other words, Tendulkar is stretched beyond the experience of the golfer. He is not nearly as much in control, and must instead fit into a group and act within the confines of a team. Also, the ball is moving, hard and sometimes mischievous. It says much about Tendulkar as a man and as a sportsman that he has survived these expectations, because it cannot be much fun to bat with a billion people demanding a ton. Tendulkar has lived with these pressures throughout his career. Indeed they are part of his greatness. Has any sportsman known pressures such as this and still managed to remain friendly and successful? Tendulkar has made no demand except upon himself. He could have asked for the sea and the sky, but has instead concentrated on scoring runs and winning matches.

Tendulkar and Shane Warne are *the* cricketers of this age. Murali cannot be included because of the controversies over his action. Cricket is lucky that its champions take their game to its edges: Warne with prodigious spin, combativeness and imagination, Tendulkar with the range and force of his strokeplay. Brian Lara is next on the list because he has played some of the greatest innings the game has known. But he is inconsistent and accordingly lags behind. Perhaps his later years will be his most productive, though this would be unusual for a batsman relying on touch. Sensibly, Lara has reduced his backlift, belated recognition of his fallibility. Tendulkar has always known he is human, though it has not always been easy to convince his more devoted followers of this fact. Tendulkar has put his heart and soul into his cricket. He has not cheated the game or himself or his team or supporters. He is a great sportsman already, though he is not yet all he can be, not yet the finished product. His greatness as a batsman can be told from his record and the respect he commands among players past and present. But there is work still to be done. He must find the confidence to dominate the entire game as he has so often dominated its bowlers. Perhaps it is beyond his range, though he is a remarkable young man. His reputation is secure, his record is unimpeachable. Certainly he is a great cricketer but India needs more even than that, needs him to throw caution to the wind and emerge as a leader.

Tendulkar is a modern master of the willow. He is a product of this impatient, often imprudent and frequently exciting age, a batsman of his times. Better than most contemporary sportsmen, though, he respects and reflects the past. In an age of improvisation, he has built a game largely founded upon the tried and trusted methods that appear in the old books used in schools and by coaches as they try to put their charges on the right path. This is a house with strong foundations. Since he is a batsman for eternity, Tendulkar can be judged by historical as well as fashionable devices. Many things are held against him, but then holes can be found in any career. People find the things they want to find. Even the Don did not win every series he played. Indeed, England and Australia were nip-and-tuck till war took its terrible toll of the old country. Sunny Gavaskar is remembered for his great days, yet he had his failures against the West Indians in their pomp. Bradman, Hammond, Jack Hobbs and the rest were treated more kindly by their critics and were not as often called upon to play in the public eye. Almost every match Tendulkar plays is for his country, with millions watching on television and the outcome depending on his performance. No cricketer has it easy, because batting is difficult and one mistake can bring a man down. But a cricketer's life was surely gentler in those days, with months and evenings out of the spotlight.

Far from regretting that Tendulkar has not scored more runs and won even more matches for his country, a demand that has been made of no batsman since Bradman, and certainly not of Richards or Peter May (everyone knows that it is bowlers who win Test matches, and since Kapil Dev there has only been Anil Kumble, and him only in the subcontinent), the game's followers should rather be thankful for his temperament, consistency and record. No batsman from the subcontinent has been as productive overseas, except perhaps Gavaskar with his triumphs in the Caribbean and Down Under. No batsman has scored as many hundreds in 50-over cricket; and still Sachin manages to construct a technique suitable for the longer game; and still he manages to keep his head.

Others might find chinks in his armour. Doubtless he could be more assertive, and time may bring its authority. Clearly he could score even more runs, though he will not face weak attacks from India or West Indies or post-war England as did Bradman. But we would not wish him to be a machine and must not judge him by the standards of romantic memory for then he must fail. Those who played with or against the great batsmen of the last 25 years, as I did, hold Tendulkar in high regard. Most put him above anyone since Bradman. Of course it is hard to think about Hobbs, George Headley, Victor Trumper and the giants of the past, but Sachin has the technique, the record, and the power to sit beside any of them, and he has done it for a long time and despite pressures calculated to break a lesser man. Because he has a squeaky voice, looks like a boy still, and is polite rather than volcanic, we are inclined to underestimate him. When all the talk subsides, there is just a bat and a ball, just notches in the scorebook, and Sachin has lots of these in his account, and none of them badly made. He has been the most civilised player of his generation and has combined perfection of technique with a desire to attack and to entertain. Nor is the cement dry upon his career, for there are great innings to be played and the afternoon and evening of his time in cricket may prove to be his best. There is room for improvement as he gives his team the character and leadership that are needed to prove conclusively that India is a force in the game and that the Australians can be beaten. This is Sachin's last and most important task. The runs are on the board, but the epic is only half-complete.

The Technician

THE SMALL ENFORCER	Mukul Kesavan, *Wisden Asia Cricket*, September 2002

It is a strangely conflicted mixture of rigorous self-denial and cathartic violence that makes up Tendulkar's craft.

Batsmen aren't remembered only for their shots; you remember them for their mannerisms, their stance, their physical presence. I remember Sunil Gavaskar for the military snap with which he shouldered arms, both pads together, bat raised high. I can't recall him shaping to play and then withdrawing the bat: there was a clean, lucid certainty to everything he did, which made him *the* great classical batsman of our time. I remember him for the compact grace that informed his presence at the crease, from taking guard to settling into his stance.

Sachin Tendulkar is different. He's about as tall as Gavaskar; they're both Bombay batsmen, and compared to someone like Brian Lara, Tendulkar seems correct, even orthodox, but he and Gavaskar are chalk and cheese. Tendulkar can produce the most wonderful shots but you wouldn't call him a beautiful batsman. Graceful he is not, in any conventional reading of the term. His most repetitive tic at the crease has been described by the writer Ruchir Joshi as his "signature crotch yank as he adjusts his abdomen guard".

He can look oddly clumsy for a great batsman: when the ball keeps low, Tendulkar will jack-knife into an exaggerated half-squat, like someone who has just discovered that he urgently needs to go. When he plays forward, he is correct but always in a slightly over-produced way: his defensive play just lacks the clockwork economy of Gavaskar's technique. In any case, with Tendulkar the ratio of bat to body makes it hard for him to look pretty: he's so small and the bat's so big that it looks more like an accomplice than an instrument. V. V. S. Laxman, long and languid, pulls and hooks in his easy upright way; when Tendulkar pulls, he looks like a small enforcer with a big cosh.

Tendulkar has a claim to being the greatest batsman in the world because he is that rare thing: an original. Gavaskar at his best used to make the classical prescriptions come to life; Tendulkar's genius lies in the impossible shots he hits off perfectly good balls. Not impossible in the sense of outrageous and chancy: men like Sanath Jayasuriya own that corner of the market; no, impossible because he hits shots mortal cricketers wouldn't attempt, and because he makes those shots look safe, even plausible, when they are not.

I have in mind the range of off-drives he plays to balls pitched on a good length or short of a good length without much width on offer. He seems to stand up straight without doing much with his front foot. The bat comes down in a little arc and then stops well short of a follow-through. The scene ends with incredulous bowler staring at Tendulkar and cover fielder trotting off on peon duty, resigned to this game of fetch. Something similar happens with that attenuated straight-drive that shaves the stumps at the bowler's end on the way to the boundary. It's not the straightness of it (straight-drives, after all, are meant to be hit straight!) but the lack of obvious effort or risk that makes the shot a bowler-killer. When Lara hits you straight, the bat describes such a flamboyant arc that it's like being lashed with a whip; Tendulkar's down-the-wicket shot is more like being heavily nudged by a barn door. When he hits that straight-drive, his bat is at once shield and bludgeon, and as the ball speeds past the blameless bowler, Tendulkar must seem both irresistible force and immovable object.

And then there are those other shots: the upper-cuff over slips and gully, the inside-out shot driven through, or over, cover; the paddle-sweep hit so perpendicularly that it finishes as a reverse straight-drive completed on one knee; the pull off the front foot hit brutally over midwicket; the trajectory-defying flick that turns the ball on the off stump or outside, through midwicket – what these strokes have in common is that they are difficult and dangerous shots, methodically and safely played. That's why bowlers in their follow-through sometimes stare at Tendulkar as if he had grown another head: he makes unlikely shots look reasonable. It's this straight-bat magic that got Graeme Hick to turn out to captain his county, Worcestershire, against India in an unimportant tour match once: he said he just wanted to stand at slip and watch Tendulkar play.

Tendulkar's remarkable repertoire of shots, his style of play, grows out of a particular temperament and a peculiar talent. Tendulkar himself has often said that he is by nature an attacking batsman. This is true, but in itself it tells us little about what makes him special. Jayasuriya is an attacking batsman by instinct, as are Ricky Ponting and that cheerful murderer, Adam Gilchrist; and they're very different from Tendulkar. Gilchrist, on present form, is the best batsman in the world. With a batting average over 60 and a strike-rate that makes bowlers feel they're bowling in the highlights segment of the evening news, Gilchrist on form can make Tendulkar look low-key. The difference between the two isn't one of talent – indeed, if Gilchrist can bat like this and stay at 60-plus, he and not Tendulkar will be remembered as the great turn-of-the-century batsman.

The difference is temperamental. Gilchrist bats in a wholly carefree way; coming in at No. 6 or 7 in Test matches, he subjects all bowlers, in every situation, to his brand of assault and battery. Perhaps it has to do with the confidence of coming in low in the batting order of a great team; perhaps being a wicketkeeper-batsman with more than one string to his bow frees him from the fear of failure. Whatever it is, it makes his demeanour at the crease very different from Tendulkar's.

No Indian cricketer, not Tendulkar, not even the inimitable Kapil Dev, has survived cricketing glory in this country over a whole career without becoming careworn, and Tendulkar isn't a product of the Bombay school of batsmanship for nothing. However different they may be from each other, the great Bombay batsmen have distrusted extravagance or flourish. Like Gilchrist, Tendulkar will, most times, try to impose himself on the bowling; unlike him, he will discriminate between bowlers, change his game to suit the moment, come up with novelties like a grandmaster discovering a new wrinkle in an old gambit.

In the First Test of India's 2001-02 tour of South Africa, Tendulkar hit one of the great hundreds of recent years. At the start of that innings, he hit Makhaya Ntini for 16 runs in an over, with three boundaries. One of these was tipped over slips simply because there was no third man. It seemed a zero-percentage play given how many slips there were, but it became the trademark shot of that particular innings. They kept bowling short outside the off stump to him, and he kept cuffing the ball in the air down to third man for four. And he did this, as he does everything, in a calculated, methodical way, and in so doing he made a bizarre shot seem like business as usual. Right through this masterful knock, Tendulkar continuously showed intent, an aggression unalloyed by doggedness or care. It was a rare moment in his recent career where we were allowed to see genius expressing itself unburdened by responsibility.

Tendulkar padded-up is usually a mass of inhibitions. His face is carefully inexpressive, but through the visor you can see his eyeballs virtually disappearing into his skull, so massively concentrated is he through an innings. In the course of every long innings he plays, you can see the tension build and then find release in shotmaking. The weight of responsibility, the fear of letting his side and his country down, will sometimes have him leaving every ball bowled an inch outside the off stump alone, as he did against Glenn McGrath in Australia in 1999-2000 before exploding into a flurry of shots once he was set. That innings was cruelly terminated by an umpire (this happens to Tendulkar a lot – not many umpires want to give genius the benefit of the doubt), but most innings he plays are a bit like that one – his runs come in clusters, not in a steady stream; his innings are made up of explosive episodes.

Unlike Gavaskar, inevitability isn't the hallmark of a long innings by Tendulkar. A century by him is an odd mixture of calm and storm. His greatest innings, of course, specially his hundreds in one-day matches, are simply single, long, violent spasms. They have become rarer, those extended bursts of berserker brilliance, because he is too much the Bombay batsman to be recklessly prodigal. So sometimes you'll see him curb his shotmaking, mainly in the interest of the team but also because he wants to prove to himself and to his audience that he can play with puritanical self-denial. The perfect example of a knock like this was his century in Chennai during the Third Test against the Australians when they toured India in early 2001. It was a dour, unlovely innings, all Bombay solidity, but it won India the match.

So much for temperament; what is Tendulkar's special talent? Every bowler who has ever sent down an over to him says the same thing when asked for a sound bite on what makes Tendulkar arguably the best batsman in the contemporary game. To a man, they say this: "He picks up the length of the ball earlier than anyone in the modern game, so he has more time than his peers to make the shot." There is such unanimity on this that it must be true. Till a year and a half ago, Tendulkar used the time that his eye bought him in the cause of aggression. He would get into position early for that perpendicular paddle-sweep, skip down the wicket for the lofted drive over straight mid-on, or advance while making room to drive a spinner inside-out over extra cover. His batting average soared, and it took the combined efforts of McGrath, Australian umpiring, and some wretched luck (the miraculous catch that Ponting took at the Wankhede Stadium off Tendulkar's pull after it ricocheted off short leg's back is a prime example) to bring him down to earth.

Even so, his career Test average had risen to 58 and was threatening to touch 60 when Nasser Hussain came to town. Hussain had a plan for Tendulkar, a plan of great simplicity. The way to keep Tendulkar from scoring runs was to bowl wide of him. Karl Marx memorably said that everything in history happened twice: first as tragedy and the second time as farce. Well, in this replay of leg theory, a boy born in Madras played Douglas Jardine, a left-arm spinner stood in for Harold Larwood, and Tendulkar, against his will, was cast as Don Bradman. Amazingly, the ploy sort of worked: it frustrated Tendulkar to the extent of getting him stumped for the first time in his Test career. And the reason it worked was this: Tendulkar tried to wait the bowlers out as Gavaskar might have done, but this game of patience and attrition didn't come naturally to him. At the same time, being a Bombay batsman and not being Gilchrist, he hated the thought of being forced into unorthodoxy and extravagance. It was the same story in the First Test of the 2002 tour of England, when run-saving sweeper fielders and cynically wide bowling goaded him into error. In between these two contests with England was a run of single-figure scores during the tour of the West Indies. No permanent damage was done, as a fine 92 in the Trent Bridge Test showed, but his dismissal in the nineties will have dimmed his aura a watt or two.

Right now, Tendulkar is a great batsman who doesn't scare the opposition. It's as if the fact that he sees the ball so early has begun to work against him: he has almost too much time to play the ball and he uses it to think and fret instead of using it to attack the bowling. There is a tense premeditation to his play these days, which is different from the calculated aggression we used to see earlier. Viv Richards said after Tendulkar's failures on the tour of the Caribbean that Tendulkar didn't seem to be enjoying his cricket. Perhaps he is right. Perhaps the master should learn from his protégé: perhaps Tendulkar could take a leaf out of Virender Sehwag's carefree book. He could stop being Atlas and just go with the flow.

The Phenomenon

A SINGULAR ICON   Mike Marqusee, *Wisden Asia Cricket*, September 2002

Of all the emotions evoked by spectator sport, there is one that, for me, supersedes all others. Aware as I have been from an early age that my own sporting prowess was negligible, I have often been touched, when gazing at top-flight competitors, by a sensation of awe. There is so much they do with ease that the rest of us can never hope to accomplish even with the most prolonged, dedicated and scientific preparation.

But the great thing here is that this awe does not leave us feeling belittled or inadequate. On the contrary, the wonder and marvel at what one of our fellow human beings can do is life-enhancing: the intricate co-ordination of mind and matter, strength and speed, the welding together of eyes, feet and hands in the heat of the moment, all driven by a single competitive purpose, yet somehow making a thing of beauty beyond that single purpose. At their best, great sporting geniuses challenge and extend our notion of what is humanly possible. Normally when this happens outside the sporting realm, it is experienced as disturbing or threatening, but somehow, within that redemptively trivial domain, it is irresistibly seductive.

So thank you, Sachin Tendulkar, for giving me as many of those delicious awe-filled moments as any sporting genius of my time. Tendulkar is one of that narrow stratum of elite sports stars that people will clamour and even make great sacrifices to watch, regardless of their national identity. If you care for cricket, you must love Sachin (and yes, that feeling can be found across Pakistan as well). In this regard, his peers are few – and mostly found in other sports, and certainly in other lands.

Like Tendulkar, Michael Jordan and Tiger Woods dominate their chosen sports both statistically and stylistically, and like Tendulkar they are a source of joy to fans of every stripe. From an early age, all three have been compelled to cultivate their extraordinary gifts in the spotlight of a powerful and ubiquitous mass media, in an industry whose commercial, cultural and political importance has swollen to outrageous dimensions in the last two decades. Of course, Don Bradman or George Best had their difficulties with the press, and sport has never been a stranger to big business. But in recent times, economic and technological changes have transformed the scale and nature of these pressures. The social context in which the likes of Tendulkar, Jordan or Woods have explored their inner potentialities has altered profoundly.

To achieve greatness in sport has always required exceptional powers of concentration. That is truer now than ever. Can we be sure that the geniuses of the past would have been able to sustain their best form in the relentless glare of today's global celebrity culture? Or that they would have succeeded in negotiating the numerous pitfalls accompanying a degree of wealth and renown previously undreamed of?

Today, Tendulkar, Woods and Jordan are all hugely profitable brand names – and it is not always easy to reconcile the demands of being a walking corporate logo with those of being a fallible, needy, ordinarily inconsistent human being. No doubt, all three have had to pay a high personal price for their exorbitant rewards. In this regard, they serve as apt reflectors of their era – its exaltation of individual success (even in team games), its neurotic fear of personal failure, and its fond embrace of an ethic of single-minded self-improvement. "Just do it" is the message these icons are used to pumping out to the rest of us – the vast majority of whom, I'm afraid, simply cannot do it.

Compared to the riches reaped by Jordan and Woods, Tendulkar's stash seems modest, though in India, or indeed in global cricket, it represents something of a breakthrough. All three have proved adroit in handling their financial success, cautious and canny in dealing with the powers-that-be, circumspect, dignified but also accessible to the media. Significantly, all three are studiously neutral when it comes to political controversy of any kind. None, however, can escape the tangle of contradictory meanings woven around the deities of modern sport.

As an African-American basketball player, Jordan embodies one of the most familiar of sports stereotypes. But as an African-American multi-millionaire, Jordan is also one of the least representative of celebrities, as far away from his community of origin as it is possible to get. Yet it is precisely because of his anomalous social status that he has become – in the age of neo-liberal triumphalism – a powerfully symbolic figure. Thanks to his association with multinational footwear giant Nike, Jordan is recognised in countries that can barely distinguish basketball from *kabaddi* as a symbol of individual success in a deregulated, global marketplace.

Woods carries a similar cachet, but with the crucial difference that he does so in a sport in which the great players were previously all white. Busting golf's racial straitjacket has proved a tricky operation. Woods self-consciously defines his ethnicity as a rainbow amalgam of African, Thai, Native American and white. That is undoubtedly an honest self-description from a thoughtful person; but as it happens, it also eases his passage into a particular North American sporting culture where being "black" is decidedly a disadvantage.

African-American sport celebrities have for many generations carried a complex burden of representation – expected to symbolise both the homogenised American mainstream and the distinctive African-American nation-within-a-nation. In earlier eras, individuals as diverse as Joe Louis and Muhammad Ali, Jesse Owens, Jackie Robinson, Wilma Rudolph and Arthur Ashe all found their careers profoundly shaped by American racism and the struggle against it. Thanks not least to their efforts, black sports stars of more recent vintage have reaped hitherto unimaginable rewards for their talents. They have also continued to face the challenges of an enduring racial divide, though in subtler forms than in the past. Jordan and Woods are both global icons, but the connotations of their iconship vary both between the USA and the larger world, and within the colour-conscious USA itself.

Some of what makes all three of these living Olympians distinctive is revealed by a comparison with another contemporary sporting hero, David Beckham, England's innovatively coiffed football captain. Without for a moment underestimating the Indian media's appetite for sensationalism, it can be safely said that Britain's tabloid celebrity culture has a peculiar brutality and coarseness, one mirrored sometimes by its football crowds. Neither Tendulkar, Jordan nor Woods has ever had to endure the kind of mega-decibel sexual and scatological abuse hurled at Beckham by thousands of English football fans. (You have to remember that within the breast of the average English football fan, hatred of Manchester United rivals support for the national team.) Then again, none of the aforementioned triumvirs has married a high-profile pop star or posed as a fashion icon. It's probably unfair on Beckham, but there are times when he does seem an apt symbol of Tony Blair's brain-dead Britain, or at least of its febrile, philistine cult of the rich and famous.

Though he is as much a household name as the others, Beckham does not, and would never claim to, dominate his sport as they have dominated theirs. He has always been more fallible, and therefore perhaps more human and approachable. And while there is no doubt that Jordan, Woods and Tendulkar will be remembered as the defining performers of their eras, it is not at all clear how history will end up viewing Beckham.

Nonetheless, like Jordan and Woods, Beckham is now something of a multinational enterprise, a globally recognised brand name. He endorses products in Singapore, Malaysia and Eastern Europe. In this respect, it is Tendulkar who is the exception. As a saleable icon, he remains confined to his national market and its diasporic extensions. No one in North America, continental Europe or East Asia is going to pay good money to put his name on a pair of trainers or sunglasses. Even within the cricket world, companies sponsor him specifically because they seek access to the South Asian, and in particular the Indian, market.

Of course, in itself, that's no mean demographic. But Tendulkar's uniqueness resides in his peculiar importance within that vast market. Jordan, Woods and Beckham may cross more boundaries, but nowhere do their performances carry the weight of expectation that Tendulkar's carry in India. Nowhere are they the focus of the kind of fervour that greets Tendulkar when he strides to the crease at the Wankhede, Eden Gardens, or the Chidambaram Stadium. It has been argued that Tendulkar is the beneficiary and victim of a specifically Indian culture of hero-worship, but in my view this theory severs Tendulkar from his times, and therefore obscures his significance.

Tendulkar has flourished during a long drought for Indian cricket. In a team that has persistently underachieved, especially away from home, he has had to shoulder an enormous burden. Often it seemed left to Tendulkar alone to salvage national pride. Somehow he has risen above the scandals and the corruption and the incompetence swirling around him. In a demanding context, he has conducted himself with probity and dignity.

It's the image that Jordan and Woods aspire to, and which they work carefully to craft, but one wonders how successful they would have been if they found themselves in Tendulkar's shoes. After all, if Woods or Jordan or Beckham fail, sports fans in the USA or even in Britain have a variety of other world-beaters to whom to switch their emotional affiliation. When Tendulkar stumbles, Indian sports fans find the cupboard nearly bare (which is not to deny the excellence of other Indian sports performers, but merely to note the over-riding and disproportionate importance of cricket in India in comparison with other sports).

Nevertheless, the intensity of the Tendulkar cult in India is about much more than just cricket. Unwittingly and unwillingly, he has found himself at the epicentre of a rapidly evolving popular culture shaped by the intertwined growth of a consumerist middle class and an increasingly aggressive form of national identity. National aspirations and national frustrations are poured by millions into his every performance. It's a tribute to his strength of personality that he has not burst apart under the pressure.

As the inheritor of the classical tradition of Mumbai batsmanship, Tendulkar has seamlessly blended power and grace, efficiency and elegance, conscientious craftsmanship and quicksilver improvisation. He is the greatest runmaker the one-day format has yet produced, as well as a complete master of the long-established disciplines of Test-match batting. More importantly, he stands at the intersection of the two forms of the game; through him we have seen one enrich and extend the other. He is a modern man playing a modern game in a modern style in the modern world – and that's what makes him of supreme importance to his fellow Indians. He's a homegrown genius excelling in a global game, a world-beater bred in the heart of Mumbai's status-hungry middle class.

During this summer's football World Cup, there was much talk in Britain about the immense burden of expectation that Beckham carried whenever he stepped forward to take a penalty for England. As I tried to point out to football's somewhat parochial devotees, Beckham's World Cup burden was as nothing compared to the weight Tendulkar has carried throughout his career. I also tried to indicate that this weight was more than just a question of numbers. Yes, Tendulkar belongs with the Jordans, the Woodses and the Beckhams as a high-value icon of personal success in a globalised economy. But his specific historical significance resides in his relationship to India and in India's relationship to the world.

In a sense, for non-Indians like myself, the joy of Tendulkar comes unadulterated. The awe he inspires belongs to no culture, carries no nationalist overtones, and is at once both intimately personal and transparently universal.

The Superhuman

SACHIN, THE BRINGER OF JOY   Tunku Varadarajan, *Wisden* 2014

Every Indian fan – and many a non-Indian – has in his head a personal montage of Sachin Tendulkar, the finest sportsman produced by India and, arguably (but not contentiously so), cricket's most complete batsman. This is not to say he was better than Donald Bradman. But Bradman played in an era when there were immensely fewer demands on a cricketer's time, body and mind. And, over a 24-year career, Tendulkar played 200 Tests at 59 different grounds, plus 463 one-day internationals at 96. Bradman's 52 Tests took place at only ten venues, all in Australia or England, allowing him a cosy familiarity with conditions that Tendulkar – except at a few marquee venues in India – never enjoyed. Add to that the pressure of a fanatical, sometimes insane, nation, and one cannot be denied at least this observation: cricket and country asked more of Tendulkar than they ever did of Bradman, or of anyone else.

But back to the montage. My own has five images. The first is from November 1989 when, as a 16-year-old who looked rather younger, Tendulkar was about to make his Test debut, in Karachi. He is flanked in a winsome photograph by Kapil Dev and Mohammad Azharuddin. The veterans are smiling their trademark smiles – Kapil's manly and toothy, Azhar's reliably goofy – and each has a proprietary arm draped around Tendulkar's shoulders. They are proud of their ward, who regards the camera almost bashfully, his hair a lush mop of black curls. A boy among men he was, his callow face yet to be bloodied by a Waqar Younis bouncer; even as he grew older, a vital part of him stayed boyish. It's possible his countrymen kept him from full manhood, their worship freezing him in time.

The second image is from Lord's, eight months later. England are looking for quick second-innings runs to set up a declaration after Graham Gooch's endless 333 and Kapil's cavalier quartet of sixes off Eddie Hemmings to save the follow-on. Allan Lamb skies one back over the head of the bowler, leg-spinner Narendra Hirwani, and a coltish Tendulkar, sprinting in from wide long-off, covers 40 yards and clings on one-handed, low to his right. It is one of the best running catches imaginable, the more so because India could no longer win: Tendulkar was propelled entirely by personal pride. Dazzled by his batting, we tend to overlook the fact that – until M. S. Dhoni – he was the fittest, most naturally athletic cricketer to play for India.

The third is bitter, but defines Tendulkar just as aptly. Chennai, January 1999, and India – with four wickets in hand – are 17 runs away from a rare Test victory over Pakistan. Tendulkar, on 136, has just pulled Saqlain Mushtaq deftly to the fence. And then he throws it all away, caught at deep mid-off. India lose by 12, which confirms what their fans have started to suspect: Tendulkar, for all his gifts and statistical irrefutability, doesn't deliver when it really matters. He is the oak that creaks. In one sense, this matters little to his countrymen, for their gods are never infallible (as a cursory glance at Hindu mythology confirms). Yet even in his moment of fallibility, Tendulkar showed physical courage: his back was in such excruciating pain that he batted with a brace, after three injections.

Image four is seared on the brain. Again, it is Pakistan, this time during the 2003 World Cup in South Africa. Shoaib Akhtar, bulging with muscle and ego, steams in at Centurion like a demented bull for the second over of India's reply to a testing Pakistan total. The ball is short, fast and wide, and Tendulkar scythes it over square third man for six. It is an entirely instinctive stroke, the acme of unorthodoxy. Shoaib's next two balls disappear for four – a silken flick through midwicket, an on-drive of sheer purity. Both are in utter contrast to the six: Tendulkar is butcher and Brahmin. It is this duality, this ability to switch instantly from the brutal to the serene, which made him such an irrepressible one-day player. Not blindly wedded to the straight bat (though he was primarily a purist), he had the eye, strength and flexibility of technique to play shots that would have made Viv Richards proud.

The last image is of Tendulkar being held aloft by team-mates after India beat Sri Lanka in the 2011 World Cup final at Mumbai. His face is ecstatic as he is carried around the ground by Virat Kohli and other young guns. They are unbridled in their affection – no, their love – for Tendulkar, an individual genius who is also a team-player and a player-patriot, a mentor, an elder statesman, and an icon, as much to colleagues and opponents as he is to spectators. A senior Indian cricket writer tells me that the country gained new respect for Kohli – hitherto seen as a brash young man, even a borderline lout – when he said: "Sachin has carried the burden of the nation for 21 years. It is time we carried him." Suddenly, Kohli seemed to have something in common with the whole of India. His quote humanised him.

You will notice that there is no image here from Tendulkar's last, unarguably moving, day in Test cricket, at Mumbai in November 2013.

Allan Donald, an old adversary, once said: "I don't think I've seen a hungrier batsman." Sometimes there is an imperceptible line between hunger and greed; and to many who watched Tendulkar linger in Test cricket for his last two years, fused like a cussed tenant to his position at No. 4, there was a sense that he was not being entirely selfless, that he should have announced his retirement after dismounting from Kohli's shoulders in Mumbai, a World Cup in his kit-bag. In India, this thought could only be whispered. Nor could it be said too forcefully that Tendulkar had become obsessed with playing 200 Tests, that he had (not for the first time) allowed a personal landmark to cloud his judgment.

Will there ever be another cricketer like him? Given the way the sport is evolving (or possibly disintegrating), it is almost certain no one will play as many Tests. His retirement, then, marks the end of a statistical era, the transition from BT to AT, from Before Tendulkar to After Tendulkar. Even the notion of this shorthand offers a nod to his status as an Indian divinity, a status that those from other countries presumably found disconcerting. For it is unlikely Tendulkar would have received the same obeisance had he been born elsewhere.

An English Tendulkar would have been made to wait for his Test debut until 22 or 23, and retired much earlier, his native self-deprecation having trumped any temptation to linger while younger players awaited their turn; adulation, in any case, isn't an English art. The rugged mateship inherent in the cultures of Australia, New Zealand and South Africa, where there is less of a gulf between player and fan, would have served as an antidote to Tendulkar-worship. West Indies and Sri Lanka have laid-back island cultures, where no man is bigger or prouder than the next, and his popularity depends on his accessibility to fellow citizens. In Pakistan too (for all its reverence of Imran Khan) there is an unwillingness to raise a mortal to superhuman status – a result, no doubt, of Islam.

Tendulkar, then, is an Indian phenomenon: a gifted man born in a land where boys can have adulthood thrust upon them quickly, yet retain a structure of family support well into later life. In fact, Tendulkar is not so much the product of India as of his family: a middle-class boy born to profoundly collaborative parents. His professor father, improbably for a bookish type, was happy for his son to spend more time on cricket than on his studies. And his family arranged for him to live with an uncle and aunt in a different quarter of his native Mumbai to shorten the commute to nets. It mattered not that the boy wasn't living with his mother and father: young Sachin was saving three hours a day in travel time!

His family's greatest gift was a cricketing cocoon. Sachin entered into it aged 11 (when, cherished and precocious, he was entrusted to his coach, Ramakant Achrekar) and emerged from it only on November 16, 2013, the day of his retirement. For three decades – to the exclusion of all else – he was able to eat, sleep, breathe and play the game. His older brother, Ajit, devoted his life to Sachin's cricket, removing him from the demands of a humdrum world. His wife Anjali, a wealthy and grounded woman six years his senior, took charge of the cocoon when she married him in 1995; he was 22. In contrast to the tumult in the lives of his great batting rival Brian Lara, or his schoolfriend Vinod Kambli, who also played for India but lacked the discipline that can be instilled only at home, Tendulkar never had to worry about anything but cricket.

Did it make him a one-dimensional human being? C. L. R. James's famous question acquires some piquancy when applied to Tendulkar, for it was evident he knew cricket – and knew only cricket. He had no apparent philosophy that was unrelated to the playing and practice of the game. He was a technician, not a thinker. In interviews he was often banal, as if saying to his interlocutors: "Please, just let my bat do the talking." His English and Hindi are imperfect (perhaps because he neglected his schooling), and he reached inevitably for platitudes and diplomatic niceties, as if suspicious of anyone who wasn't hurling a ball at him. There is no big social issue on which he has taken a public stand – this, in a country awash with worthy causes, any one of which would have received a glorious boost had Tendulkar lent his name.

And yet Indian cricket grew gradually stronger for his single-mindedness. Tendulkar was their first player to be held in awe by other sides – and even feared. The awe came early. When, not yet 19, he flayed Australia in a Test at Perth, Merv Hughes told Allan Border: "This little prick's going to get more runs than you, AB." When Border retired two years later, he did so with a Test-record 11,174 runs; and 13 years after that, in November 2007 against Pakistan at Delhi, Tendulkar would prove Hughes right. He would overhaul Lara the following October, since when Tendulkar has always been top of the tree; his Test tally of 15,921 may never be broken.

Every bowler raised his game when charging in at Tendulkar; if only there were some way of factoring that extra effort into the value of his runs. For Indian fans, opposition bowlers became defined by their showdowns with him. James Anderson – who dismissed Tendulkar nine times in Tests, more than anyone – wasn't just James Anderson: he was James-Anderson-when-bowling-to-Tendulkar. And so it was with Courtney Walsh, Glenn McGrath, Muttiah Muralitharan and Dale Steyn. Donald, quoted in Vimal Kumar's *Sachin: Cricketer of the Century*, offered an example of the phenomenon: "My fondest memory of Sachin is bowling him through the gate in the Durban Test. There is no question about the fact that it was the best-ever ball that I bowled in

Test cricket." At the spectrum's less rarefied end, Michael Vaughan has dined out on the off-break that once sneaked through Tendulkar in a Test in Nottingham; it was the man who mattered, as much as the delivery.

Despite this, his retirement does not leave Indian cricket noticeably weaker. After all, the batting line-up had been carrying him for two years, the result of Tendulkar being allowed to choose the time of his own retirement. He played on for 23 Tests after the 2011 World Cup final, averaging a downright un-Tendulkarish 32, as against nearly 57 until then. Just as tellingly, he became more susceptible to the straight ball: in that final phase, he was either bowled or lbw in 49% of his innings; until then, the figure had been 34%. But what Indian cricket – or, more specifically, Indian batting – now has is a fearlessness that was missing in the BT years. Self-belief is Tendulkar's greatest bequest to his country's cricket. To everyone else he gave something of equal consequence: joy, and pleasure – the pleasure that comes from watching a simple, unaffected man perform beautiful feats with the bat, year after year after year.

Chapter 2

The Ten Best Innings

"W ho cares about the tussle for Championship points if a Ranji be glancing to leg?" wrote Neville Cardus in 1921, when cricket-lovers could just about get away with preferring style over substance. But Tendulkar's followers were a demanding lot: sometimes even a century was not enough, let alone a delicate flick through midwicket. If he couldn't win India the game, what was the point?

When wisden.com drew up a list in 2001 of the 100 greatest Test innings, not one of Tendulkar's made the cut, not even his first Test hundred, when he saved the game at Old Trafford, nor his 114 at Perth in 1991-92; the poetry of a fighting century, in a hopeless cause, by a 19-year-old was not enough. The computer-generated logic was cut-throat: none of Tendulkar's innings had, at that point, culminated in a victory overseas for India.

If there were a similar list now, would any of his innings make it? His exhibition of discipline and denial at Sydney in 2003-04, perhaps, or his unbeaten 103 in a fourth-innings run-chase against England at Chennai in 2008-09?

Choosing Tendulkar's ten best innings is like trying to decide van Gogh's ten greatest masterpieces. There are some shoo-ins, the equivalents of "Starry Night" and "Café Terrace in Arles", celebrating life's beauty: the 169 at Cape Town in 1996-97, or the 143 at Sharjah in 1997-98. Then there are the ones where the artist's inner struggle is apparent: for van Gogh's "Old Man in Sorrow", read Tendulkar's epic struggle to 136 with an injured back, followed by the agony of a narrow defeat by Pakistan at Chennai in 1998-99. Some innings had to miss out: the 120 not out against

Kenya in Bristol during the 1999 World Cup just days after his father's funeral in Mumbai, and the 134 in the Coca-Cola Cup final against Australia at Sharjah in 1998-99. Those innings that did qualify are ranked in chronological order alone.

Tendulkar's best innings, like van Gogh's masterpieces, showcase his evolution as an artist – from destroyer to accumulator to the destructive accumulator. There is no better example of this than his 200 not out – the first double-century in a one-day international – against South Africa, and the world's best bowling attack, in Gwalior.

As Rahul Bhattacharya, tracing Tendulkar's progression from dazzler to ruthless run machine, wrote in Wisden Asia Cricket in 2002: "What masterpieces will he paint? What masterpiece will he himself end up becoming? We will follow every move. Whoever said watching paint dry is boring?"

A GENIUS TEMPERED   Rahul Bhattacharya, *Wisden Asia Cricket*, April 2002

Madhav Mantri is 80, and behind thick, black-framed glasses his eyes glint, and his toothless smile spreads like a warm glow, as he talks of a man with 13 saved-up one-rupee coins in a plastic packet. This is no staggering amount, but these are important rupees. They taught Sachin Tendulkar to not lose his wicket. As is well documented now, he got to pocket a coin placed on top of middle stump by his coach Ramakant Achrekar if it remained in its original location at the end of a net session.

Tendulkar learned his lessons well and fast. He played for Mumbai and India while boys around him played the fool, and on the 1990 tour to England, for which Mantri was manager, he scored a century that must be regarded as one of our nation's greatest. He was then a shade above 17, his country was in a heap of trouble trying to survive a Test. On the last day, in climes unknown to him, he took it upon himself to protect his wicket so that his team might hold their heads high. The following day after breakfast at the hotel, he sat by Mantri's feet – because he was always taught to respect his elders – and asked whether he had made any mistakes during his innings. How do you answer that?

Soon, he was conquering the world. Sometimes, his greatness was being assessed by his ability to lose, not just preserve, his wicket. In a county match during Tendulkar's time with Yorkshire, Martin Crowe reckoned he had "bowled the ball of my life on a cabbage-patch of a wicket". It hit a bump just short of a length between middle and off stumps, rocketed off towards the slips and Sachin got a nick to it. "No one in the world," according to Crowe, "would have got near it."

And so, for much of the 1990s, Tendulkar dazzled us with his ever-present incandescence. At Perth, aged 18, he was so courageous and skilful while taking on a bullying five-man pace attack in a sparkling century that Richie Benaud lamented there weren't at least a hundred thousand at the stadium. At Cape Town in 1996, his 169 made a dire situation and a dark series worth the pain. At Chennai in 1998, his assault on Shane Warne elevated a cricket battle to something higher, as those who were present will doubtless tell their grandchildren. He could make life worth living.

So when you first admit to yourself that you are no longer stirred by his play like you once were, that, whisper it, you wouldn't mind Virender Sehwag facing the bulk of the first 15 overs of a one-dayer, it seems a thought worth banishing. Like the moment you first realised Superman was a lie. Eventually, the resistance ends. What can you say – the thrill is gone.

Tendulkar is scoring more runs than before and is more consistent, among the most consistent there has been, but he doesn't excite the senses quite like he used to. It is not uncommon; batsmen, great batsmen too, are human; they grow older, wiser, more cynical if you like, and so become acutely aware of every pothole on every road. Minimising risk becomes an obsession which only a handful haven't succumbed to.

See the magnificent George Headley. When, on one occasion in Australia, he was trapped out on the glance – among his more favoured shots – he decided to "cut it out". So he wouldn't glance again? asked C. L. R. James. "Sure I glance, but I take care to find out first if any of these traps are being laid."

Jack Hobbs, he played his career in two separate parts. Before the war of 1914, he was said to be "quick on the attack on swift feet, strokes all over the field, killing but never brutal", and after the resumption of cricket in 1919, to be "as serenely poised as any ever witnessed on a cricket field" according to Neville Cardus in the 1963 *Wisden*. Despite the later prolificacy, Hobbs himself liked Mark I.

But every great has his own method. Age or experience wouldn't change Viv Richards or Garry Sobers. Among cricket's, let alone Sobers's own, greatest and most spectacular innings is his 254 as captain of the Rest of the World against Australia at Melbourne in 1971-72; Sobers was then into his 18th year of international cricket. Richards was past 34 when he smashed 100 off 56 balls against England at home in Antigua early in 1986; well over 35 when he got a run-a-ball 109 not out in the fourth innings at Delhi; and close to 37 when he slammed 146 in 150 balls at Perth in 1998-99. Their teams, of course, won all those matches.

* * *

Tendulkar has opted to take the risk out of his batting. Four years back, he was still the best in the world, but of all the words used to describe him – sensation, genius, technically perfect – you might never have called him a run machine. He was unpredictable in a manner machines cannot be. The Tendulkar of today is ruthless in a way only a machine could be. He does not lose his head against mediocre bowling, and he does not think himself to be bigger than any situation.

His average in 33 Tests since (and including) the monumental home series against Australia in early 1998 is 68.59, and in that period he has scored 14 centuries, the same as in almost twice the number of Tests previously. The new ratio is a mind-boggling one century per 2.36 Tests.

In the same four-year period mentioned above, Tendulkar has scored two rip-roaring, match-winning and utterly memorable double-hundreds. For Mumbai. Anyone who wasn't at the Brabourne on February 25, 1998, when he plundered 204 not out in 192 balls to defeat the Australians within three days and set the agenda for the entire series to follow hasn't *really* been exposed to the full might of Tendulkar. Nobody who was at the Wankhede for the semi-final of the Ranji Trophy, 1999-2000, when he made 233 not out and squeezed out 41 runs alongside Nos 10 and 11 (each of whom made ducks) to edge Mumbai past Tamil Nadu's first-innings total, will claim that Tendulkar has played a more decisive innings in cricket. God, he was free and unfettered and overall fab. His two Test double-hundreds, against New Zealand and Zimbabwe, couldn't hold a candle to these.

In a sense, the new Tendulkar is more complete. Technically, not much has changed, except according to one veteran coach who wishes to remain anonymous, a tendency to play the forward defensive alongside, rather than in front of, his left leg; possibly a product of a less-sure mindset. Yet, he is no Plain Jane accumulator. He is subtle – more sensitive than any contemporary to a match situation or field placement; delicate – full of paddles, dabbles, uppercuts; merciless – not bored on any surface or by any opposition; but, he is humble – more prepared than ever before to give a bowler his due.

Previously, only the rarest of situations and bowlers could demand this. When he played out five entire overs of Glenn McGrath without scoring a run at the end of a tense day at Adelaide in 1999-2000 (McGrath's figures for the spell were 8–7–1–0), he was not only denying psychological points to the man who likes to send out memos to his targets, he was also programming what he calls "his computer" for the new conditions in his first innings of the tour. As the days rolled by, he was tucking in to McGrath and his band, and had it not been for what came across as a devious and pointed umpiring campaign, Tendulkar would have shone even brighter.

Too many chaps can claim that reverence now. In the second innings of India's loss at Harare last year, Andy Blignaut managed 23 dot-balls out of 26 that he bowled to Tendulkar (perhaps so thrilled was Blignaut with his subsequent Man of the Match, that he retired at a ripe 23). At Delhi last month, Ray Price, like fellow Zimbabwean Blignaut, could bowl 60 balls at him for nine runs – and two wickets. In a one-dayer against Kenya, a fellow called Joseph Angara sent down two maidens, and then bowled him through the gate to end a three-run innings from 24 balls.

Tendulkar does not chew up spinners and spit them out quite like he used to, because he doesn't step out to them like he did earlier. Against Warne last year, he was almost as effective as in 1998, but hardly as brutal. In one-day cricket, you won't see him break a bowler's heart as much as surprise him with his ability to score quickly without apparent effort. He is so good at stealth, yet it isn't his greatest ally. As Sanjay Manjrekar points out, a 60 or 70 can often be a whole lot more than a century.

Still, there are passages where Tendulkar takes us places that only he can. See Day One at Bloemfontein against South Africa last November, or the second session on Day Three at Ahmedabad against England a month later. They were the work of a man willing to strut his stuff, and these were periods of cricket that most Indians live for, and for which, somewhere in the world, there are new fans born every day.

Despite what the numbers say, the Tendulkar of today is selling himself short, because he is batting below what he was meant to by the Gods. He has managed to master, because he is a genius, shots that don't come naturally to him. But need he trade that for what he was born with? Should he be a victim of circumstance? Should he think of himself as Atlas? It has not worked for India thus far: what a weaker bowling needs is quicker runs so that they have longer to take 20 wickets; what an often-spineless batting requires is to be shown that opposition bowlers are only human. When he doesn't tear apart Zimbabwe home or away, he is not showing the way; he is under-achieving.

So too when he doesn't seal matches off his own bat. Which is why when he tells Harsha Bhogle on his TV show that not taking India past the wire often enough is not only a regret, but doing so now has become something of a mission, it is a most significant statement. He has taken a first and enormous step: that of acknowledging. If the past is anything to go by, he will probably meet his target.

* * *

Tendulkar is great and so has a legacy to leave behind. As John Wright mentions, a hundred hundreds would be Bradmanesque: Tendulkar's version of 99.94. But mustn't he bequeath something far greater than a number? Every generation has its stars, and every generation has its immortals. The immortals need no numbers. Theirs is a less tangible, more encompassing aura.

W. G. Grace was credited by Neville Cardus with having "invented what we now call modern cricket... his bulk and stride carried cricket into the highways of our life". C. L. R. James summed up what Headley gave to cricket: "Just at the time when the game was about to sink into its present defensive spell... he restored it to the glamour of its best days." Cardus, almost identically, observed that Sobers maintained the "*art* of cricket at a time which day by day... threatens to change the game into (a) real industry or (b) a sort of out-of-door Bingo cup jousting".

The spirit of Victor Trumper still burns brightly, because he so tingled the senses that at least one Englishman was moved to pray for Trumper to score a century and Australia to lose the match. There was Viv Richards in the 1980s, who fashioned an entire team in his helmetless, black-is-might swagger, and Brian Lara in the '90s, who was a hero and a victim of his unfathomable excesses, and we will never forget either of them.

Bradman, leave him aside, he only sculptured the everlasting, insurmountable ideal that every Australia citizen and every cricketer the world over will always aspire to.

Tendulkar. He has filled stadiums relentlessly – he once even emptied one, when a rioting crowd at the Eden Gardens was disbanded because they couldn't bear to watch him lose his wicket in a collision which could only be termed unfortunate. He has had gold medallions released in his honour and he has roused the nation's parliament because a match referee thought him to be lifting a seam. He has demonstrated to the world a consistency in run-scoring never seen since the Second World War and a technical well-roundedness not seen since Barry Richards in the 1970s. He has been a role model, not merely for Indian cricketers but for every Indian, and he has been, for a decade, the very face of not just Indian cricket, but of India herself.

On April 24, 2002, he will be 29, at his ripest, and in the middle of perhaps the third-but-last phase of a fascinating journey. (Another tenure as captain, and a final stage as the ultimate wise old pro are probably still to come.) These are the days that will shape his legend.

So, what will be his legacy? How will he be remembered? Will he kindle a twinkle in our eyes like he does in Mantri's today? Will he awaken inside the stomach the grim and defiant tricoloured pride that the name Gavaskar does?

More importantly, how will he remember himself? Will he be tinged with regret, as Hobbs was, when on his 70th birthday he was driven to remark upon his evolution: "You could play cheeky shots and make 50 or 60 and feel life was worth living. Then came the exasperation when they started counting your hundreds, publishing averages, and it was all figures."

Will he one day reminisce about his youth as Headley once did: "When I think of the things I used to do, I tremble and marvel at myself"?

Will he dance the way he used to? Will he, in the words of his favourite, Mark Knopfler, put his hand on the lever and say, let it rock and let it roll? Will he allow himself the freedom to be the very boldest, the very best he can be? What masterpieces will he paint? What masterpiece will he himself end up becoming? We will follow every move. Whoever said watching paint dry is boring?

Wisden's Top Ten

119* v ENGLAND, 1990	Graham Otway, *Wisden* 1991

A photograph by Ben Radford from the final afternoon of the Old Trafford Test in 1990 perfectly captures the boy-among-men essence of Tendulkar's teenage exploits (he scored five centuries, four of them overseas, before he turned 20). A 17-year-old walks back to the pavilion, having made his first Test century and saved India from almost certain defeat in the Second Test. Yet to grow any facial hair, he is at the centre of the frame, surrounded by moustachioed men who look twice his age, and in some cases are. Yet the faces of the English cricketers – Allan Lamb, Robin Smith, Eddie Hemmings and John Morris – tell of an understated awe as they walk behind Tendulkar, applauding him all the way back. His first century had come six months after he missed out on becoming the youngest Test centurion, in Napier.

Of the six individual centuries scored in this fascinating contest, none was more outstanding than Tendulkar's, which rescued India on the final afternoon. At 17 years and 112 days, he was only 30 days older than Mushtaq Mohammad was when, against India at Delhi in 1960-61, he became the youngest player to score a Test hundred. More significantly, after several of his colleagues had fallen to reckless strokes, Tendulkar held the England attack at bay with a disciplined display of immense maturity.

Leading an unchanged side, Graham Gooch put on 73 untroubled runs with Michael Atherton in the first hour, and India soon resorted to their leg-spinners, Narendra Hirwani and Anil Kumble. They slowed down England's progress, but could do little to prevent a 225-run opening partnership. In scoring 116, Gooch became the first English batsman for 19 years to record centuries in three successive Test innings, but on the day he was eclipsed by his junior partner. In five and a half hours, Atherton carefully constructed 131. Smith batted for just over four hours, passing his century during a last-wicket partnership of 60 with Devon Malcolm as England reached 519.

The loss of three quick wickets for 57 to the seam movement of Angus Fraser, in the final hour of the second day, placed India in immediate peril. On Saturday, however, they were rescued in style by their captain, Mohammad Azharuddin, and Sanjay Manjrekar. In a breathtaking 281-minute stay for 179, Azharuddin hit 21 fours and a six. After he had miscued a drive off Fraser to Atherton, the second new ball accounted for most of the remaining Indian batting, although Tendulkar, after taking 54 minutes to get off the mark, gave warning of his talents in scoring 68 from 136 balls to reduce the England lead to just 87.

As England's second innings began on the fourth morning, Gooch suffered a rare failure in a rich summer, departing for seven. But Atherton added a further 74 to his first-innings hundred, and a winning position was achieved through the efforts of Lamb – his 109 from 141 balls, followed by Smith's unbeaten 61, allowed Gooch to declare 25 minutes into the final day.

To win and square the series, India were offered a minimum of 88 overs in which to score 408, two runs more than their own record for the highest winning total by a side batting second in a Test. From the seventh ball of their innings, when Navjot Sidhu was brilliantly caught off Fraser by the substitute, Chris Adams, at short leg, it looked a tall order. On a slowly wearing pitch Hemmings produced just enough deviation to have both Manjrekar and Azharuddin caught in the leg trap – but it was the gay abandon of three senior Indian batsmen which might have set Tendulkar a bad example. Shastri dragged a wide ball on to his stumps, Dilip Vengsarkar offered no stroke to Chris Lewis, and Kapil Dev sallied down the pitch to Hemmings.

When the all-rounder, Manoj Prabhakar, joined Tendulkar, India were 183 for six and there were two and a half hours of the match remaining. Gooch crowded the bat and shuffled his bowlers like a croupier, but England were to be denied by their own mistakes. Hemmings put down a simple return catch when Tendulkar was ten, and Gooch failed to get a hand at second slip to a chance offered by Prabhakar. England could ill-afford such lapses, and the pair had seen India to safety when the game was halted with two of the final 20 overs still to be bowled.

Tendulkar remained undefeated on 119, having batted for 224 minutes and hit 17 fours. He looked the embodiment of India's famous opener, Gavaskar, and indeed was wearing a pair of his pads. While he displayed a full repertoire of strokes in compiling his maiden Test hundred, most remarkable were his off-side shots from the back foot. Though only 5ft 5in tall, he was still able to control without difficulty short deliveries from the English pacemen.

England

*G. A. Gooch c More b Prabhakar	116	– c More b Prabhakar		7
M. A. Atherton c More b Hirwani	131	– lbw b Kapil Dev		74
D. I. Gower c Tendulkar b Kapil Dev	38	– b Hirwani		16
A. J. Lamb c Manjrekar b Kumble	38	– b Kapil Dev		109
†R. C. Russell c More b Hirwani	8	– (7) not out		16
R. A. Smith not out	121	– (5) not out		61
J. E. Morris b Kumble	13	– (6) retired hurt		15
C. C. Lewis b Hirwani	3			
E. E. Hemmings lbw b Hirwani	19			
A. R. C. Fraser c Tendulkar b Kumble	1			
D. E. Malcolm b Shastri	13			
B 2, l-b 9, w 1, n-b 6	18	L-b 15, n-b 7		22

1/225 (1) 2/292 (3) 3/312 (2) (160.5 overs) 519
4/324 (5) 5/366 (4) 6/392 (7)
7/404 (8) 8/434 (9) 9/459 (10) 10/519 (11)

1/15 (1) (4 wkts dec, 81 overs) 320
2/46 (3)
3/180 (2) 4/248 (4)

Kapil Dev 13–2–67–1; Prabhakar 25–2–112–1; Kumble 43–7–105–3; Hirwani 62–10–174–4; Shastri 17.5–2–50–1. *Second innings*—Kapil Dev 22–4–69–2; Prabhakar 18–1–80–1; Hirwani 15–0–52–1; Kumble 17–3–65–0; Shastri 9–0–39–0.

India

R. J. Shastri c Gooch b Fraser	25	– b Malcolm		12
N. S. Sidhu c Gooch b Fraser	13	– c sub (C. J. Adams) b Fraser		0
S. V. Manjrekar c Smith b Hemmings	93	– c sub (C. J. Adams) b Hemmings		50
D. B. Vengsarkar c Russell b Fraser	6	– b Lewis		32
*M. Azharuddin c Atherton b Fraser	179	– c Lewis b Hemmings		11
S. R. Tendulkar c Lewis b Hemmings	68	– not out		119
M. Prabhakar c Russell b Malcolm	4	– (8) not out		67
Kapil Dev lbw b Lewis	0	– (7) b Hemmings		26
†K. S. More b Fraser	6			
A. Kumble run out	2			
N. D. Hirwani not out	15			
B 5, l-b 4, n-b 12	21	B 17, l-b 3, n-b 6		26

1/26 (2) 2/48 (1) 3/57 (4) (119.2 overs) 432
4/246 (3) 5/358 (5) 6/364 (7)
7/365 (8) 8/396 (9) 9/401 (10) 10/432 (6)

1/4 (2) 2/35 (1) (6 wkts, 90 overs) 343
3/109 (3)
4/109 (4) 5/127 (5) 6/183 (7)

Malcolm 26–3–96–1; Fraser 35–5–124–5; Hemmings 29.2–8–74–2; Lewis 13–1–61–1; Atherton 16–3–68–0. *Second innings*—Malcolm 14–5–59–1; Fraser 21–3–81–1; Hemmings 31–10–75–3; Atherton 4–0–22–0; Lewis 20–3–86–1.

Umpires: J. H. Hampshire and J. W. Holder.

THE BOY WHO CONQUERED ENGLISH HEARTS

R. Mohan, *Wisden* 1991

India were let down by their lack of cold-blooded professionalism, most obvious when they failed in the task of batting just under four sessions for the draw at Lord's. Under the pressure of having to remain at the wicket, rather than being able to bat with uninhibited aggression, they succumbed more easily than one would have imagined, while at the same time continuing their spectacular strokeplay. It was after the senior batsmen had displayed the same lack of commitment on the final day at Old Trafford that Sachin Tendulkar completed his conquest of English hearts, saving his side from defeat and scoring the sixth century of the match. There should be many more Test hundreds for Tendulkar; what made his first so special were the circumstances in which he made it, as a 17-year-old coming to the rescue of his country. Yet those who had seen him stand up to a barrage of bouncers from the Pakistani fast bowlers at Sialkot the previous winter would have had no doubts about his genius, or his capacity to set an example to colleagues old enough to be father figures. He had already shown his character in the first innings at Manchester when, after waiting nearly an hour for his first run, he went on to regain his one-day touch, and he had dazzled the crowd at Lord's with an unbelievably athletic catch of the sort that only players of his age can attempt.

---

114 v Australia, 1992   Dicky Rutnagur, *Wisden* 1993

The five-Test series against Australia, played just before the 1992 World Cup, was a miserable one for India. They reached Perth trailing 3–0, having managed a single draw, thanks to a 196-run stand between Ravi Shastri and Sachin Tendulkar at Sydney. That Test was the start of Tendulkar's love affair with the Sydney Cricket Ground – he scored 148 not out, his second Test hundred, and went on to make three more centuries there. But it is his hundred at Perth, the world's quickest wicket in the 1990s, against a fast-bowling attack featuring Craig McDermott and Merv Hughes, that is regarded as one of his bravest and finest.

Tom Moody made a triumphant return as the final Test brought another resounding victory. The fast-medium Paul Reiffel was preferred to a spinner on the WACA pitch and he assisted in the demolition of India's second innings by Mike Whitney, who returned match figures of 11 for 95.

Though India took only four wickets on the first day, they restricted Australia to 222 runs. But as the ball lost its shine, the last four wickets added 87.

India's bedrock was a captivating 114 from Tendulkar from 161 balls with 16 fours, the bulk of them square-cuts. He came in at 69 for two and was ninth out at 240, after 228 minutes, and a record ninth-wicket stand for India against Australia, of 81, with Kiran More. On the third morning, as he ran out of partners, he scored his second 50 from 55 balls. While Merv Hughes and Whitney shared the bowling honours, Craig McDermott's two wickets took him past the series record for an Australian against India. In his second spell of Australia's second innings, Kapil Dev claimed his 400th wicket when Mark Taylor was lbw. With Australia's overall lead just 105, the match was still wide open, until David Boon, Dean Jones and Moody – who shared 173 for the fourth wicket – put it out of India's reach.

India were left a minimum of 107 overs to chase 442. Kris Srikkanth and Sidhu started briskly, and on the final morning took their stand to 82, India's highest opening partnership of the series. Yet less than two hours after Reiffel broke it with his maiden Test wicket, Australia were winners. Whitney, brought on 40 minutes before lunch, toppled seven batsmen in 8.5 overs, while conceding 26 runs. Five of his victims were caught in the arc between wicketkeeper and gully, as were both of Reiffel's, including the prize wicket of Tendulkar.

Australia

M. A. Taylor c Srikkanth b Kapil Dev	2	– (2) lbw b Kapil Dev	16
W. N. Phillips c More b Prabhakar	8	– (1) c Kapil Dev b Srinath	14
D. C. Boon c Sidhu b Prabhakar	107	– c Kapil Dev b Prabhakar	38
*A. R. Border c Srikkanth b Kapil Dev	59	– (8) not out	20
D. M. Jones c Srikkanth b Raju	7	– (4) not out	150
T. M. Moody c Vengsarkar b Prabhakar	50	– (5) c More b Kapil Dev	101
†I. A. Healy c More b Srinath	28	– (6) c More b Raju	7
M. G. Hughes c Srikkanth b Srinath	24	– (7) c Tendulkar b Srinath	11
P. R. Reiffel c More b Prabhakar	9		
C. J. McDermott c Srikkanth b Prabhakar	31		
M. R. Whitney not out	1		
B 1, l-b 7, n-b 12	20	L-b 4, n-b 6	10

1/10 (2) 2/21 (1) 3/138 (4)   (125.5 overs) 346
4/145 (5) 5/232 (6) 6/259 (3)
7/290 (7) 8/303 (8) 9/338 (9) 10/346 (10)

1/27 (1)   (6 wkts dec, 113.3 overs) 367
2/31 (2)
3/113 (3) 4/286 (5) 5/298 (6) 6/315 (7)

Kapil Dev 40–12–103–2; Prabhakar 32.5–9–101–5; Srinath 25–5–69–2; Tendulkar 5–2–9–0; Raju 23–6–56–1. *Second innings*—Kapil Dev 28–8–48–2; Prabhakar 32–4–116–1; Srinath 29.3–4–121–2; Raju 24–5–78–1.

India

K. Srikkanth c Boon b McDermott	34	– c Jones b Whitney	38
N. S. Sidhu c Healy b Hughes	5	– c Jones b Reiffel	35
S. V. Manjrekar c Jones b Hughes	31	– c Healy b Whitney	8
S. R. Tendulkar c Moody b Whitney	114	– c Moody b Reiffel	5
D. B. Vengsarkar c Taylor b Hughes	1	– c Moody b Whitney	4
*M. Azharuddin c Healy b McDermott	11	– lbw b Whitney	24
S. L. V. Raju c Taylor b Whitney	1	– (10) c Healy b Whitney	8
Kapil Dev c Hughes b Whitney	4	– (7) lbw b Whitney	0
M. Prabhakar c Reiffel b Whitney	0	– (8) c Healy b McDermott	3
†K. S. More c Healy b Hughes	43	– (9) c Taylor b Whitney	1
J. Srinath not out	5	– not out	1
L-b 14, n-b 9	23	L-b 11, n-b 3	14

1/25 (2) 2/69 (1) 3/100 (3)   (89.5 overs) 272
4/109 (5) 5/130 (6) 6/135 (7)
7/159 (8) 8/159 (9) 9/240 (4) 10/272 (10)

1/82 (2) 2/90 (1)   (55.1 overs) 141
3/97 (4) 4/103 (5) 5/111 (3) 6/111 (7)
7/126 (8) 8/129 (9) 9/134 (6) 10/141 (10)

McDermott 21–6–47–2; Hughes 26.5–5–82–4; Reiffel 17–5–46–0; Whitney 23–4–68–4; Moody 2–0–15–0. *Second innings*—McDermott 20–8–44–1; Hughes 12–2–25–0; Reiffel 11–2–34–2; Whitney 12.1–3–27–7.

Umpires: A. R. Crafter and T. A. Prue.
Referee: P. B. H. May.

169 v SOUTH AFRICA, 1997 Dicky Rutnagur, *Wisden* 1998

The Second Test of India's tour to South Africa in 1996-97 led to another scintillating show from Tendulkar in a losing cause, as the Indian batsmen struggled to adjust to the local pace and bounce. After an innings defeat in Durban, Tendulkar's India fared better at Newlands. A glorious partnership between him and Azharuddin failed to avert another Indian defeat on foreign soil. But, for one sunny afternoon in Cape Town, under the gaze of Table Mountain, the outcome seemed of little relevance.

A stand of 222 between Tendulkar and Azharuddin not only averted another abbreviated Test, but also illuminated the game with its sheer brilliance and aggression in the face of adversity. It occupied just 40 overs. Azharuddin, scoring 115 in 110 balls, with 19 fours and a six, provided the major share. But Tendulkar kept going to save India from following on and was last out, after nearly six hours, to an outstanding catch by Adam Bacher at deep midwicket.

India were 58 for five when Tendulkar and Azharuddin came together, replying to South Africa's highest total since isolation, which included three centuries. The first, from Gary Kirsten, took nearly five hours. Javagal Srinath and Venkatesh Prasad had bowled splendidly when fresh but, once they tired, the attack was innocuous, and a firm, true pitch encouraged aggression.

Lance Klusener launched a spectacular century – 102 in 100 balls, the fastest recorded in terms of balls by a South African Test player. He had not finished. Before the close, Klusener ran out Woorkeri Raman and had experimental opener Rahul Dravid playing on. Nightwatchman Prasad lasted only one ball against Paul Adams. In the first over next morning, Sourav Ganguly steered Allan Donald to second slip. V. V. S. Laxman, after an uneasy half-hour, deflected Shaun Pollock down the leg side.

That was the start of the Tendulkar–Azharuddin stand, whose tone belied India's desperate plight. Azharuddin, free of the responsibilities of the captaincy, played the more exotic – and often unorthodox – shots; Tendulkar was more orderly, but attacked in a grand manner. In a six-over spell after lunch, Klusener was hit for 30 and South Africa were forced on to the defensive. Azharuddin constantly took risks and, with the stand at 197, Hansie Cronje held a skimming drive at extra cover, but, landing on his elbows, lost his grip. A run later, Tendulkar played a square cut to gully which a juggling Andrew Hudson muffed. But an over or two of restraint caused Azharuddin to fret, and he ran himself out with India 50 short of saving the follow-on. Tendulkar averted it with two wickets standing.

India's recovery continued as they captured three wickets for only 33, but partnerships between Hudson and Daryll Cullinan and then Brian McMillan and Pollock played them out of the match. Cronje's declaration, 426 ahead, left South Africa a minimum of 118 overs to bowl India out, but they needed only 67.

South Africa

A. C. Hudson c Mongia b Prasad	16	–	b Srinath	55
G. Kirsten run out	103	–	lbw b Ganesh	0
A. M. Bacher c Mongia b Srinath	25	–	lbw b Srinath	0
D. J. Cullinan c Mongia b Prasad	77	–	(5) b Kumble	55
*W. J. Cronje c Mongia b Srinath	41	–	(6) c Dravid b Kumble	18
B. M. McMillan not out	103	–	(7) not out	59
S. M. Pollock c Tendulkar b Prasad	1	–	(8) not out	40
†D. J. Richardson c Dravid b Srinath	39			
L. Klusener not out	102	–	(4) c Dravid b Srinath	12
B 5, l-b 9, n-b 8	22		B 4, l-b 12, w 1	17

1/37 (1) 2/89 (3) (7 wkts dec, 162.5 overs) 529
3/203 (2) 4/251 (4)
5/291 (5) 6/299 (7) 7/382 (8)

1/6 (2) (6 wkts dec, 72 overs) 256
2/7 (3)
3/33 (4) 4/127 (5) 5/133 (1) 6/155 (6)

A. A. Donald and P. R. Adams did not bat.

Srinath 38–8–130–3; Prasad 36–1–114–3; Ganesh 23.5–6–93–0; Kumble 51–7–136–0; Ganguly 9–1–24–0; Raman 5–1–18–0. *Second innings*—Srinath 18–5–78–3; Ganesh 10–3–38–1; Prasad 7–1–16–0; Kumble 25–4–58–2; Ganguly 2–0–5–0; Raman 10–0–45–0.

India

W. V. Raman run out	5	–	c Richardson b Pollock	16
R. Dravid b Klusener	2	–	(3) c Richardson b Adams	12
S. C. Ganguly c McMillan b Donald	23	–	(4) c McMillan b Pollock	30
B. K. V. Prasad b Adams	0	–	(10) st Richardson b Adams	15
*S. R. Tendulkar c Bacher b McMillan	169	–	c Klusener b McMillan	9
V. V. S. Laxman c Richardson b Pollock	5	–	(7) not out	35
M. Azharuddin run out	115	–	(6) c Hudson b Donald	2
†N. R. Mongia lbw b Adams	5	–	(2) b Donald	2
A. Kumble c Richardson b Donald	2	–	(8) c Richardson b Adams	14
J. Srinath b Pollock	11	–	absent injured	
D. Ganesh not out	2	–	(9) b Donald	1
L-b 9, n-b 11	20		L-b 1, w 2, n-b 5	8

1/7 (1) 2/24 (2) 3/25 (4) 4/33 (3) (92.2 overs) 359
5/58 (6) 6/280 (7) 7/298 (8)
8/315 (9) 9/340 (10) 10/359 (5)

1/7 (2) 2/26 (1) (66.2 overs) 144
3/44 (3) 4/59 (5)
5/61 (6) 6/87 (4) 7/115 (8) 8/121 (9) 9/144 (10)

Donald 24–3–99–2; Pollock 23–2–76–2; Adams 18–5–49–2; Klusener 12–1–88–1; McMillan 6.2–0–22–1; Cronje 9–5–16–0. *Second innings*—Donald 18–5–40–3; Pollock 12–2–29–2; Klusener 9–3–13–0; McMillan 11–4–16–1; Adams 16.2–4–45–3.

Umpires: D. B. Hair and R. E. Koertzen.   Third umpire: C. J. Mitchley.
Referee: B. N. Jarman.

155* v AUSTRALIA, 1998   Dicky Rutnagur, *Wisden* 1999

Rarely has a contest between two individuals been the focus of as much attention in a team game: Sachin Tendulkar v Shane Warne was the battle royale of the Border–Gavaskar Trophy in 1997-98. Tendulkar had spent days preparing for Warne by getting the former Indian leg-spinner Laxman Sivaramakrishnan to bowl round the wicket into the rough outside leg stump. In the Mumbai v Australia game at the Brabourne Stadium that preceded this Test, the signs were ominous for the tourists: Mumbai won by ten wickets on the back of Tendulkar's double-century, and Warne's figures read 16–1–111–0. Tendulkar was just warming up.

In On Warne, *Gideon Haigh tells the story of Tendulkar's innings in the First Test at Chennai, as Warne – having captured his wicket cheaply on the first day – was brought on to bowl to him straightaway in the second innings. After Tendulkar hit three fours in the first over, Warne told his captain Mark Taylor: "Tubs, we're stuffed."*

Tendulkar went on to have a remarkable series. He scored 79 in the Second Test at Kolkata (Warne went wicketless again) as India won by an innings and 219 runs, and 177 in the Third at Bangalore, where Australia managed a consolation victory.

The head-to-head contest between Sachin Tendulkar and Shane Warne was the key to this opening encounter. Warne's quick conquest of Tendulkar in the first innings gave Australia the initial advantage. But Tendulkar retaliated so devastatingly in the second, scoring 155 not out, that India were able to declare with a lead of 347, and 105 overs to bowl Australia out on a spinners' pitch. They had three men out overnight and won in comfort on the final afternoon.

On the first day, Tendulkar had been as much a victim of Warne's guile as of his own daring. He drove his first ball with scorching power past the bowler. But the fifth dipped as he rushed forward, and turned to take the edge of his flailing bat; Taylor completed a marvellous slip catch. In the second innings, however, when Tendulkar scored his third and highest century in seven Tests against Australia, he was as severe on Warne as on the rest. Warne followed up his first-innings four for 85 with a deflating one for 122. Tendulkar's belligerence was awesome and his shot-placement enthralling.

Both sides batted erratically at their first attempt. After an opening stand of 122 between Sidhu and Nayan Mongia, three Indian wickets went down for eight and the last five for ten. They were saved because Dravid batted four hours and built respectable stands with Azharuddin and Kumble. Warne and the tall debutant off-spinner Gavin Robertson skilfully exploited the batsmen's indiscretions. Each picked up four wickets.

In reply, Australia stumbled to 137 for six: only Mark Waugh, who lasted three hours, batted with distinction. They were hauled back into the game by the indomitable Ian Healy. He made a fighting 90, and put on 96 with Robertson, splendidly accomplished for a No. 10. They looked so much at ease as they set up a lead of 71 that the pitch seemed to have dozed off.

This impression stayed when India resumed on the third evening. Warne had already been softened up by Sidhu before Tendulkar came in at 115 for two. He and Dravid almost doubled that. Then, when Australia rather fortuitously prised Dravid out, Azharuddin joined Tendulkar to pound a wilting attack for another 127 runs in even time, a stand reminiscent of their epic in Cape Town 14 months earlier. In all, Tendulkar batted for 286 minutes and 191 balls, and struck 14 fours and four sixes.

Azharuddin's declaration gave Australia 15 overs on the fourth evening, in which India grabbed three wickets. These disasters extinguished Australia's hopes of winning.

India

†N. R. Mongia c Healy b Kasprowicz	58	– lbw b Blewett	18
N. S. Sidhu run out	62	– c Ponting b Robertson	64
R. Dravid c Robertson b Warne	52	– c Healy b Warne	56
S. R. Tendulkar c Taylor b Warne	4	– not out	155
*M. Azharuddin c Reiffel b Warne	26	– c S. R. Waugh b M. E. Waugh	64
S. C. Ganguly lbw b Robertson	3	– not out	30
A. Kumble c S. R. Waugh b Robertson	30		
J. Srinath c Taylor b Warne	1		
R. K. Chauhan c Healy b Robertson	3		
Harvinder Singh not out	0		
S. L. V. Raju b Robertson	0		
B 8, l-b 6, n-b 4	18	B 18, l-b 6, n-b 7	31

1/122 (1) 2/126 (2) 3/130 (4)   (104.2 overs) 257
4/186 (5) 5/195 (6) 6/247 (7)
7/248 (8) 8/253 (9) 9/257 (3) 10/257 (11)

1/43 (1)   (4 wkts dec, 107 overs) 418
2/115 (2)
3/228 (3) 4/355 (5)

Kasprowicz 21–8–44–1; Reiffel 15–4–27–0; Warne 35–11–85–4; Robertson 28.2–4–72–4; M. E. Waugh 1–0–4–0; S. R. Waugh 4–1–11–0. *Second innings*—Kasprowicz 14–6–42–0; Reiffel 9–1–32–0; Robertson 27–4–92–1; Warne 30–7–122–1; Blewett 10–2–35–1; M. E. Waugh 9–0–44–1; S. R. Waugh 8–0–27–0.

Australia

*M. A. Taylor c Mongia b Harvinder Singh	12	– (2) c Srinath b Kumble	13
M. J. Slater c Dravid b Kumble	11	– (1) b Srinath	13
M. E. Waugh c Ganguly b Raju	66	– (5) c Dravid b Kumble	18
S. R. Waugh b Kumble	12	– (6) c Dravid b Raju	27
R. T. Ponting c Mongia b Raju	18	– (7) lbw b Raju	2
G. S. Blewett lbw b Chauhan	9	– (3) c Dravid b Kumble	5
†I. A. Healy c Ganguly b Raju	90	– (8) not out	32
P. R. Reiffel c Dravid b Kumble	15	– (4) c Azharuddin b Raju	8
S. K. Warne c Tendulkar b Kumble	17	– c Kumble b Chauhan	35
G. R. Robertson c Mongia b Srinath	57	– b Chauhan	0
M. S. Kasprowicz not out	11	– c Srinath b Kumble	4
B 1, l-b 6, n-b 3	10	B 4, l-b 3, n-b 4	11

1/16 (2) 2/44 (1) 3/57 (4) 4/95 (5)   (130.3 overs) 328
5/119 (6) 6/137 (3) 7/173 (8)
8/201 (9) 9/297 (7) 10/328 (10)

1/18 (1) 2/30 (3)   (67.5 overs) 168
3/31 (2) 4/54 (5) 5/79 (4)
6/91 (7) 7/96 (6) 8/153 (9) 9/153 (10) 10/168 (11)

Srinath 17.3–3–46–1; Harvinder Singh 11–4–28–1; Kumble 45–10–103–4; Chauhan 25–3–90–1; Raju 32–8–54–3. *Second innings*—Srinath 6–4–9–1; Harvinder Singh 2–0–9–0; Chauhan 22–7–66–2; Kumble 22.5–7–46–4; Raju 15–4–31–3.

Umpires: G. Sharp and S. Venkataraghavan.   Third umpire: K. Murali.
Referee: P. L. van der Merwe.

143 v AUSTRALIA, 1998 Wisden 1999

Unfortunately for Australia and Warne, the Tendulkar headache persisted even after the Border–Gavaskar Trophy, as the two teams, plus New Zealand, headed to Sharjah for a triangular tournament. This is where the cult of Tendulkar reached a new level, thanks to two match-winning innings against Australia, two days apart – the first hundred to qualify for the final, the next to win India the trophy. His 134 in the final, on his 25th birthday, helped chase down a challenging 273. But it was the first of his centuries that came to be regarded as one of the finest one-day innings of all time: a virtual one-man show in a card that recorded scores of 17, 35, 14, 1, 23 and 5 from his team-mates. With the local climate interrupting the game, Indians still refer to it as Tendulkar's "desert sandstorm" innings.

At stake was whether India or New Zealand would join Australia in the final. Spectators and organisers were eager to avoid an all-Antipodean final, but Australia were less keen to oblige. Michael Bevan, scoring his third century in one-day internationals, and Mark Waugh took advantage of a true pitch and slipshod fielding. India then had two targets: 285 to win the match, 254 to qualify on run-rate. After a dust storm accounted for four overs, these were revised to 276 and 237. Their success was thanks to a glorious 143 from Tendulkar. His highest score in limited-overs internationals (and the third-highest for India) took 131 balls and included nine fours and five sixes. India lost the match, but achieved their main objective.

Australia

†A. C. Gilchrist c Mongia b Harvinder Singh	11	T. M. Moody c Azharuddin b Prasad	5
M. E. Waugh c Ganguly b Tendulkar	81	S. K. Warne not out	7
R. T. Ponting st Mongia b Harbhajan Singh	31	L-b 4, w 6, n-b 1	11
D. R. Martyn b Kumble	1		
M. G. Bevan not out	101	1/17 (1) 2/84 (3)	(7 wkts, 50 overs) 284
*S. R. Waugh run out	10	3/87 (4) 4/177 (2)	
D. S. Lehmann b Prasad	26	5/197 (6) 6/250 (7) 7/271 (8)	

M. S. Kasprowicz and D. W. Fleming did not bat.

Prasad 8–0–41–2; Harvinder Singh 7–0–44–1; Kumble 10–0–41–1; Harbhajan Singh 8–0–63–1; Ganguly 2–0–15–0; Kanitkar 6–0–33–0; Laxman 4–0–16–0; Tendulkar 5–0–27–1.

India

S. C. Ganguly lbw b Fleming	17	H. H. Kanitkar not out	5
S. R. Tendulkar c Gilchrist b Fleming	143	L-b 5, w 3, n-b 4	12
†N. R. Mongia c M. E. Waugh b Moody	35		
*M. Azharuddin b Moody	14	1/38 (1) 2/107 (3)	(5 wkts, 46 overs) 250
A. Jadeja c Gilchrist b S. R. Waugh	1	3/135 (4) 4/138 (5)	
V. V. S. Laxman not out	23	5/242 (2)	

A. Kumble, Harvinder Singh, B. K. V. Prasad and Harbhajan Singh did not bat.

Fleming 10–0–46–2; Kasprowicz 9–0–55–0; Warne 9–0–39–0; Moody 9–0–40–2; S. R. Waugh 9–0–65–1.

Umpires: S. A. Bucknor and I. D. Robinson. Third umpire: Javed Akhtar.
Referee: Talat Ali.

136 v PAKISTAN, 1999 Qamar Ahmed, *Wisden* 2000

If Tendulkar were allowed to rewrite the script of just one match in a career featuring 200 Tests and 463 one-day internationals, this would be it. Struggling with back spasms, he took India to within inches of the finishing line, only to fall to Saqlain Mushtaq. India lost the Test by 12 runs, and a devastated Tendulkar could not bring himself to attend the post-match presentation – the only time in a 24-year career that he never collected his Man of the Match award. Instead, he locked himself in the dressing-room, and cried. In his autobiography, he wrote: "My world seemed to collapse around me and I just couldn't hold back the tears... My back was in horrible shape and mentally I was at a serious low." India went on to square the series in the next Test, at Delhi, but Pakistan's win in the Asian Test Championship a month later secured an informal decider.

The first Test between India and Pakistan for nine years began amid massive security, after vandalism by Hindu extremists had forced the Indian Board to transfer the match from Delhi to Chennai. The Chidambaram Stadium was guarded by 3,000 police and military officials. Well before the end of the game, though, the talk was not of politics but of thrilling cricket.

A nail-biting finish on the fourth day saw India, chasing 271, slump to 82 for five – two of the wickets controversially given out by umpire Steve Dunne. When Tendulkar and Mongia combined to add 136 for the sixth wicket, however, they seemed to be on their way to victory. Then Mongia was caught for 52. Still Tendulkar kept going, despite a back strain, and India were only 17 from their target when he holed out at mid-off, trying to hit Saqlain Mushtaq out of the ground. He had batted 405 minutes and scored 136, his 18th Test hundred, including 18 fours. But India's last three wickets added only four more runs; Saqlain finished them off with five for 93, giving him ten for 187 in the match. The Pakistanis bowed to the ground in prayer and embarked on a lap of honour, to a standing ovation from the Chennai crowd, whose sporting behaviour won much praise.

On the opening day, Pakistan chose to bat and were struggling at 91 for five. They fought back through Yousuf Youhana and Moin Khan, who both hit fifties. Wasim Akram added a lusty 38 before Kumble polished off the tail for figures of six for 70.

Sadagoppan Ramesh, who was making his Test debut on his home ground, and Laxman put on a brisk 48 for India that evening, but both were dismissed by Wasim within half an hour of play resuming. Then

Saqlain took the first of his 20 wickets in this series when his tantalising length accounted for Tendulkar; the batsman dashed down the wicket, mis-hit and scooped a catch to backward point for a third-ball duck. But Dravid and Ganguly helped India towards a narrow 16-run lead before the spinners finished them off.

Shahid Afridi took the last three wickets with his leg-breaks, and the third day belonged to him as a batsman – he disproved the theory that he was merely a limited-overs man by batting more than five hours for 141, striking 21 fours and three sixes, helped mainly by Inzamam-ul-Haq and Salim Malik. At 275 for four, Pakistan looked impregnable. But after tea, six wickets fell for 11.

That left India needing 271, with the odds against them; their best fourth-innings total to win a home Test was 256 for eight against Australia in 1964-65. Thanks to Tendulkar's century, they almost got there, but Pakistan were victors by a mere 12 runs.

Pakistan

Saeed Anwar lbw b Srinath	24	– lbw b Prasad	7
Shahid Afridi c Ganguly b Srinath	11	– b Prasad	141
Ijaz Ahmed, sen. lbw b Kumble	13	– c and b Kumble	11
Inzamam-ul-Haq c and b Kumble	10	– c Laxman b Tendulkar	51
Yousuf Youhana lbw b Tendulkar	53	– b Tendulkar	26
Salim Malik b Srinath	8	– c Dravid b Joshi	32
†Moin Khan c Ganguly b Kumble	60	– c Mongia b Prasad	3
*Wasim Akram c Laxman b Kumble	38	– c Joshi b Prasad	1
Saqlain Mushtaq lbw b Kumble	2	– lbw b Prasad	0
Nadeem Khan c Dravid b Kumble	8	– not out	1
Waqar Younis not out	0	– c Ramesh b Prasad	5
L-b 5, n-b 6	11	B 1, l-b 4, n-b 3	8

1/32 (2) 2/41 (1) 3/61 (4) 4/66 (3)   (79.5 overs) 238   1/11 (1) 2/42 (3)   (71.2 overs) 286
5/91 (6) 6/154 (5) 7/214 (7)   3/139 (4) 4/169 (5) 5/275 (6) 6/278 (7)
8/227 (8) 9/237 (10) 10/238 (9)   7/279 (2) 8/279 (9) 9/280 (8) 10/286 (11)

Srinath 15–3–63–3; Prasad 16–1–54–0; Kumble 24.5–7–70–6; Joshi 21–8–36–0; Tendulkar 3–0–10–1. *Second innings—*Srinath 16–1–68–0; Prasad 10.2–5–33–6; Kumble 22–4–93–1; Joshi 14–3–42–1; Tendulkar 7–1–35–2; Laxman 2–0–10–0.

India

S. Ramesh lbw b Wasim Akram	43	– c Inzamam-ul-Haq b Waqar Younis	5
V. V. S. Laxman lbw b Wasim Akram	23	– lbw b Waqar Younis	0
R. Dravid lbw b Saqlain Mushtaq	53	– b Wasim Akram	10
S. R. Tendulkar c Salim Malik b Saqlain Mushtaq	0	– c Wasim Akram b Saqlain Mushtaq	136
*M. Azharuddin c Inzamam-ul-Haq b Saqlain Mushtaq	11	– lbw b Saqlain Mushtaq	7
S. C. Ganguly c Ijaz Ahmed, sen. b Shahid Afridi	54	– c Moin Khan b Saqlain Mushtaq	2
†N. R. Mongia st Moin Khan b Saqlain Mushtaq	5	– c Waqar Younis b Wasim Akram	52
A. Kumble c Yousuf Youhana b Saqlain Mushtaq	4	– (9) lbw b Wasim Akram	1
S. B. Joshi not out	25	– (8) c and b Saqlain Mushtaq	8
J. Srinath c Ijaz Ahmed, sen. b Shahid Afridi	10	– b Saqlain Mushtaq	1
B. K. V. Prasad st Moin Khan b Shahid Afridi	4	– not out	0
B 2, l-b 2, n-b 18	22	B 8, l-b 10, n-b 18	36

1/67 (2) 2/71 (1) 3/72 (4) 4/103 (5)   (81.1 overs) 254   1/5 (1) 2/6 (2) 3/50 (3)   (95.2 overs) 258
5/156 (3) 6/166 (7) 7/188 (8)   4/73 (5) 5/82 (6) 6/218 (7)
8/229 (6) 9/246 (10) 10/254 (11)   7/254 (4) 8/256 (9) 9/256 (8) 10/258 (10)

Wasim Akram 20–4–60–2; Waqar Younis 12–2–48–0; Saqlain Mushtaq 35–8–94–5; Shahid Afridi 7.1–0–31–3; Nadeem Khan 7–0–17–0. *Second innings—*Wasim Akram 22–4–80–3; Waqar Younis 12–6–26–2; Shahid Afridi 16–7–23–0; Saqlain Mushtaq 32.2–8–93–5; Nadeem Khan 13–5–18–0.

Umpires: R. S. Dunne and V. K. Ramaswamy.   Third umpire: A. V. Jayaprakash.
Referee: C. W. Smith.

98 v PAKISTAN, 2003

The build-up to this marquee clash at the 2003 World Cup had begun a year in advance, when the ICC announced the draw. Tendulkar captured the mood: for days before the game, he had trouble sleeping. India had won each of their three previous World Cup encounters with Pakistan. And, while this group-stage match was not crucial to their qualifying chances, it was vital to the morale of a nation whose cricket-loving public had made one thing quite clear: lose any other game, but not this one.

Though the players played down the first clash between India and Pakistan since June 2000, it remained the tournament's most feverishly talked-up match. Almost incredibly, the cricket lived up to the hype. Under a hot sun and in front of a crammed stadium (and a TV audience implausibly guesstimated at a billion) Tendulkar played an astounding innings – perhaps the best of the tournament, and undoubtedly one of his best in one-day internationals. Chasing 274, on a shirtfront but against a testosterone-propelled pace attack, he hit a vivid and memorable stream of shots, none so perfect as the cut six and the two fours – one swirled into the leg side, one pushed down the ground – which concluded Shoaib Akhtar's first over. By the 12th, India had reached 100; Tendulkar, missed on 32 and struggling with cramp, went on to 98 from 75 balls. After the storm came calm, as Dravid and Yuvraj Singh eased home to maintain India's pristine World Cup record (four wins out of four) against Pakistan. All along it had been a batsman's match, started by Saeed Anwar, whose century, full of dextrous, angle-batted shots, contained only seven boundaries. It took the ball of the game – a rapid Ashish Nehra yorker – to remove him. Younis Khan provided a late, impish flourish, along with Rashid Latif, who was hit on the helmet and could not keep wicket. But the 28 extras in India's innings were not so much an indictment of Taufeeq Umar's keeping as of the experienced fast bowlers who billowed in with passion but not discipline. The win guaranteed India's progress and nudged the door further open for England.

Pakistan

Saeed Anwar b Nehra	101	†Rashid Latif not out	29
Taufeeq Umar b Khan	22	Wasim Akram not out	10
Abdul Razzaq c Dravid b Nehra	12	B 2, l-b 7, w 11, n-b 7	27
Inzamam-ul-Haq run out	6		—
Yousuf Youhana c Khan b Srinath	25	1/58 (2) 2/90 (3)	(7 wkts, 50 overs) 273
Younis Khan c Mongia b Khan	32	3/98 (4) 4/171 (5)	
Shahid Afridi c Kumble b Mongia	9	5/195 (1) 6/208 (7) 7/256 (6)	

*Waqar Younis and Shoaib Akhtar did not bat.

Khan 10–0–46–2; Srinath 10–0–41–1; Nehra 10–0–74–2; Kumble 10–0–51–0; Ganguly 3–0–14–0; Sehwag 4–0–19–0; Mongia 3–0–19–1.

India

S. R. Tendulkar c Younis Khan b Shoaib Akhtar	98	Yuvraj Singh not out	50
V. Sehwag c Shahid Afridi b Waqar Younis	21	B 1, l-b 3, w 19, n-b 5	28
*S. C. Ganguly lbw b Waqar Younis	0		—
M. Kaif b Shahid Afridi	35	1/53 (2) 2/53 (3) 3/155 (4)	(4 wkts, 45.4 overs) 276
†R. Dravid not out	44	4/177 (1)	

D. Mongia, A. Kumble, Zaheer Khan, J. Srinath and A. Nehra did not bat.

Wasim Akram 10–0–48–0; Shoaib Akhtar 10–0–72–1; Waqar Younis 8.4–0–71–2; Shahid Afridi 9–0–45–1; Abdul Razzaq 8–0–36–0.

Umpires: R. E. Koertzen and D. R. Shepherd.   Third umpire: B. F. Bowden.
Referee: M. J. Procter.

241* v AUSTRALIA, 2004   Matthew Engel, *Wisden* 2005

Each of Tendulkar's best innings seems to bring out a unique facet of his batting, whether it is explosive violence, patient accumulation, quiet domination or exemplary discipline. The double-century in Sydney not only took India close to winning their first Test series in Australia, it was an almost superhuman display of self-denial outside off stump. As Ricky Ponting points out in the foreword, it is one thing to make a plan, quite another to stick with it while scoring 241 not out.

In strict cricketing terms, this should be remembered for the way India batted Australia out of the game, ensuring a drawn series, maintaining their hold on the Border–Gavaskar Trophy and consolidating their presumed new position as No. 1 contenders to Australia's crown. But cricket was a secondary feature of this extraordinary occasion, a mere backdrop. The contest was compelling enough, but it was taken over – hijacked almost – for a farewell the like of which cricket, normally a diffident kind of sport, had never seen.

Steve Waugh's 168th and positively last Test (no one would dare attempt a comeback after this) turned into one long wallow, starting with adulatory wraparound newspaper souvenir supplements and culminating in Waugh being chaired round the SCG by his team-mates. John Williamson's nostalgic anthem "True Blue" competed with the roars of a record last-day crowd, many waving red rags, Waugh's customary comfort-object. No one had ever left the cricketing stage like this; no one had dared.

The Indians? They just dominated the Test match. Ganguly called correctly and condemned Australia to the field on a belting wicket, in extreme heat, with a weakened attack and less than 72 hours after the previous Test.

It was tough for Australia on the first day, which started with a blistering 72 from Sehwag and an outbreak of no-balls from Brett Lee. But there were even more ominous features for Australia. They were set intently, behind the grille of his helmet, and they belonged to Tendulkar. Shrewd observers of the series sensed that he might impose himself in this Test, though no one would have guessed quite how. Tendulkar had thought through his problems to the point of cutting out one of his most distinguished strokes, abandoning the cover-drive and instead just waiting for the chance to hit to leg. He maintained this policy for 613 minutes and 436 deliveries, scoring an unbeaten 241, his highest first-class score and perhaps the highest ever made by a man still nowhere near his own top form. Twenty-eight of his 33 fours and 188 of his runs came on the leg side. His 32nd Test hundred matched Waugh; only Sunil Gavaskar, on 34, remained ahead. He was also the fourth man to reach 9,000 Test runs, two days ahead of Brian Lara in Cape Town.

Tendulkar put on 353, an Indian fourth-wicket record, with Laxman, whose 178 was of a different order: a lovely innings, full of perfectly timed caresses. The crowd never gave the partnership the credit it deserved, partly because they were obsessed with Waugh, partly because the over-elaborate Sydney scoreboard's failings meant only statisticians noted the 300 stand.

When Laxman was out, it was 547 for four, which in a normal series would be deemed unassailable. But Australia had scored 556 in Adelaide and lost, and Ganguly rightly decided to bat on and on, 39 minutes into the third day.

It was yet another sign, however, that India were now playing cricket every bit as ruthlessly as Australia. When Ganguly finally gave over, at 705 for seven – India's highest Test total, and the second-highest conceded by Australia – the response was predictably savage. The Australian openers put on 147. The third-day crowd were mostly interested in Waugh, who scored a cameo 40, after which they streamed out. Waugh himself was still intent on business and refused to doff his helmet, sensing this was not his real farewell innings. Less noticed, Simon Katich became the fourth centurion of the game next day with an innings of lithe grace and huge promise, thus restricting India's lead to 231.

Again, Ganguly was criticised by pundits for not enforcing the follow-on, though again he was right: avoiding any risk of defeat before thinking of victory. Dravid and Tendulkar extended the lead to 442 before Kumble set to work again, sharing the new ball on the fourth evening. At 196 for four there was some danger of an Aussie defeat, but that presupposed a failure by Waugh. Not here, not today. He never quite got the century all Australia wanted, but he batted with the ease and grace of a man at the peak of his career. Then, cricket being cricket, Waugh finally slipped away.

India

A. Chopra b Lee	45	– c Martyn b Gillespie		2
V. Sehwag c Gilchrist b Gillespie	72	– c Gillespie b MacGill		47
R. Dravid lbw b Gillespie	38	– not out		91
S. R. Tendulkar not out	241	– not out		60
V. V. S. Laxman b Gillespie	178			
*S. C. Ganguly b Lee	16			
†P. A. Patel c Gilchrist b Lee	62			
A. B. Agarkar b Lee	2			
I. K. Pathan not out	13			
B 4, l-b 5, w4, n-b 25	38	L-b 3, w 1, n-b 7		11

1/123 (2) 2/128 (1) (7 wkts dec, 187.3 overs) 705 1/11 (1) (2 wkts dec, 43.2 overs) 211
3/194 (3) 4/547 (5) 2/73 (2)
5/570 (6) 6/671 (7) 7/678 (8)

A. Kumble and M. Kartik did not bat.

Lee 39.3–5–201–4; Gillespie 45–11–135–3; Bracken 37–13–97–0; MacGill 38–5–146–0; Waugh 2–0–6–0; Katich 17–1–84–0; Martyn 9–1–27–0. *Second innings*—Lee 12.2–2–75–0; Gillespie 7–2–32–1; MacGill 16–1–65–1; Bracken 8–0–36–0.

Australia

J. L. Langer c Patel b Kumble	117	– c Sehwag b Kartik		47
M. L. Hayden c Ganguly b Kumble	67	– c Dravid b Kumble		30
R. T. Ponting lbw b Kumble	25	– c and b Pathan		47
D. R. Martyn c and b Kumble	7	– c sub (Yuvraj Singh) b Kumble		40
*S. R. Waugh c Patel b Pathan	40	– c Tendulkar b Kumble		80
S. M. Katich c Sehwag b Kumble	125	– not out		77
†A. C. Gilchrist b Pathan	6	– st Patel b Kumble		4
B. Lee c Chopra b Kumble	0			
J. N. Gillespie st Patel b Kumble	47	– (8) not out		4
N. W. Bracken c Agarkar b Kumble	2			
S. C. G.MacGill not out	0			
B 6, l-b 9, w3, n-b 20	38	B 6, l-b 7, w2, n-b 13		28

1/147 (2) 2/214 (1) 3/229 (3) (117.5 overs) 474 1/75 (2) (6 wkts, 94 overs) 357
4/261 (4) 5/311 (5) 6/341 (7) 2/92 (1) 3/170 (4)
7/350 (8) 8/467 (6) 9/473 (9) 10/474 (10) 4/196 (3) 5/338 (5) 6/342 (7)

Agarkar 25–3–116–0; Pathan 26–3–80–2; Kumble 46.5–7–141–8; Kartik 19–1–122–0; Ganguly 1–1–0–0. *Second innings*—Agarkar 10–2–45–0; Kumble 42–8–138–4; Pathan 8–1–26–1; Kartik 26–5–89–1; Tendulkar 6–0–36–0; Sehwag 2–0–10–0.

Umpires: B. F. Bowden and S. A. Bucknor. Third umpire: P. D. Parker.
Referee: M. J. Procter.

103* v ENGLAND, 2008 Scyld Berry, *Wisden* 2009

His century against England in the highest fourth-innings run-chase on the subcontinent was Tendulkar's redemption song. Nearly a decade after his innings against Pakistan in 1999 at the same ground had ended in a flood of tears, Tendulkar had an answer for those critics who claimed he was guilty of not playing enough match-winning innings. His unbeaten 103, just days after the Mumbai terrorist attacks, was like balm for a distraught nation.

A historic occasion, and a magnificent match, culminated in the highest fourth-innings run-chase ever to succeed in an Asian Test, enabling India to win with about an hour to spare. The start came only two weeks after the terrorist attack on Mumbai, and the Test was staged amid "presidential-style" security, but by the end the most famous of all Mumbaikars had gone some way to erasing the memories. In a century he dedicated to all Indians, Sachin Tendulkar masterminded the run-chase after Sehwag had snatched the initiative from England's grasp with batting of equal brilliance.

England went into the game without a warm-up (their first-class game in Vadodara had been cancelled when they flew home after the Mumbai attack) and after only three days of nets in Abu Dhabi. Their lack of match-practice, it could be argued, was decisive, but England's captain Kevin Pietersen and his players never advanced it as an excuse.

Andrew Strauss's last cricket had been in the Stanford tournament (for Middlesex) six weeks before, but he attributed his success – he became the first England batsman to hit a century in each innings of a Test on the subcontinent – to this very freshness of mind. He had been notably decisive about England's duty to return to India, and the same certainty informed his batting. On a slow pitch, where the odd ball leapt alarmingly throughout, he crafted a game plan that played to his strengths: the cut, whenever the ball was short, and the sweep to spin bowling of a full length, without risking the front-foot drive. If a criticism could be made, it was that neither he nor Paul Collingwood forced the pace after reaching hundreds in England's second innings.

It was, nevertheless, a fine achievement for England to win so many sessions until Sehwag overwhelmed them. Strauss and Alastair Cook put together their fourth century opening partnership in eight Tests, and England reached 164 for one at tea on the first day before Zaheer Khan began their demise.

England's first-innings collapse was partially arrested by Matt Prior, in his first Test for a year, and India then struggled to 102 for five. M. S. Dhoni called it "a bad day at the office" when he fronted up for the second-evening press conference.

After Laxman and Tendulkar had been caught and bowled in successive overs from checked drives (Tendulkar was Andrew Flintoff's 200th Test wicket for England), Dhoni made his fifth fifty in six Test innings to take India within striking distance, but it was widely considered that a lead of 75 would be decisive on a disintegrating pitch. Only the pitch did not disintegrate. It had been prepared for a 20-over game in the Champions League cancelled because of the Mumbai attack and, although copious dust arose from the red earth, it just about held together.

England slipped to 43 for three when Yuvraj Singh trapped Pietersen with his first ball. England needed their highest fourth-wicket partnership in Asia, 214 from Strauss and Collingwood, to recover. Together they batted out the third day, added 72 runs off 24 overs next morning, and should have been in a position to ram home England's advantage on the fourth afternoon. But the longer England's innings went on, the more Zaheer Khan and his partner in reverse-swing, Ishant Sharma, slowed them down until Pietersen set India 387 in what would have been 126 overs had his side achieved the required over-rate.

England had been diffident about ramming home the advantage; Sehwag was not. He climbed into the opening bowlers (James Anderson's first two overs cost 15, Steve Harmison's first four 33), mesmerised them into bowling short and wide, and spread the field – which was never brought in again to save singles, allowing India's batsmen to rotate the strike and keep the score ticking over. Only one six had come in the first three innings; Sehwag hit four, upper-cutting Harmison over third man, swinging a full toss from Monty Panesar for six and driving him for another, then pull-driving Graeme Swann. Two balls later, Sehwag missed a sweep at an off-break turning out of Zaheer's footmarks, but his 83 from 68 balls had asserted India's mental dominance once and for all.

Requiring a further 256 on the final day, India were always ahead of the rate. It might not have suited England that Dravid went early when he was so out of form (he had also missed a straightforward slip catch). Gautam Gambhir saw off Flintoff's opening blast on the final day before steering to gully, and after lunch Laxman pushed a leaping off-break to forward short leg, but that was the end of England's victory bid.

Scoring a hundred in a successful fourth-innings run-chase was, according to Tendulkar, something he had wanted, the one achievement missing from his CV: in consequence, he rated his hundred as "up there" and "one of the best". It was a masterclass in its conception – of what shots to play, and how often – and in its execution, especially of the sweep in all its forms. Pietersen changed his bowlers with the greatest frequency but never found a pair to stem the flow. Yuvraj did not allow himself to be wound up second time round, and was only reined in when he restrained himself in order to allow Tendulkar to reach three figures. It was a Test which contained some superlative batting, in various styles – and Strauss deserved a share of the match award for shaping the game, before Sehwag redesigned it and Tendulkar unveiled his masterpiece.

England

A. J. Strauss c and b Mishra	123	– c Laxman b Harbhajan Singh		108
A. N. Cook c Khan b Harbhajan Singh	52	– c Dhoni b Sharma		9
I. R. Bell lbw b Khan	17	– c Gambhir b Mishra		7
*K. P. Pietersen c and b Khan	4	– lbw b Yuvraj Singh		1
P. D. Collingwood c Gambhir b Harbhajan Singh	9	– lbw b Khan		108
A. Flintoff c Gambhir b Mishra	18	– c Dhoni b Sharma		4
J. M. Anderson c Yuvraj Singh b Mishra	19	– (10) not out		1
†M. J. Prior not out	53	– (7) c Sehwag b Sharma		33
G. P. Swann c Dravid b Harbhajan Singh	1	– (8) b Khan		7
S. J. Harmison c Dhoni b Yuvraj Singh	6	– (9) b Khan		1
M. S. Panesar lbw b Sharma	6			
L-b 7, n-b 1	8	B 10, l-b 13, w 2, n-b 7		32

1/118 (2) 2/164 (3) 3/180 (4)   (128.4 overs) 316   1/28 (2) 2/42 (3)   (9 wkts dec, 105.5 overs) 311
4/195 (5) 5/221 (1) 6/229 (6)   3/43 (4) 4/257 (1)
7/271 (7) 8/277 (9) 9/304 (10) 10/316 (11)   5/262 (6) 6/277 (5) 7/297 (8) 8/301 (9) 9/311 (7)

Khan 21–9–41–2; Sharma 19.4–4–32–1; Harbhajan Singh 38–2–96–3; Mishra 34–6–99–3; Yuvraj Singh 15–2–33–1; Sehwag 1–0–8–0. *Second innings*—Khan 27–7–40–3; Sharma 22.5–1–57–3; Mishra 17–1–66–1; Yuvraj Singh 3–1–12–1; Harbhajan Singh 30–3–91–1; Sehwag 6–0–22–0.

India

G. Gambhir lbw b Swann	19	– c Collingwood b Anderson		66
V. Sehwag b Anderson	9	– lbw b Swann		83
R. Dravid lbw b Swann	3	– c Prior b Flintoff		4
S. R. Tendulkar c and b Flintoff	37	– not out		103
V. V. S. Laxman c and b Panesar	24	– c Bell b Swann		26
Yuvraj Singh c Flintoff b Harmison	14	– not out		85
*†M. S. Dhoni c Pietersen b Panesar	53			
Harbhajan Singh c Bell b Panesar	40			
Zaheer Khan lbw b Flintoff	1			
A. Mishra b Flintoff	12			
I. Sharma not out	8			
B 4, l-b 11, n-b 6	21	B 5, l-b 11, n-b 4		20

1/16 (2) 2/34 (1) 3/37 (3)   (69.4 overs) 241   1/117 (2)   (4 wkts, 98.3 overs) 387
4/98 (5) 5/102 (4) 6/137 (6)   2/141 (3)
7/212 (8) 8/217 (9) 9/219 (7) 10/241 (10)   3/183 (1) 4/224 (5)

Harmison 11–1–42–1; Anderson 11–3–28–1; Flintoff 18.4–2–49–3; Swann 10–0–42–2; Panesar 19–4–65–3. *Second innings*—Harmison 10–0–48–0; Anderson 11–1–51–1; Panesar 27–4–105–0; Flintoff 22–1–64–1; Swann 28.3–2–103–2.

Umpires: B. F. Bowden and D. J. Harper.   Third umpire: S. L. Shastri.
Referee: J. J. Crowe.

"I PLAY FOR INDIA. NOW MORE THAN EVER."

David Hopps, *Wisden* 2009

England's 2008-09 tour of India was one of the most politically significant in cricket history. From the moment that the vibrant Indian city of Mumbai fell prey to Islamist extremism, and a shaken touring party flew home without playing the last two one-day matches because of safety fears, arguments resounded about whether they should return to fulfil the two Tests before Christmas. That they did go back was a decision that did them great credit. The prime minister, Gordon Brown, called them "brave and courageous".

From the time that the first TV pictures of the Mumbai atrocities were seen, and England's cricketers – then staying in Bhubaneshwar – looked in disbelief at rolling news footage of fires, gunfights, explosions and bloodied bodies being pulled from the Taj Mahal Hotel, where they had stayed only a fortnight earlier, the two scheduled Tests took on a magnitude far beyond a sporting contest. After much agonising, England did fly back to play – and their choice was widely praised for the defiant message that normal life must proceed however wicked the terrorism...

The First Test in Chennai was a classic in which England, despite defeat, could take pride. This time there really was inestimable value in turning up, in taking part. But when India, against all expectations, stole the game from England's grasp by successfully chasing 387, Kevin Pietersen's captaincy looked exposed. His dissatisfaction with coach Peter Moores's input deepened.

For others, India's victory smacked of karma – the Hindu philosophy of cause and effect – as a foot-perfect, match-winning, unbeaten hundred was scored by Sachin Tendulkar, Mumbai's most celebrated figure. It was a draining innings, but one of complete authority, expressed not by flamboyant flourishes so much as concentration, repetition and accuracy; more than that, it was a suitable reminder that Mumbai was, despite the foreigners caught up in it, essentially an Indian tragedy.

The most resonant image throughout the Chennai Test had been that of Tendulkar, looking drawn and suppressing his emotions as he perched on an armchair for a TV advert that felt more like an address to the nation. He ended it by vowing: "I play for India. Now more than ever." And play he most certainly did. It was the first time he had scored a match-winning century in the fourth innings of a Test. He called afterwards for perspective, acknowledging that he could not assuage the hurt of those who had lost loved ones, but the symbolism was powerful.

200 v SOUTH AFRICA, 2010 Ken Borland, *Wisden* 2011

When Tendulkar began with four dot-balls, there was little sign that history was in the offing at Gwalior. In the end, it was only appropriate that the world's greatest one-day batsman made international cricket's first limited-overs double-century. It was also part of a heady year for Tendulkar, which already included four Test hundreds in six innings. Overall in 2010, he scored 1,766 runs in 14 Tests and two one-day internationals at an average of 84.09.

Sachin Tendulkar produced a dazzling display of top-class strokeplay to become the first man to score a double-century in a one-day international, and sealed India's series victory. He needed just 147 balls, having reached his 46th one-day hundred (to go with 47 in Tests) in 90, and he collected 25 fours and three sixes. From the outset, Tendulkar looked on course for something special. After the early loss of Sehwag, he raced to his fifty in 37 balls, driving superbly square of the wicket; with Dinesh Karthik ensuring his senior partner had plenty of strike, India breezed to 219 for two in the 34th over. Tendulkar had 124 at that stage, and he forged on remorselessly, his placement so perfect, his timing so precise that South Africa were simply blown away. Dhoni's pyrotechnics – seven fours and four sixes off 35 balls – ensured the innings ended in a blur, even though cramp meant Tendulkar was running out of puff towards the end. He passed the previous one-day international record of 194 (shared by Saeed Anwar of Pakistan and Zimbabwe's Charles Coventry) in the 46th over, before being briefly becalmed as Dhoni flailed away. But a single steered behind point off the third ball of the final over brought up the historic 200, amid a tremendous hullabaloo from the capacity crowd. South Africa's batsmen had little stomach for the daunting chase, focusing too much on the overall target rather than building partnerships, although A. B. de Villiers made an excellent century, full of elegant drives.

India

V. Sehwag c Steyn b Parnell	9
S. R. Tendulkar not out	200
K. D. Karthik c Gibbs b Parnell	79
Y. K. Pathan c de Villiers b van der Merwe	36
*†M. S. Dhoni not out	68
L-b 3, w 5, n-b 1	9
1/25 (1) 2/219 (3) (3 wkts, 50 overs)	401
3/300 (4)	

V. Kohli, S. K. Raina, R. A. Jadeja, P. Kumar, A. Nehra and S. Sreesanth did not bat.

Steyn 10–0–89–0; Parnell 10–0–95–2; van der Merwe 10–0–62–1; Langeveldt 10–0–70–0; Duminy 5–0–38–0; Kallis 5–0–44–0.

South Africa

H. M. Amla c Nehra b Sreesanth	34	D. W. Steyn b Sreesanth	0
H. H. Gibbs b Kumar	7	C. K. Langeveldt c Nehra b Jadeja	12
R. E. van der Merwe c Raina b Sreesanth	12		
*J. H. Kallis b Nehra	11	L-b 5, w 8, n-b 4	17
A. B. de Villiers not out	114		
A. N. Petersen b Jadeja	9	1/17 (2) 2/47 (3) 3/61 (1) (42.5 overs)	248
J. P. Duminy lbw b Pathan	0	4/83 (4) 5/102 (6) 6/103 (7)	
†M. V. Boucher lbw b Pathan	14	7/134 (8) 8/211 (9) 9/216 (10)	
W. D. Parnell b Nehra	18	10/248 (11)	

Kumar 5–0–31–1; Nehra 8–0–60–2; Sreesanth 7–0–49–3; Jadeja 8.5–0–41–2; Pathan 9–1–37–2; Sehwag 5–0–25–0.

Umpires: I. J. Gould and S. K. Tarapore.   Third umpire: S. S. Hazare.
Referee: A. J. Pycroft.

TENDULKAR'S 200, BALL BY BALL

0000 4402 14 01 004020 04001 2421 1 4104 1 0004[†]1 0020 11
2040 410 1 211 011 014 111 00410 0100 1200 11 00101 11
0111[‡] 40410 1 001 614 11 040041 1140 404 4[§]1 401 021 116
146 124 1 211 221 101 01 1[¶]

50 dot-balls, 56 singles, 13 twos, 25 fours, 3 sixes. There were three overs in which Tendulkar did not face a ball.

† 51 from 37 balls; ‡ 100 from 90 balls; § 151 from 118 balls; ¶ 200 from 147 balls.

THE SAINT

Greg Baum, *Wisden Asia Cricket*, November 2003

The two keenest appreciations of Sachin Tendulkar were made from vantage points that could not have been more opposite to each other, and together serve as an incontrovertible cross-reference to his greatness. The first was Sir Donald Bradman's famous remark to his wife during the 1996 World Cup that Tendulkar put him in mind of how he himself batted.

The second is the widespread understanding in the cricket community that match-fixers will not successfully get on with their crooked business until Tendulkar is out, and an anecdotal account of how Tendulkar once unwittingly ruined a fix by batting too blissfully well.

It must be understood that neither reflection would have been made lightly. Sir Donald was not given to hyperbole or glibness, but rather was precise in everything he did and said. Nor would the fixers have bothered with throwaway lines.

Together, these tributes convey immutable impressions of Tendulkar that accord with less quantifiable, more aesthetic understandings of the glory of his batsmanship. Here is a man capable of changing the course of any game. Here is a man incorruptible in the face of the venal temptations that so many of his peers could not resist. Outside the laws or outside the off stump, he could not be lured. Here is a man not susceptible to human failing in any endeavour, a man not so much invincible as invulnerable.

Here is a man whose name is synonymous with purity, of technique, philosophy and image. If Ian Botham can be seen as the Errol Flynn of cricket, or Viv Richards as the Martin Luther King, or Shane Warne as the Marilyn Monroe, or Muttiah Muralitharan as the hobbit, Tendulkar is surely the game's secular saint.

Right from the beginning, he appeared to be touched by divinity. He came among us as a boy-god, unannounced. He was 16 and was hit on the face in his first appearance, but neither flinched nor retreated a step. Nothing thenceforth could harm him, temporal or otherwise. He was short and stocky – like all the best – and mop-topped and guileless to behold. He has scarcely changed since.

Tendulkar was born with extravagant natural talent, but he was also driven and indefatigable. When a boy, he would bat from dawn to dusk, and even a little beyond. As with all the greats, he came not from another dimension, nor the mystical east, but from the nets. By such dedication, he came to understand intimately his own gift, and at length to lavish it upon others.

His movements at the crease are small but exact. He said once that he did not believe in footwork for its conventional purpose, because the tempo of Test cricket did not permit a batsman the textbook indulgence of getting to the pitch of the ball. Rather, he thought of footwork as a means of balancing himself up at the crease so that each shot was hit just as he meant it. He scores predominantly through the off side, an unusual characteristic for such a heavy run maker, but of course he can play every shot.

Tendulkar's method promotes an air of calm, reassurance and poise at the crease. Brian Lara's batting is characterised by explosion and violence, and Steve Waugh's by grim resolve, but Tendulkar's ways are timeless. His battles with Shane Warne, genius versus genius, have been for the ages. It is said that the common element to concepts of beauty among all peoples is symmetry, a balance between all the parts. So it is with Tendulkar's batting.

How easily he carries the hopes and takes responsibility for the well-being of untold millions on that impossible subcontinent; in this, he is also divine. All eyes are upon him, day and night, but no scandal has attached itself, not in his private life nor in his cricket endeavours. Across the land, he is the little man on the big posters and hoardings, creating a kind of reverse Big Brother effect; he is not watching them, but they are watching him. Still he stands tall.

Sometimes petty criticism is made that he fails India in its hours of need, but it is not borne out by the figures, and besides, no one man could take upon his shoulders all of India's needy hours. Just 30, he has already made more than 50 international centuries.

When called upon, he also bowls intelligently, if sparingly. He is sure in the field. There is even about him, as there was about many saints, something of the ingénu. He is not a natural captain for the modern era because he can lead only by example. He does not have a charismatic presence in a cricket stadium, but rather fills it in a different way, as the one certainty in a sea of doubt. Batting is the most fraught of sporting pursuits because even for the best the end is only ever one ball away. Tendulkar seems to turn that verity upon itself.

As Tendulkar put Bradman in mind of himself, so he puts others in mind of Bradman. Once I was on a night train winding down from Simla to Kalka that stopped halfway for refreshments at a station lit by flaming torches. On a small television screen wreathed in cigarette smoke in the corner of the dining room Tendulkar was batting in a match in Mumbai. No one moved or spoke or looked away. The train was delayed by 20 minutes. Not until Tendulkar was out could the world resume its normal timetables and rhythms.

Chapter 3

The Early Years: 1989 to 1996

I t is fitting that Sachin Tendulkar's first appearance in Wisden took place before his international career had even begun. The 1989 Almanack portentously features an appreciation of The Little Master. "He looked neat, 5ft 4¾in tall, and strong in the legs and forearms," wrote Tony Lewis. "His kit was clean, his appearance smart… preparation perfect for the pursuit of runs. He kept his eye on the ball and swayed either side of the high bounce, but when the ball was pitched up he was immediately forward to drive it straight."

In fact, Lewis was summing up the career of India's original Little Master – Sunil Gavaskar – who retired in March 1987. Less than a year later, Tendulkar scored 326 not out in a school match during a 664-run partnership with Vinod Kambli. In 1989, both these feats made it into the Almanack, as life had come full circle. While one Little Master was retiring, another had already snuck his way in, announcing himself the heir.

RECORD PARTNERSHIP   *Wisden 1989*

A world-record partnership of 664 runs unbroken was compiled by two schoolboys during the Harris Shield tournament for Bombay schools. Vinod Kambli, a 16-year-old left-hander, and 14-year-old Sachin Tendulkar were playing for Shardashram Vidyamandir (English) against St Xavier's High School at the Sassanian Ground (Azad Maidan) in Bombay on February 23, 24, 25, 1988. Kambli hit three sixes and 49 fours in his innings of 349 not out and followed it up by taking six wickets for 37, bowling off-breaks, as St Xavier's were dismissed for 145, leaving Shardashram Vidyamandir the winner by 603 runs. Tendulkar's 326 not out contained one six and 48 fours. Details of the innings are as follows.

Shardashram Vidyamandir (English)

A. Ranade c N. Dias b Sanghani		42
†R. Mulye c Bahatule b Sanghani		18
V. G. Kambli not out		349
*S. R. Tendulkar not out		326
1/29 2/84	(2 wkts dec.)	748

Did not bat: A. A. Muzumdar, P. Bhiwandkar, M. Phadke, S. Sinha, S. Jadhav, R. Bashte and S. Ambapkar.

Bowling: A. Sanghani 22–1–98–2; S. Sasnur 14–0–79–0; M. Walawalkar 22–0–161–0; J. Kothari 7–0–38–0; S. Bahatule 27–0–182–0; S. Saherwala 2–0–31–0; K. Apte 26–149–0.

INTERNATIONAL DEBUT

And so it was that Tendulkar came to make his debut for Bombay in the Ranji Trophy in December 1988, at the age of 15, while continuing to play school cricket. A century in his first game for Bombay, followed by a double-hundred and a century in the Under-19 Cooch Behar Trophy, meant he was ripe for selection by the Indian team. But he was overlooked for the tour of the West Indies early in 1989 because the selectors were worried about exposing a 16-year-old to the pace of Ambrose, Bishop, Marshall and Walsh. India could hardly have done worse: they lost the four-Test series 3–0. As Dicky Rutnagur wrote in the 1990 Wisden: "For the first time since his retirement, India truly felt the absence of Sunil Gavaskar."

Meanwhile, Tendulkar continued to score prolifically in domestic cricket. The selectors decided he was ready to face Imran Khan, Wasim Akram and Waqar Younis in the four-Test tour of Pakistan in November 1989. At 16 years and 205 days, he became India's youngest Test cricketer. They managed to draw all four Tests, thanks to solid batting partnerships, the poor fitness of the Pakistani bowlers and, just as significantly, neutral umpires. Both teams also adopted a defensive approach. But Tendulkar, with two half-centuries, made a keen impression. "Sixteen-year-old Sachin Tendulkar showed that age is no consideration in Test cricket when a batsman is brimming with talent," wrote R. Mohan in the 1991 Almanack. "He made runs at critical stages to bolster a fiercely motivated side playing under a new captain in Krishnamachari Srikkanth."

In his very first innings, though, Tendulkar admitted, he was all at sea against Wasim and Waqar. "I began to doubt my ability to bat and questioned whether I was ever going to be good enough to play at the international level."

Pakistan v India

First Test, at Karachi, November 15–20, 1989

Pakistan 409 (Imran Khan 109*, M. Prabhakar 5-104) and **305-5 dec.** (Salim Malik 102*);

India 262 and **303-3** (S. V. Manjrekar 113*)

Drawn.

Tendulkar: 15 and DNB

R. Mohan, *Wisden* 1991

The intrusion of a zealot who became involved in a scuffle with the Indian captain, Srikkanth, provided a contentious moment on the opening day and led to the strengthening of security at the National Stadium. For Pakistan it was a day of consolidation, with Shoaib Mohammad setting the trend for slow but steady scoring.

It was Imran Khan who injected the dynamism Pakistan were looking for in his unbeaten 109. India, in desperate trouble at 85 for six against the wiles of Wasim Akram and the pace of the newcomer, Waqar Younis, staged a recovery through Kapil Dev and Ravi Shastri.

Pakistan were batting again by the third day, but were unable to force the pace. The declaration left India to make 453 off 102 overs or bat through four sessions to save the match. Sanjay Manjrekar, the find of India's tour to the West Indies, led their defensive action, reaching his second Test century.

This was Kapil Dev's 100th Test, and with his third wicket he became the fourth bowler to take 350 Test wickets. He also became the first bowler to play in 100 Tests. At the other end of the spectrum, Sachin Tendulkar made his debut at the age of 16 years 205 days.

At the next Test in Faisalabad, India were in a spot of trouble on a lively pitch at 101 for four before a 143-run stand between Tendulkar and Manjrekar rescued them; batting at No. 6, Tendulkar made 59 from 172 balls before he fell to Imran. He made 41 in the Third Test at Lahore, but it was in the Fourth at Sialkot that he proved his mettle against quality bowling. Walking in to bat at 38 for four in the second innings, Tendulkar had his nose bloodied by a Waqar bouncer after it deflected on to his face from his helmet. Not bothered by the blood all over his shirt, the opposition sledging him, the team doctor's concerns about his well-being, or banners from the crowd instructing the kid to go home and drink milk, Tendulkar said: "Main khelega" [I will play].

Pakistan v India
Fourth Test, at Sialkot, December 9–14, 1989
India 324 (Wasim Akram 5-101) and **234-7**;
Pakistan 250 (V. Razdan 5-79).
Drawn.
Tendulkar: 35 and 57

R. Mohan, *Wisden* 1991

Although a green and seemingly lively pitch held something for the fast bowlers, India were not hard pressed to compile a reasonable total after being put in. Indeed, Pakistan were the side in greater trouble against the moving ball – Vivek Razdan, playing in his second Test, surprised Ramiz Raja and Shoaib Mohammad with his pace and then came back to wind up the innings. India were 74 ahead.

On the third day, more time had been lost when those witnessing only the second Test to be played in Sialkot revealed a tendency to pelt the Indian fieldsmen with orange peel and some harder missiles. A draw seemed the obvious result. But on the afternoon of the fourth day the match sprang to life when Wasim and Imran reduced India to 38 for four. They were rescued by Navjot Sidhu and Tendulkar, who stood firm in a century stand, even though the youngster was bounced repeatedly by the Pakistan pacemen. At one stage umpire John Holder had to warn Wasim for intimidatory bowling. Tendulkar batted for three and a quarter hours for his second fifty of the series. The contest, which had promised much when wickets were falling the previous afternoon, petered out, and the umpires called the match off at tea.

After the Test series, India were to play an exhibition match in Peshawar and four one-day internationals. A limited-overs debut was not on the cards, but Tendulkar played the unofficial exhibition match. Batting with Srikkanth, he made 53 off just 18 balls, including six sixes – four off leg-spinner Abdul Qadir's bowling. So impressed was Srikkanth with Tendulkar's attacking batsmanship, he is rumoured to have said: "The little bugger must play." And that is how Tendulkar came to make his limited-overs debut. While he scored a duck in his first one-day international at Gujranwala, Tendulkar established himself in the Indian middle order with a couple of fifties against Sri Lanka the following month. But it would take a few more years until he was able to claim the opener's role and assert his authority as a limited-overs batsman.

MISSING OUT ON HIS FIRST TEST HUNDRED

A month after the Pakistan tour, India travelled to New Zealand to play three Tests. In the Second Test "Sachin Tendulkar batted with the poise of a player twice his age," according to the 1991 Almanack. "At Napier, 80 not out overnight, he seemed destined to become the youngest batsman to score a Test century, but he added only eight more the next morning." Tendulkar was caught at mid-off by John Wright, who went on to coach India a decade later. While Tendulkar was disappointed to miss out on the record at the time, he blamed India's future coach for depriving him of his first Test century as the dismissal became a long-standing joke between the two.

New Zealand v India
Second Test, at Napier, February 9–13, 1990
India 358-9 dec. (D. K. Morrison 5-98);
New Zealand 178-1 (J. G. Wright 113*).
Drawn.
Tendulkar: 88

Dick Brittenden, *Wisden* 1991

The match was ruined by rain. No play was possible on the first day because of a drenched outfield, and on the second, which started an hour late and finished early because of bad light, only 52 overs were bowled. When the fifth day was abandoned after rain spread under the covers, the game simply slipped into obscurity. Woorkeri Raman fell to Richard Hadlee without scoring, but Manoj Prabhakar and Manjrekar added 92.

On the third day Prabhakar carried through to 95. Mohammad Azharuddin was shackled by the slow pace of the completely grassless pitch and Dilip Vengsarkar was out second ball. Tendulkar, however, made the match his own. He looked considerably older than his 16 years as, with strong driving and deft placements, he reached 80 by the close, off 258 balls. With the perky Kiran More, he had added 128 for an Indian seventh-wicket record against New Zealand. Tendulkar began the fourth day with the prospect of becoming the youngest Test century-maker. But after a four off Danny Morrison and an all-run four from a superb drive in the next over, he went to the well of Morrison's bowling once too often and offered a straightforward catch to mid-off.

TENDULKAR'S NURSERY

Lawrence Booth, *Wisden Cricket Monthly*, August 2002

The pads almost touch the navel, the gloves extend halfway up the arm and the bat handle brushes the nose. A small left-hander, no more than 13, pounds his bat into the bone-dry red dust while an even smaller left-arm seamer scuttles in as if he's struggling against a conveyor belt. The ball shoots along the ground and a piercing appeal goes up. A pint-sized umpire shakes his head sternly. You sense he enjoys the power, but you also sense he knows that ball hit the pad just outside the line of off.

It's a warm February evening and Shivaji Park, situated beyond the shanty towns as you drive north from the centre of Mumbai, is alive with the sound of youthful hope and oohs and aahs, most of them in the local dialect of Marathi. They call it the nursery of Indian cricket, which is a proud claim but one with history on its side. Sachin Tendulkar took his first tentative steps towards immortality here, and 17 other Indian Test cricketers – including former captain Ajit Wadekar, Sandeep Patil, Subhash Gupte and Vijay Manjrekar – once called it home. There's a shiny plaque in the pavilion to prove it.

But Shivaji Park isn't about plaques and pavilions. It's about India's very public love affair with cricket, and it makes a spine-tingling sight. As the sun prepares to set, there are several mini-matches going on at once, not to mention all the net sessions and the 20 or so groundsmen getting the wickets ready for the next day. Mumbai doesn't produce as many Test cricketers as it used to – only Tendulkar, Ajit Agarkar and Wasim Jaffer of the current crop are locals – but there is still a clamour for space.

It makes for a peculiarly Indian conjunction of chaos and order, a bit like its roads. Square leg in one game can shake hands with third man in another, yet everyone knows their place and only the casual observer is confused. Like a real nursery, it's colourful, loud and full of kids who want to be the centre of attention. More than that, they want to be the next Sachin.

This is not just because he walks on water. It also has something to do with the fact that Mumbai traditionally produces batsmen like the Caribbean once produced fast bowlers. Locals still remember with pride the 1971 Indian side which won 1–0 in England, because six of its top seven – Sunil Gavaskar, Ashok Mankad, captain Ajit Wadekar, Dilip Sardesai, Farokh Engineer and Eknath Solkar – were from these parts. (Gundappa Viswanath, from Karnataka, was the odd man out.)

The urge is still to bat rather than bowl, and Shivaji Park, with its variable, sometimes non-existent bounce, is a great place for a 12-year-old to hone his reflexes. The wrist is a vital joint in India, and the whip through midwicket is to Shivaji Park what the forward defensive is to the Lord's nets.

Najesh Churi was coached by Ramakant Achrekar, who also coached Tendulkar in his formative years. Churi even captained Sachin in three games for Shivaji. Churi ("in my late 30s") is in charge of six teams – four of them school sides – which practise six days a week and play limited-overs on Sundays. The crowds don't flock to the matches as much as they used to, which is partly the fault of TV and football – the English Premiership has been on Indian screens for a couple of years now, and Shivaji Park even contains a set of goalposts. But Churi explains in broken English that young cricketers still come from all over India to sample the Shivaji experience.

When Tendulkar served his apprenticeship here, he stayed with his uncle because he lived nearer the park than his parents did, even though their home in Bandra was only 15 minutes away by car. Churi talks about one 12-year-old who came all the way from Madhya Pradesh more than 300 miles away, stayed alone as a paying guest, and went home once a year, as if it was the most natural thing in the world.

But Shivaji Park is not a conventional place, which may explain why India has turned out some wonderfully unconventional cricketers.

In his first three years of international cricket, the young Tendulkar had already been severely tested with tours to Pakistan, New Zealand and England. Two fifties in Pakistan, an 88 in New Zealand and 119 not out against England meant Tendulkar was adequately prepared to fight the Australians in their backyard. While the 114 at the WACA in the Fifth

Test is regarded as a fine lesson in playing fast bowling, it helped that Tendulkar had got his bearings in the Third Test at Sydney. "The outstanding Indian batsman was Tendulkar, whose 148 not out in the Third Test was so largely responsible for giving India a glimpse of victory and whose 114 at Perth saved them an even quicker rout in the Fifth," wrote Dicky Rutnagur in the Almanack review of India's tour.

Australia v India

Third Test, at Sydney, January 2–6, 1992

Australia 313 (D. C. Boon 129*) and **173-8**;

India 483 (R. J. Shastri 206, S. R. Tendulkar 148*).

Drawn.

Tendulkar: 148*; 1-2

Dicky Rutnagur, *Wisden* 1993

Deferring to the Sydney pitch's reputation as a turner, Australia took aboard the uncapped leg-spinner Shane Warne. India put Australia in, a hard pitch and a clear sky notwithstanding.

The Indians not only batted and bowled better than Australia; their fielding and running between wickets were so vastly improved that they were unrecognisable. But for the loss of 94.1 overs to bad light and rain on the third and fourth days, they would have won. Kapil Dev dismissed Allan Border for the third time in the series, and three wickets from Prabhakar pinned back Australia to 269 for eight.

Shastri and Vengsarkar batted stoically through the shortened third day. In the morning Craig McDermott removed Vengsarkar and Azharuddin in one over with the new ball, but Australia did not claim another wicket until tea when Shastri, having reached his first double-century in a Test, fell to a tired shot at Warne. He had shared India's highest ever fifth-wicket partnership (196) against Australia with Tendulkar, who later became the youngest man to score a Test century in Australia. His mature and fluent innings lasted 298 minutes.

India batted on into the fifth day. The pace bowlers reduced Australia to 55 for three, and then Shastri took three wickets to make the score 114 for six. The collapse was checked by Border, assisted first by Merv Hughes and then by Warne, who helped block out the last seven minutes.

A STINT WITH YORKSHIRE

Yorkshire had their work cut out when Tendulkar became their first overseas signing: getting him to score runs was important, but getting the local public to warm to him was just as necessary. And that is how the 19-year-old came to pose with a flat cap, frothing pint, White Rose anorak and a bat, at Headingley. His only season with an English county was disappointing by his standards, but Yorkshire fell in love with him – he had to ask for his name to be removed from the sponsored car when he started to get mobbed quite regularly – and Tendulkar later said the summer of 1992 "was one of the greatest four-and-a-half months I have spent in my life".

POSING WITH A PINT OF TETLEY'S

John Callaghan, *Wisden* 1993

Yorkshire's decision to break with cherished tradition and sign an overseas player brought some commercial success, checking the worrying decline in membership. However, the county endured a disastrous season on the field, emphasising that there are no easy or short-term answers to long-standing problems…

Australian fast bowler Craig McDermott, the original choice as Yorkshire's first officially recognised "outsider", broke down during the winter and required an operation for groin trouble, so, with little room for manoeuvre, the club turned their attentions at the last minute to Sachin Tendulkar. The 19-year-old Indian's appearance on the scene at least silenced all those who, from a distance, accused Yorkshire of being racist, and he proved extremely popular with the public and fellow-players. Tendulkar collected his runs with a good deal of style, scoring quickly in the limited-overs competitions and being prepared to apply himself diligently in the Championship, but he lacked the experience to dominate. Additionally, Martyn Moxon made a mistake in not moving him up the order from No. 4 to open the innings in the Sunday League. Tendulkar topped 50 in eight of his Championship innings, yet he managed only one century, which won the match against Durham. He also completed a Sunday League century, but, having arrived too late to influence Yorkshire's Benson and Hedges Cup prospects seriously, he departed unexpectedly early, missing the last four Championship fixtures to play domestic cricket in India…

LIMITED-OVERS TRAILBLAZER

While he had made his mark in Test cricket right at the start, it would be a few years before Tendulkar would establish his presence in the limited-overs game. One of the best fielders in the Indian side, especially in the first half of his career, he usually seemed to have a trick or two up his bowling sleeve too. Over the years, Indian captains often turned to him to change the course of a game. And, quite often, Tendulkar managed to make something happen. It was no different during the 1993 Hero Cup semi-final. India went on to win the final – against West Indies – but had it not been for Tendulkar's over in the semi, they would almost certainly have missed out.

India v South Africa
Hero Cup, Semi-final, at Calcutta, November 24, 1993 (day/night)
India 195;
South Africa 193-9.
India won by two runs.
Tendulkar: 15; 1–0–3–0

India's second successive win over South Africa was a much tighter affair. The match was the first played under lights at Eden Gardens.

It was also the first match in India to feature a video replay umpire: S. K. Bansal made his mark early on when he sent back Vinod Kambli, then Manoj Prabhakar, both run out by Daryll Cullinan. Azharuddin pulled his team round with Praveen Amre's help, but India failed to reach 200. South Africa came to the last five overs needing 45, which was down to seven when they lost Dave Richardson. They entered the final over – Tendulkar's first – looking for six, but they managed only three, and Fanie de Villiers became the seventh run-out of the game.

Had it not been for an injury to a team-mate, Tendulkar might have had to wait even longer to open the batting in limited-overs cricket. As it turned out, the wait still lasted 70 one-day internationals. His arrival on the scene as an attacking opening batsman was the start of a new trend, two years before the strategy was successfully adopted by Sri Lanka at the 1996 World Cup.

New Zealand v India
Second one-day international, at Auckland, March 27, 1994
New Zealand 142;
India 143-3.
India won by seven wickets.
Tendulkar: 82

Qamar Ahmed, *Wisden* 1995

Tendulkar played a blazing innings of 82 from 49 balls, with 15 fours and two sixes, and India achieved a thumping victory in less than half their allocated 50 overs. Opening because of Navjot Sidhu's neck strain, Tendulkar put on 61 with Ajay Jadeja in nine overs, and 56 in six with Kambli. He smashed three fours and a six off Gavin Larsen's first over, and Kambli was just as hard on Morrison.

Ken Rutherford had chosen to bat, but half the side went for 34. Adam Parore and Chris Harris staged a minor recovery, with 52 for the sixth wicket, but off-spinner Rajesh Chauhan destroyed the tail.

It took Tendulkar fewer than ten games, after he was promoted to the opener's slot, to score his first limited-overs century.

Australia v India
Singer World Series, Game three, at R. Premadasa Stadium, Colombo, September 9, 1994 (day/night)
India 246-8 (S. R. Tendulkar 110);
Australia 215.
India won by 31 runs.
Tendulkar: 110

R. Mohan, *Wisden* 1996

Tendulkar's maiden century in 78 one-day internationals was fashioned from a blazing assault in the first hour. He raced to 50 in 43 balls, knocking first the pace bowlers and then Warne – with two sixes in an over – out of the attack. His 110 from 132 balls should have been the platform for a huge total; India reached 100 in the 18th over. It never quite materialised after he played over a yorker from McDermott, but India won calmly, with Prabhakar challenging Tendulkar for the match award. He took a return catch off Mark Taylor, two further wickets, another catch and two run-outs. Australia's only substantial partnership was 67 from Mark Waugh and David Boon.

BEST YEAR SO FAR

Tendulkar had an astonishing 1996, scoring over 2,200 runs in Test and limited-overs cricket. A productive World Cup was followed by a tour of England, where India lost the Test series 1–0, although fine centuries from

Tendulkar and Sourav Ganguly in the first innings of the Third Test provided just a tiny glimmer of hope in India's attempt to square the series. On the back of his performances at the World Cup, and during the English summer, Tendulkar was one of Wisden's *Five Cricketers of the Year.*

Long before 300-plus scores became routine in 50-over cricket, it was Tendulkar who established the record for India.

India v Pakistan
Pepsi Cup, Game four, at Sharjah, April 15, 1996
India 305-5 (S.R. Tendulkar 118; N. S. Sidhu 101);
Pakistan 277.
India won by 28 runs.
Tendulkar: 118; 2-40

Colin Bryden, *Wisden* 1997

India passed 300 for the first time in one-day cricket to set up a satisfying win. It was rooted in a 231-run stand between Tendulkar and Sidhu, an Indian all-wicket record in limited-overs internationals. India started slowly: Tendulkar was intent on building an innings after scoring just three in India's two defeats. The tempo rose as he put on a classical display; Sidhu punished the slow bowlers, and both reached three figures. Pakistan had two overs deducted for their slow over-rate, but replied with spirit. They were 172 for two in the 26th over when Aamir Sohail, on 78 from 76 balls, was furious to be run out – by his runner, Rashid Latif. Sohail's dismissal, followed up by accurate bowling from Anil Kumble, gave the upper hand to India again.

India v England
Third Test, at Nottingham, July 4–9, 1996
India 521 (S. C. Ganguly 136, S. R. Tendulkar 177) and **211**;
England 564 (M. A. Atherton 160, N. Hussain 107 ret. hurt).
Drawn.
Tendulkar: 177 and 74

David Field, *Wisden* 1997

Reports that showers would seriously disrupt the final Test proved to be incorrect, but the forecast that a flat and slowish pitch would prevent a result was more accurate. The match was duly drawn, although England persevered commendably to dismiss India in 69 overs on the fifth day.

India were bowled out 168 ahead, bringing down the curtain on a match graced by the batting artistry of Tendulkar and Ganguly.

Azharuddin won the toss for the third time and elected to bat on a cloudy, blustery day. The home side quickly claimed the wickets of Vikram Rathore and Nayan Mongia. But that was no prelude to an Indian collapse, though it threatened when Tendulkar gave a chance before scoring; Michael Atherton failed to hold it at gully. Instead, Tendulkar and the cool, stylish Ganguly settled in to bat beautifully for the rest of the first day and, by the close, the partnership was an unbeaten 254. Tendulkar completed his tenth Test hundred, and fourth against England, with 15 fours.

Determined bowling had kept India to 521, a formidable total, but less than England had feared. In reply, Atherton gave a hard chance to Azharuddin at slip on 34; Alec Stewart, on the other hand, looked unlucky to be given caught behind after a hard-fought fifty.

That brought in Nasser Hussain, who epitomised the confident batsman. He scored 25 from his first 16 balls and completed his second hundred in three Tests, although some Indian fieldsmen were convinced he had been caught behind off Tendulkar when 74. England had averted the follow-on just before the close, consigning the match to stalemate.

By 1996, Tendulkar had become a force to reckon with – in Test and one-day cricket. While Brian Lara had cornered the records, his lack of both consistency and a calm temperament were apparent. These were two areas where Tendulkar was head and shoulders above most of his contemporaries, thanks to the values he inherited from his parents, and the stubborn grit – or "khadoos" nature – of the Bombay school of batsmanship.

FIVE CRICKETERS OF THE YEAR: SACHIN TENDULKAR

Mike Selvey, *Wisden* 1997

It was one brief moment in time. The World Cup, India versus West Indies in Gwalior, and a single stroke of such exquisiteness that the old maharajah surely would have had it carved in ivory and placed on a plinth. In essence, it was no more than a leg-side flick to the boundary and, in a competition that gorged itself on hitting, might have been worth only transient acclaim. But this was a gem: a length ball from a high-class pace bowler met initially with a straight blade, and then, at the last nanosecond, turned away with a roll of the wrist and such an irresistible alliance of power, timing and placement that first of all it eluded the fingertips of a midwicket fielder diving to his right, and then it did the same to the boundary runner haring and plunging to his left. Skill, technique, confidence, awareness, vision: pure genius, and four more runs to Sachin Tendulkar.

The young man is probably the most famous and feted man in India, outglitzing even the stars of Bollywood movies. With endorsements over the next five years estimated to be worth at least $US75m, he is also the highest earner in cricket. He has become public property in a country of enthusiasms that can spill over into the fanatical, but has managed to maintain a dignified, mature outlook, remaining aware of his responsibilities while protecting his privacy. When he married Anjali, a doctor, he rejected massive sums from satellite TV for live coverage, keeping the ceremony a family affair. He knows his worth, and is wealthy beyond the dreams of almost a billion Indians, but he is not a grabber. His father, a university professor, imparted a sense of perspective and a work ethic.

Tendulkar averages over 50 in Tests and is the supreme right-hander, if not quite the finest batsman, on the planet. He is a focused technician, who offers a counterpoint to Brian Lara's more eye-catching destruction, fuelled on flair and ego. He has, it seems, been around for ever. In the Third Test at Trent Bridge last summer, he scored 177, the tenth century of his Test career and his second of the series: yet remarkably, at 23, Tendulkar was younger than any member of the England team, with only Dominic Cork and Min Patel born even in the same decade. His figures have been achieved despite a lack of Test cricket, particularly at home. Seven of his centuries had been scored before his 21st birthday, a unique record. Had India not rationalised their Test match programme so much that, prior to last summer, they had played just one three-match series, heavily affected by rain, against New Zealand, in the previous 18 months, there is no telling what he might already have achieved. With time on his side and a return to a full Test programme, he could prove Sunil Gavaskar right and rewrite the records.

SACHIN RAMESH TENDULKAR was born in Bombay on April 24, 1973, and, since childhood, has trodden a steady, almost inevitable, path to greatness. He attended the city's Sharadashram Vidyamandir school, where the Harris Memorial Challenge Shield, a competition for Under-17s, provided the chance to bat for hours. From the age of 12, when he scored his first century for the school and came to notice as a special talent, he indulged himself. When 14, he compiled not-out scores of 207, 326 and 346 in the space of five innings, one of them contributing to an unbroken partnership of 664 with Vinod Kambli, a record in any form of cricket.

He was 16 years and 205 days old when he made his Test debut, in November 1989, in the National Stadium in Karachi – for a young Indian, perhaps the most fiery baptism of all. The following year, at Old Trafford, he hit his first Test century – not a scintillating innings, but an exercise in technique, concentration and application beyond his tender years, which saved a game that might have been lost. Had it come 31 days earlier, he would have been the youngest century-maker in Test history. During the winter of 1991-92, he went to Australia, where they still talk in awe of the centuries he scored in Sydney and in Perth.

A few days after his 19th birthday, Tendulkar came back to England: to Yorkshire, no less, as the county's first overseas player. It would have been a massive responsibility for anyone, let alone a teenager from India, and it did not quite work. Tendulkar assumed the mantle conscientiously, and posed with cloth cap and pint of bitter, impressing colleagues and supporters alike with his understanding of public relations. But, in the end, he failed to come to terms with the county game, scoring only one century and barely scraping past 1,000 runs in his only season. Hindsight would tell him that it was part of his education, but a mistake none the less.

In 1996 he returned to England, a teenage prodigy no longer, but a seasoned Test batsman fit to stand alongside his first hero, Gavaskar. The pair have much in common: Gavaskar was slight of build and, of necessity, a supreme judge of length. Tendulkar, too, is short. There is a lot of bottom hand, but he drives strongly, on the rise, such is his strength of wrist and the control in his hands, while he is devastating off his legs, pulls well and – given good bounce – can cut wide bowling to ribbons. If the delicate and unexpected talents of Sourav Ganguly provided a distraction last season, then Tendulkar's two hundreds in three Tests were ample demonstration of the team's premier batsman leading from the front. The first of them – at Edgbaston, where he made 122 out of 219 – was a stunning display of virtuosity in adversity.

In August, aged 23, Tendulkar succeeded Mohammad Azharuddin as captain of his country. Had he craved it and pursued it with a passion, he would surely have got the job earlier, perhaps even while a teenager. Rather, it was a position that was being held in abeyance until the time was right. His leadership has a firm base of experience to it now. His first Test in charge was against Australia. He made ten and nought but India won, just as one almost assumed they would. Some things just seem part of a wider plan.

Chapter 4

The World Cups: 1992 to 2011

This is the story of boyhood dream bookended by the two most famous dates in Indian cricket history, 28 years apart: June 25, 1983, and April 2, 2011. "I started playing cricket because I felt that I should have this beautiful trophy in my hands," Sachin Tendulkar told me in an interview the day after India won the 2011 World Cup. "It took long, but I never gave up. I continued chasing my dream."

And chase it he did: from the ten-year-old prankster-boy who celebrated India's 1983 World Cup win with a jig in his parents' flat, to the 38-year-old puckish man who tucked flowers behind his ears and danced without inhibition at 2 a.m. on April 3, 2011. Champagne and tears flowed. There, he was hoisted on the shoulders of his team-mates, waving the Indian tricolour and living his lifelong dream, spanning three decades and a record-equalling six World Cups. It was, he said, "the greatest moment of my cricketing journey".

There was no doubt this would be Tendulkar's last World Cup. Do sportsmen get their fairytale finishes? Muhammad Ali lost his fourth and final bid for the heavyweight title to Larry Holmes in 1980, the only fight he ever lost by knockout; Diego Maradona tested positive for drugs in the 1994 World Cup – his last; and Tiger Woods prowls forlornly on golf courses in search of another major. The god who writes sporting scripts isn't always benevolent. But who was to tell Tendulkar that? Who was to tell a 38-year-old man-child that his dreams were outrageous?

He never listened, not to his doctors, physiotherapists, critics or fans. His dream finish at the Wankhede – his temple since he was 14 – was the stuff of legend. No, he didn't make a century, just 18 quiet runs. No, he *didn't take any wickets, because by then his battle-weary body refused to traipse to his every whim. And yet here he was, after a gut-wrenching semifinal at Eden Gardens in 1996, a devastating personal loss in 1999, a so-near-yet-so-far heartbreak in 2003, a humiliating first-round expulsion in 2007. And then 2011. Ah, 2011! The greatest-ever one-day batsman had finally climbed Everest.*

SACHIN THE INNOCENT   Siddhartha Vaidyanathan, *The Nightwatchman*, Spring 2013

February 27, 1996. Sachin Tendulkar stands in the middle of Mumbai's Wankhede Stadium, his home ground, a pulsing floodlit amphitheatre that sways to his command. He scans the field, dotted with Australian fielders, splotches of mustard sauce in a vast expanse of green. His palms grasp a plank of balsa that points heavenwards. Damien Fleming, goat-eed, hustles in from the Tata End. Tendulkar pats his bat against the earth once, then twice. The crowd's chant crescendoes. Another pat and Tendulkar is ready; ready for mischief.

There are many Tendulkars: the upstart keelhauling Qadir in Peshawar; the trooper scurrying twos and threes from the middle order in Sydney; the mutineer promoted to open at Auckland; the seraph overwhelming Australia in Sharjah; the impetuous virtuoso blasting McGrath in Nairobi; the Zen-master rattling Shoaib and Wasim in Centurion; the peerless technician thwarting Gul and Asif at Lahore; the sorcerer's 175 at Hyderabad; and the path-breaker charting the course for the first one-day double-hundred in Gwalior. And we've barely scratched the surface.

And then there is *that* Tendulkar. Those who watched him between March 1994, when he first opened, and April 1998, when he walked on water, know this avatar, a pixie who hopped across television screens. Spry and indulgent, he was always ready with a prank. His bat traversed dangerous arcs. He opened up his stance and swished across the line. He charged fast bowlers, slog-swept leg-spinners and lofted off-spinners inside-out. He even hooked. Here was a ballet artiste on a jagged boulder on the edge of a steep cliff. Of course he slipped now and then – and that was to have consequences – but when he came off, it was unworldly.

The Mumbai escapade was a keystone. Tendulkar was 22, eligible for alcohol and marriage, but still the youngest member of the team. He was the linchpin of the line-up but still the most free-spirited batsman. He was yet to have captaincy thrust upon him. This was the last phase of his batting childhood. He was innocent, insatiable and incorrigible; consummate, adventurous and borderline reckless. And he was glorious.

India are chasing 259. Fleming starts with away-swing, then quickly shifts to curling it in. A half-arsed appeal for lbw is drowned out by an intimidating hum from the stands.

Tendulkar examines his bat, a Vampire, as if to indicate an inside edge. The next ball, also angled in, is overpitched. Tendulkar shuffles his front foot and the bat meets the ball delicately.

As the ball races to the long-on fence his head, shielded by a navy blue helmet, stays still; the Wills stickers, plastered on his sleeve and chest, shimmer. The Vampire is a study in verticality, giving us a clear sight of the sponsor logo plastered across the bat face… except there is no sponsor logo. The Vampire is stark naked.

This is one of cricket's great marketing ironies: the highest-paid cricketer (of his time and all time) did not have a bat contract at the start of the 1996 World Cup. His 523 runs, at 87.16, were harvested with a bare piece of wood. Sixteen years later he would reveal, in an interview with *Time* magazine, that he was approached with a deal before the Australia match. "But I had already played the first two matches without a sticker on the bat: I was used to the way it looked, and didn't want to change that in the middle of the tournament; didn't want the distraction."

Where superstition ended, derring-do took over. "I had this stickerless bat which I used for fielding and catching practice," said Ajit Wadekar, who managed India in that World Cup, in an interview with Mumbai tabloid *Mid-Day*. "Sachin somehow liked the feel of it. Of course, it was slightly lighter than the bats he normally uses. He asked me if he could have it and I had no problems in giving it to him."

McGrath bowls three maidens in a row. Ruthless with his line, he cramps Tendulkar for room: short of a length moving out, short of a length moving in. Many of these exchanges finish with a cautious push back to the bowler. Then, an in-cutter that thuds into the pads. McGrath shrieks in appeal. Umpire David Shepherd says no, with the look of a man who has just resolved a serious dilemma. Replays show how harrowing the dilemma could have been.

These were early days in the Tendulkar–McGrath–Warne chronicles, only the fourth one-day international when the three shared the same tinderbox. The first was at the Austral–Asia Cup in Sharjah (Tendulkar fell early to McGrath, India won); the second at the Singer World Series in Colombo (Tendulkar's first ODI hundred, India won); and the third at the New Zealand Centenary Tournament in Dunedin (Tendulkar flayed a 40-ball 47, India won). Tendulkar had not yet known defeat to Australia outside Australia.

The Mumbai match was the first time he would face the duo in a global tournament. McGrath had established himself as one of the world's best opening bowlers; Shane Warne, after a glittering 1994, was the leading spinner. And Tendulkar was arguably the world's finest batsman. This would be a battle for the ages.

McGrath digs one short outside off. Bang. The screen turns technicolor. Tendulkar has pushed on to his back foot and pulled through midwicket. The ball screams to the boundary. On air Ian Chappell says that the ball was not that short at all. He talks about the speed with which Tendulkar has rocked on to his back foot. These are the first runs McGrath has conceded tonight. A gigantic pressure valve has been released.

Two balls later, Tendulkar tries to ramp a short ball over the wicketkeeper, as if prodding a broom against a cobweb. He misses. The ball is high enough to be no-balled but Tendulkar shadow-practises the shot, showing us how he ought to have played it. The next ball, short again, is pulled off the front foot, an irreverent mosquito swat that he, as Ravi Shastri says, has "dismissed from his presence".

In his pomp Tendulkar was a horizontal-bat anarchist. He pulled (off both front and back foot), slashed, late-cut and flat-batted forehands down the ground. There was puckishness to these shots. His violent pulls – when the ball threatened to crash into his face – and back-foot square cuts – often lashed off tiptoe – accentuated his littleness. Still a few years adrift of a serious back injury, he explored his range with aplomb.

Never before had India seen a batsman so technically correct dismantle bowlers with such a vast repertoire of strokeplay. Here was a classical dancer swinging to hip-hop, infusing the new art form with a correctness associated with the old. This was beautiful, racy and intoxicating.

India are 40 for two after ten. Tendulkar has scorched four fours in two overs. His shirt is unbuttoned and a chain glints in the bare V around his neck. You can feel the urgency.

McGrath strays wide, Tendulkar clatters a cover-drive (it takes Mark Waugh's brilliance to prevent a boundary). McGrath angles one in, Tendulkar responds with a juddering on-drive for four, with frightening economy of movement.

McGrath is full and straight, Tendulkar pops a leading edge back to the bowler (which is high enough and quick enough to deflect off his palms). McGrath is accurate outside off, Tendulkar is cautious with a pat to cover. McGrath drifts on to the pads, Tendulkar launches a six over midwicket. McGrath slides a wide full toss, Tendulkar consigns the ball to the extra-cover outpost.

India have reeled off 37 in three overs, including 27 off McGrath's last two. Mohammad Azharuddin seems to be telling Tendulkar to calm down. Chappell calls it "unbelievable batting". He says the counter-attack is the "most exciting" part of cricket. He says he wouldn't be surprised if the rest of India's batsmen are "intimidated" by Tendulkar.

This was batting that tested your sanity. One moment he was lofting over the infield, the next he was offering a chance. These were times when Tendulkar commanded you to jump around the room. Those were pre-DVR, pre-repeat telecast days and you didn't dare to take your eyes off the screen. You just sat there, a package of gunpowder, ready to explode.

Batsmen with similar attitudes were emerging. Sanath Jayasuriya and Mark Waugh enjoyed spectacular success as openers. Saeed Anwar was blazing a trail in Pakistan. A few years down the line every team would have at least one popcorn-bursting batsman at the top of the order. But Tendulkar started all this. Yes, there were belligerent openers before him. Yes, there were pinch-hitters who had come off. But nobody was consistent enough and successful enough to instigate a change in thinking. Tendulkar did. And that is one of his lasting legacies.

India are 56 for two after 12 when Warne, his lips zinc-creamed, is introduced. His loosening-up routine – bowling to the mid-off fielder – is long enough for both Chappell and umpire Shepherd to lose patience. Tendulkar waits. He tries to delay Warne further by checking the field. The two seem to be enjoying the foreplay.

The first ball is a long-hop. Tendulkar can tonk it anywhere square of the wicket. Strangely, even though there's a fielder at long-on, he chooses to back away and flat-bat a forehand straight over the bowler's head for four. Warne looks confused with the shot. Tendulkar raises his bat to the dressing-room and then to the crowd. Fifty off 41.

Warne's third ball is a leg-break that drifts in and spits away. Tendulkar winds up, as if to blast a straight-drive over the roof. The leading edge sails tantalisingly over mid-off, grazing Stuart Law's fingertips along the way. The fifth ball is flayed again and another edge races to third man for four. Then comes a ripped leg-break that beats his bat. "Awwwww," says Ian Healy behind the stumps. "There's anticipation every ball," says Chappell.

Warne v Tendulkar was never short of frisson. There was an audacity to Warne's tactics and a ferocity to Tendulkar's attempts at throwing him off rhythm. Those were the days when Tendulkar treated leg-spinners as if they had no moral right to breathe the same air as him. And he telegraphed his intent from the first over of a spell. He would do it again, most memorably, in a warm-up match in Mumbai and a Test in Chennai in 1998. He would do the same in a one-day series in India and a tri-series in Sharjah in the same year.

Nobody knew it then, but it remained the first and last time Warne bowled to Tendulkar in a World Cup game. Tendulkar was claimed by McGrath in 1999 and Warne by a diuretic pill in 2003, after which he never played another 50-over game for Australia.

Over the next few overs Warne sticks to a plan: he chooses to pitch on leg stump and curl in his leg-breaks. Mark Taylor stands at slip and stations a backward square leg at the edge of the inner circle. The fielding restrictions are gone and Tendulkar is content to nudge singles. Chappell talks of the respect Warne is giving Tendulkar by keeping just five fielders in the circle and adopting a restrictive line. The pressure gradually builds, in part because Sanjay Manjrekar is facing the bulk of the strike.

These were a significant few overs in the Warndulkar rivalry, when the bowler pitched on and outside leg stump while spinning the ball into his pads. He bowled differently to Manjrekar, sticking to a line that was on middle and off. This ploy to Tendulkar worked. The quiet phase added to the pressure on the team. And Warne came off the victor.

But Tendulkar would remember this. Before the 1998 home Test series he would practise with former Indian leg-spinner Laxman Sivaramakrishnan ripping leg-breaks from the rough outside leg stump. And he would go on to crush Warne's leg-stump tactic in the First Test in Chennai with a staggering slog-swept six over midwicket. The strike, Chappell maintains, changed the course of both the match and the series.

Tendulkar would pounce again a few months later, in the final of the Coca-Cola Cup in Sharjah, his ODI *pièce de résistance*, when Warne shifted to around the wicket at a critical stage of the game. Tendulkar charged down the ground and smacked a six. India won the game. Warne joked about having nightmares about Tendulkar (though it would have been totally believable had he been serious).

Australia introduce their second-string bowlers, Shane Lee, Mark Waugh and Michael Bevan. Lee pitches short and watches a flat-batted swat screaming to the ropes at long-off. Mark Waugh flights one outside off only to be swept to the boundary in front of square. Sunil Gavaskar points out that the sweep isn't a shot Tendulkar prefers against spinners. "But the pitch is affording a bit of turn and he's playing it with the turn, something which the Australians do very regularly."

Tendulkar's flat-batted forehand down the ground and the sweep in front of square were endangered species post-1999, when he suffered a back injury and turned himself into a more ruthless, risk-free batsman. You could still spot these shots once in a while but never with the same regularity. These were signatures of his naughty phase, when he pulled them out at will, intimidating the bowlers and injecting new life into the middle overs.

Mark Waugh has his collar up. His hair is neatly parted at the centre. His shades, which give him an air of mystique while fielding, have been handed to the umpire. He flights one outside off. A menacing Tendulkar prances down the ground, meets the ball on the full and clatters it back down the ground. This is an almighty biff. Waugh dares to get his hands behind the ball, risking injury. He prevents a four and, in characteristic style, brushes off the blow with a steely walk back to his mark.

Two overs later Waugh hops in to bowl again. Tendulkar begins a shimmy down the ground even before Waugh's back foot lands. This is too early. Waugh is canny enough to float it wide. Tendulkar tries a late cut. Not a pat to off. Not a desperate lunge. But a late cut! The ball eludes him. Healy whips the bails off. Umpire Steve Dunne calls a wide, but Waugh is ecstatic. For a brief moment, for those in the stadium and many others watching on television, the world stops spinning.

Tendulkar wades through a sea of murmurs on the way to the pavilion. There is no major applause, no standing ovation, nothing to prompt him to lift his bat. He takes off his gloves and helmet, brushes his forehead, rinses off the sweat from his hands, wipes his right temple against his sleeve, and walks away. It would have been fitting if, at that instant, the floodlights were switched off.

You can watch every ball of this Tendulkar innings on YouTube in a 43-minute clip uploaded by Rob Moody, the creator of the popular channel Robelinda2. Rob describes Tendulkar's innings as "fucking amazing" and follows up with eight exclamation marks.

"Took me awhile [sic] to make," writes Rob, "you can witness the sheer mastery of this great, great cricketer, he single-handedly keeps India in the contest, before he loses his cool and loses the match. Superb display of batting anyway, obliterates Glenn McGrath in the process."

This comment is reflective of two (related) narratives that were to haunt Tendulkar through his career: one, when Sachin does well, India lose, and two, Sachin doesn't do enough in big matches. Mumbai '96 was one of the early games that sowed the seeds of this perception (a week later he scored a hundred against Sri Lanka and India lost again) and over time – with every Indian defeat, with every big Tendulkar innings in vain – the roots took hold and grew into a gigantic banyan.

Now no debate on Tendulkar – often enraged dogfights online – is complete without these recurring themes. The comments below this particular YouTube video are a microcosm of most Tendulkar discussions. Some have pointed to the meagre contribution from the other batsmen and the excessive burden that Tendulkar was forced to carry. Some have called him a choker. Some have compared him to Brian Lara. Some have sworn. Others have sworn back.

Had India won, *ceteris paribus*, they would have gone on to play New Zealand in the quarter-final and West Indies in the semi. And maybe even Sri Lanka in the final where (who knows) Tendulkar could have led them to victory. Woulda, coulda, shoulda.

These are the "what ifs" that keep me awake some nights. I was 14 in 1996. This was the first match I saw with my dad, a man who was convinced cricket was "the worst opium of the masses". Even he couldn't escape Tendulkar's magnetic pull. He flew off his seat when Tendulkar thundered a six off McGrath and screamed in delight at various other points. And he didn't speak for a couple of hours after the defeat.

This was anything but a perfect Tendulkar knock. Neither was it a match-winning effort. His 84-ball 90 required large slices of luck. He wasn't up against a genuine quick bowler. And there were no adverse conditions to counter. Yet it remains my favorite Tendulkar one-day innings, a daring high-wire act where he walked the razor-thin line between recklessness and bravado.

Writing of his 254 at Lord's in 1930, an innings many consider the greatest of all, Sir Donald Bradman said: "Practically without exception every ball went where it was intended." We are yet to hear much of what Tendulkar makes of his 90 in Mumbai but, for a 14-year-old watching on TV, practically without exception every ball could have gone anywhere. The possibilities were endless. What greater thrill than that?

1992 WORLD CUP

Tendulkar's World Cup career got off to an underwhelming start on a bouncy Perth pitch. Having scored a remarkable 114 in the Fifth Test there just two weeks earlier, he managed 35 against England before being bowled by Ian Botham. India lost by nine runs, a defeat typical of a half-hearted campaign in which they were plagued by captaincy issues and fatigue, and trudged from one rout to the next. They won only two games out of nine, against Pakistan and Zimbabwe. Tendulkar, batting in the middle order, was already starting to show promise, with scores of 54 not out, 81 and 84. He had only just begun.

1996 WORLD CUP

Tendulkar's dam of one-day runs burst in his second World Cup, where he was the tournament's leading run-scorer with 523, including two centuries. Aged just 23, he had already been the mainstay of India's limited-overs batting for a couple of years. Placed in Group A, with Australia, Kenya, Sri Lanka and West Indies, India had an easy start as Tendulkar took advantage of an inexperienced Kenyan attack to race to his first World Cup century. But qualifying games against Australia and Sri Lanka – the two eventual finalists – were tough: despite an attacking 90 against Australia at his home ground in Mumbai, and 137 against Sri Lanka in Delhi, he could not prevent defeat. This World Cup was the start of a script that repeatedly played out over the next few years: Tendulkar standing alone between the opposition and defeat, a colossus among the ruins of another Indian collapse.

India v Kenya
Group A, at Cuttack, February 18, 1996
Kenya 199-6;
India 203-3 (S. R. Tendulkar 127*).
India won by seven wickets.
Tendulkar: 127*

Wisden 1997

Kenya's batsmen gave them a satisfactory launch into senior international cricket, but had to give way to one of the world's best, Tendulkar. The first part of the day belonged to Steve Tikolo, however. He scored 65 in 83 balls, hit a six and six fours, and put on 96 with his captain, Maurice Odumbe. Then the middle order rashly tried to hit out against Anil Kumble, who took three wickets in four overs. India needed only 200, and Ajay Jadeja and Tendulkar began with 100 in 20 overs, putting on 163 – India's highest for any wicket in the World Cup – before Jadeja, who had just begun to show signs of cramp, was caught on the boundary in the 33rd over. Tendulkar was then 98 and he was stuck on 99 for nine balls before completing his fifth hundred in one-day internationals. The tension seemed to be transmitted to his team-mates, Navjot Sidhu and Vinod Kambli; both struggled to get going before hitting out to find catchers in the deep. But by then Tendulkar had resumed his surge onwards, finishing on 127 from 134 balls, with 15 fours and a six. It was Nayan Mongia who hit the winning four.

India v West Indies
Group A, at Gwalior, February 21, 1996 (day/night)
West Indies 173;
India 174-5.
India won by five wickets.
Tendulkar: 70

Wisden 1997

This match was the first real test for both teams, and India won it hands down. First, they dismissed the West Indians for 173 – less than they conceded to Kenya – on a decent pitch; then, inspired again by Tendulkar, they knocked off the runs inside 40 overs. In fact, both innings followed the same pattern up to the halfway mark: two early wickets falling to the strike bowler, then a recovery checked by the loss of the captain, caught in the deep, with the total in the early nineties. But whereas Richie Richardson's departure sparked the first of two West Indian collapses – curiously, both of three wickets for eight in 12 balls – India steamed on. The key moments of the match came when Brian Lara was given caught behind fifth ball, apparently off his pad, and later when Courtney Browne dropped a skyer off Tendulkar, then 22. Tendulkar advanced to 70 from 91 balls, earning his second successive match award, before he was run out in a mix-up with Kambli, who then took charge of the closing stages. Despite some tight bowling by Courtney Walsh, West Indies' task had become hopeless. A crowd of 30,000 lit torches and firecrackers, and the smoke drifted through the floodlights as they celebrated a home victory.

India v Australia

Group A, at Bombay, February 27, 1996 (day/night)

Australia 258 (M. E. Waugh 126);

India 242 (D. W. Fleming 5-36).

Australia won by 16 runs.

Tendulkar: 90

Wisden 1997

The first floodlit international in Bombay was also illuminated by some thrilling batting. Mark Waugh became the first man to score consecutive World Cup centuries, and Tendulkar treated his home crowd to an explosive 90. At first, Waugh was overshadowed by Taylor, who galloped to 59 as they opened with 103 at five an over; Australia looked capable of topping 300. But once Taylor was caught on the boundary, the spinners Venkatapathy Raju and Kumble thwarted such ambitions. Waugh eventually went for 126 from 135 balls, having hit three sixes and eight fours, and the last seven wickets fell for 26. After six overs, India had lost two wickets to Damien Fleming, while McGrath had bowled three maidens. But Tendulkar hit three fours off McGrath's fifth over, and blazed from 12 to 56 in 25 balls, with seven fours and one six. When Fleming bowled Azharuddin, Tendulkar steadied himself slightly, then raced to 90 from 84 balls, with 14 fours and a six. He was finally stumped off a wide – delivered by his rival, Mark Waugh, trying his hand at off-spin. Until then, no one could write off India, and, though Warne bowled tightly, Manjrekar and Mongia kept them in the hunt. They were always a couple of wickets adrift, however, and Fleming ended the innings by bowling Kumble, his fifth victim, with two overs to go.

India v Sri Lanka
Group A, at Delhi, March 2, 1996
India 271-3 (S. R. Tendulkar 137);
Sri Lanka 272-4.
Sri Lanka won by 6 wickets.
Tendulkar: 137

Wisden 1997

A devastating assault by their openers ensured Sri Lanka first place in the group. They made 272 look a simple target, though Kumble made the middle order work hard for it. Victory by half-time seemed possible when Sanath Jayasuriya and Romesh Kaluwitharana smashed 42 in their first three overs – Manoj Prabhakar conceded 11 and 22 – and they had shot past 50 in five when Kaluwitharana, looking for his seventh four, gave Kumble a diving catch. Jayasuriya charged on, though his final statistics of 79 in 76 balls, with nine fours and two sixes, seemed sedate after his initial rampage. Having set off at twice the required rate, Sri Lanka gradually fell behind, as spinners Kumble and Tendulkar bowled 12 overs in harness for 48. Kumble instigated a mini-collapse as he completed the run-out of Asanka Gurusinha and then, in his next two overs, dismissed Jayasuriya and Aravinda de Silva. But Arjuna Ranatunga and Hashan Tillekeratne restarted the ignition in a stand of 131, winning with eight balls to spare. India paid for their slow progress in the morning. They began batting in light mist, after play was delayed 15 minutes by dew on the outfield, and took 25 overs to score 100. After a short rain-break, the final 11 overs brought 105, thanks to Tendulkar. His run-a-ball 137, with five sixes and eight fours, was his second century of the tournament, and he added 175 with Azharuddin, an all-wicket World Cup record for India. Ravindra Pushpakumara's last over cost 23 – but that only prefigured the carnage to come.

TRACKING BRAND SACHIN

The 1996 World Cup was where it all began: the game exploded in the subcontinent and Brand Tendulkar received its almost official stamp. It was the year Mark Mascarenhas, sports head of the Connecticut-based sports-marketing firm WorldTel, signed up Tendulkar in an unprecedented multimillion-dollar deal – a move that changed Indian cricket forever.

Richard Gillis, *Wisden* 2014

The story of Sachin Tendulkar is usually told in one currency – runs, and more runs. But there is another: in June 2013, *Forbes* listed his annual earnings at $US22m. The precise value doesn't really matter: above all, Brand Sachin has been India's confidence index throughout a period of rapid economic liberalisation. As an essentially socialist nation, crippled by the "Hindu rate of growth", gave way to a buoyant capitalism, so Tendulkar's runs enhanced its self-esteem. He was a one-man Sensex – Mumbai's stock exchange – seemingly reflecting the mood of the nation.

Like the IPL, Brand Sachin has been used to project the country as an economic powerhouse; unlike the IPL, its integrity has rarely been questioned. As with the value of traded commodities, the direction of travel is the most important thing. And since 1989, when Tendulkar made his Test debut and endorsed his first brand – Boost, a nutritional drink – his stock price has been going up and up. In all, he is believed to have lent his name to over 50 brands, earning an estimated $80m in endorsements alone. That wealth is based in particular on his popularity as an endorser of corporate brands, including Coca-Cola, Adidas, Toshiba and BP Castrol oil (alcohol and tobacco are off limits). Tendulkar is often seen as India's answer to David Beckham, or – pre-scandal – Tiger Woods. But there are stronger parallels with the packaging and selling of Arnold Palmer in 1960s USA. Palmer's America prefigured Tendulkar's India, full of economic and social optimism, with sport at its heart.

With the help of his agent Mark McCormack, Palmer defined the role of the brand ambassador, creating the blueprint used by

Indian businessman Mark Mascarenhas to build Tendulkar's profile. In 1996, Mascarenhas's WorldTel agency guaranteed his new client $7.5m a year; in 2001, that rose to $18m. Tendulkar introduced commerce to Indian sport. He changed the game. Palmer's value outlasted his career – 50 years after he last won a major, he remains in the top ten of the world's highest-earning golfers – and Tendulkar's sponsors were keen to plan ahead. "Whether he plays cricket, it will not affect our relationship," said Adidas India brand director Tushar Goculdas. Coca-Cola's Indian representative reckoned Tendulkar was "an icon of happiness, much like Coca-Cola". Property developers Amit Enterprises were planning "Sachin-branded residences"; their managing director described Tendulkar as "an evergreen brand".

His initial post-retirement activity balanced commerce with a strong social agenda: Tendulkar, whose wife Anjali is a paediatrician, became the first UNICEF ambassador for South Asia, with a focus on children's health. Recently, Aviva Life Insurance depicted him as an emblem of reliability with an advert in which the adult Tendulkar offers advice to his 16-year-old self before his maiden Test innings.

So where next? Harish Krishnamachar, senior vice-president of the Indian branch of World Sport Group, the company that manages Tendulkar's endorsements, says: "Brand Sachin has come to represent respect, consistency, humility and excellence – its stature has grown with Sachin getting the Bharat Ratna and becoming a Rajya Sabha MP. Through the brands he represents, he will be looking to share what it took to become a world-class sportsman, and how he managed to stay there for so long."

India, though, is an increasingly young nation. With half the population aged 30 or under, Tendulkar's legacy may not last for ever. Bollywood star Amitabh Bachchan is one of the most featured faces in Indian advertising, and reinvention has been the hallmark of his 45-year career. But Krishnamachar does not foresee a problem: "Sachin has built up such a stature and reputation over the years that there is no reason why the second phase of his life will not be as successful as the first."

With three wins and two defeats, India finished third in Group A. The tournament's format more or less guaranteed their entry into the quarter-finals, but Pakistan – second in their group – had to travel to India for the knockout. For Javed Miandad – the only man apart from Tendulkar to play six World Cups – it was a bitter farewell.

India v Pakistan
Quarter-final, at Bangalore, March 9, 1996 (day/night)
India 287-8;
Pakistan 248-9.
India won by 39 runs.
Tendulkar: 31

Wisden 1997

This encounter inspired high passions which boiled over back in Pakistan after India won. One fan reportedly shot his television and then himself, while captain Wasim Akram was burned in effigy. Wasim was not even playing, having ruptured his side muscles, but conspiracy theorists, fuelled by the previous year's allegations of bribery, speculated that he might have withdrawn deliberately, a charge he indignantly denied. In fact, the game looked keenly contested and turned into a thriller. India chose to bat but, though the bowlers made no gains until the 22nd over, their top batsmen never quite took control either. Tendulkar's 31 was a trifle by his standards. Sidhu, seven short of his century when Mushtaq Ahmed's flipper deceived him, steered India to an impressive-sounding 168 for two, but the scoring-rate was barely four and a half an over. It was Jadeja who played the decisive role, scoring 45 from 25 balls (four fours and two sixes), coupled with a tremendous onslaught from the tail. They smashed 51 off the last three overs. Waqar Younis bowled two of those overs for 40 runs, after his first eight had cost just 27. Meanwhile, a slow over-rate was punished by the deduction of an over from Pakistan's reply, the only such penalty in the tournament. Even so, their openers seized the initiative. Saeed Anwar had scored 48 from 32 balls, including two sixes, when he skied to Kumble; stand-in captain Aamir Sohail was 55 from 46, with one six, when he slashed wildly at Venkatesh Prasad. Pakistan made 113 for two from the vital first 15 overs, putting them way ahead of India. But Prasad grabbed two more wickets and, gradually, the scoring-rate faltered. Rashid Latif, with two big sixes in a run-a-ball 26, kept Pakistan going, but his stumping sparked a collapse to Kumble. The run-out of Javed Miandad signalled the end of Pakistan's reign as one-day champions.

For Indian cricket-lovers, the 1996 semi-final at Eden Gardens holds sad memories: once again, Tendulkar top-scored in an Indian defeat; once again, there was crowd trouble from angry fans, who set fire to the stands; once again, a talented Indian line-up subsided to a panicky collapse; and, once again, India lost a World Cup semi-final at home, their second since the defeat to England at the Wankhede in the 1987 World Cup.

India v Sri Lanka
Semi-final, at Calcutta, March 13, 1996 (day/night)
Sri Lanka 251-8;
India 120-8.
Sri Lanka won by default.
Tendulkar: 2-34; 65

Wisden 1997

Sri Lanka played brilliantly after a disastrous first over to achieve an unbeatable advantage. But the headlines were devoted to the riot which ended the match. Enraged by an Indian collapse of seven wickets for 22, some home supporters threw bottles on to the outfield and set fire to the seating. Referee Clive Lloyd took the teams off for 15 minutes, attempted a restart, and then awarded Sri Lanka the game by default. Nobody questioned the result; India needed a near-impossible 132 from 15.5 overs, with only two wickets standing. But the Indian board smarted at the word default and asked for Sri Lanka to be declared winners on run-rate.

The authorities – and many home fans – were intensely embarrassed by the trouble. Even as the match was abandoned, one Indian raised a banner reading: "Congratulation [sic] Sri Lanka – we are sorry". Some took out apologetic advertisements in the Sri Lankan press. But, like the Pakistani fans four days before, others raged against their unsuccessful players, and a guard was put on captain Azharuddin's house.

Azharuddin took much criticism for fielding first. He knew Sri Lanka preferred to chase, as they had done to beat India in Delhi, but critics argued that he should play to his team's strengths, not his opponents' weaknesses. There were few objections, however, when Kaluwitharana and Jayasuriya, Sri Lanka's celebrated pinch-hitters, both hit straight to third man in the first four balls of the game. Gurusinha soon followed, but de Silva determinedly stuck to the strategy of scoring as heavily as possible early on: he hit 22 off Prasad's first two overs. Though he was bowled in the 15th over, de Silva had scored 66, with 14 fours, off 47 balls, and Sri Lanka already had 85. Ranatunga and Roshan Mahanama (who eventually succumbed to cramp) kept up a steady five an over.

A target of 252 was not necessarily beyond India's batting heroes. However, Tendulkar was stumped and when, seven balls later, Azharuddin gave Kumar Dharmasena a return catch, the 100,000 crowd was stunned into silence. That did not last, as the collapse fuelled their fury, and no play was possible after the loss of Aashish Kapoor to de Silva's running catch in the deep.

Yet the presentation ceremony went ahead as if nothing untoward had occurred, and, against the smoking backdrop, Tony Greig conducted post-match interviews so normal they were bizarre.

1999 WORLD CUP

Despite qualifying for the Super Sixes with wins over England, Kenya and Sri Lanka, India never posed a serious threat to the likes of Australia and South Africa. For Tendulkar it was a time of personal crisis: he lost his father, Ramesh, during the tournament. He skipped the game against Zimbabwe (which India lost by three runs) to attend the funeral, and returned four days later to play what was then the most determined and emotional knock of his career – a century against Kenya at Bristol that he dedicated to the man he calls his "biggest inspiration". From that day, whenever he scored a century, Tendulkar looked skywards – a son's way of thanking his father for all he achieved.

India's only consolation in an otherwise forgettable tournament was a win against Pakistan in the Super Sixes, to preserve their unbeaten World Cup record against the old enemy.

India v Kenya
Group A, at Bristol, May 23, 1999
India 329-2 (R. Dravid 104*, S. R. Tendulkar 140*);
Kenya 235-7 (D. S. Mohanty 4-56).
India won by 94 runs.
Tendulkar: 140*

Wisden 2000

A passionate, awe-inspiring display by Tendulkar kept India in the hunt for the Super Six. He had returned from his father's funeral in India the day before. And, when he came in at 92 for two, Bristol heard a roar from the crowd that probably startled the lions in the zoo. Tendulkar started carefully, but accelerated after each landmark: 50 came off 54 balls, 100 in 84. He flicked the last ball of the innings over mid-wicket for six – his third, in addition to 16 fours – to finish on 140 from 101 balls. It was his 22nd one-day international century, but the first when he was not opening. The stand of 237 in 29 overs with Rahul Dravid, who was in lovely touch while scoring a century (almost ignored), was the highest in World Cup history – until India's next match.

Kenya's batsmen were so stunned that they failed to hit the boundary until the tenth over. But Tikolo guided them to respectability in a partnership of 118 with Kennedy Otieno. In the absence of the injured Kumble and Prasad, Debasis Mohanty, swinging the ball both ways, was the pick of the bowlers. But the day belonged to Tendulkar, who dedicated his highest World Cup score to his father's memory.

2003 WORLD CUP

India's World Cup campaign followed a 5–2 loss in New Zealand on a host of lively pitches that drew disparaging remarks from the tourists' batsmen. But, come the tournament itself, Tendulkar was in the form of his life. He didn't face a single ball in the nets throughout the competition, preferring hundreds of throwdowns – and his strategy worked a treat. His 673 runs were a new World Cup record, and meant he was the tournament's highest scorer for the second time; he also went past Javed Miandad as the greatest run-scorer in all World Cups. His tally included 152 against Namibia at Pietermaritzburg, a memorable 98 against Pakistan at Centurion, and 97 against Sri Lanka at Johannesburg. But it wasn't all smooth sailing. India's tournament got off to a shaky start, much to the anger of the fans back home, with an unconvincing 68-run win against the part-timers from the Netherlands. But it was after the match against Australia – when India were blown away for 125 – that pundits and fans properly ripped into the team.

Australia v India
Group A, at Centurion, February 15, 2003
India 125;
Australia 128-1.
Australia won by nine wickets.
Tendulkar: 36

Wisden 2004

This was the Australia the rest of the world had been dreading: an unstoppable force, which blasted away one of their most highly fancied rivals through force of reputation and a swinging ball. India, uneasy against Holland, were quivering here – all nervous edges and twitches, with no vivacious strokeplay until Harbhajan Singh briefly revelled in the freedom of a lost cause. McGrath's probing line and Lee's waspish pace created the nervy mood, but it was Jason Gillespie who snuffed out India's hopes. Instead of respite, he provided mean accuracy at first change, bowling ten overs straight through and taking three for 13. India's last hope evaporated with Tendulkar, removed by a magical slow off-cutter from Gillespie. Their top six had made 51 between them. It took Australia just 22.2 overs to overtake India's lowest-ever World Cup total, as Adam Gilchrist and Matthew Hayden entertained those of the crowd who were not burying their heads in their hands, and despairing at the apparent inevitability of it all.

After India's humiliating nine-wicket defeat, things got out of control back home, with fans burning effigies of captain Sourav Ganguly, and vandalising batsman Mohammad Kaif's home in Allahabad. The players turned to Tendulkar to restore calm. Before India's third game against Namibia in Pietermaritzburg, he read out a statement on behalf of the team: "This is to all the well-wishers in India… We ourselves are very disappointed with the kind of performances we have put up and I also understand the disappointment you have gone through. I am just here to assure all of you that we will be fighting in all the games until the last ball is bowled."

And fight they did, remaining unbeaten all the way until the final, as India put on their best showing at a World Cup since 1983. They finished the group stage and the Super Sixes in second place, just behind Australia.

While a couple of senior players thought Tendulkar should bat at No. 3 to lend more stability to the team, he eventually batted in his favourite opening position. The move paid off, especially in the run-chase against Pakistan in the Super Sixes, and in laying the foundation during the games against England, Sri Lanka and Kenya.

India v Namibia
Group A, at Pietermaritzburg, February 23, 2003
India 311 (S. R. Tendulkar 152, S. C. Ganguly 112*);
Namibia 130 (Yuvraj Singh 4-6).
India won by 181 runs.
Tendulkar: 152

Wisden 2004

India's batting blasted off at last, propelling them to their biggest victory in the World Cup (at least until they thrashed Sri Lanka in the Super

Sixes). Earlier in the week, the team had been greeted rapturously when they helped unveil a plaque at Pietermaritzburg station where, in 1893, Mahatma Gandhi had been thrown off a train because of his colour. Here at the cricket ground, their support was equally fervent. To shouts of "Sachin, Sachin", Tendulkar eased his way to 152 – his 34th one-day century – without ever producing that familiar, resounding crack of the bat. Namibia, who had chosen to field first, had the despair of dropping him on 32, although Ganguly played, if anything, with more freedom and found his form with hoisted fours and sixes. Together they added 244, their third stand of more than 200 in one-day internationals. Jan-Berrie Burger then injected some fire to Namibia's reply – hitting four fours and a six – but after he had gone their biggest success was managing to bat out more than 42 overs.

England v India
Group A, at Durban, February 26, 2003 (day/night)
India 250-9;
England 168 (A. Nehra 6-23).
India won by 82 runs.
Tendulkar: 50

Wisden 2004

This time it was England who fell foul of the toss of a coin and a zesty young fast bowler. Beginning the match with a dicky ankle and 30 wickets in 32 one-day internationals, Ashish Nehra snatched six for 23 and wiped out England's chase with searing pace and swing – much as James Anderson had done to Pakistan. It was, at the time, the third-best analysis in World Cup history – and the best away from the green fields of Headingley. It was also a kick in the guts for England, who had earlier managed to subdue India after a booming overture worth 75 from the first 11 overs. It was Andrew Flintoff who silenced the innings: Virender Sehwag got a leading edge and Tendulkar, in ineffable form and hitting with silky ferocity, cut to point just after drinks. After that, the next ten overs produced 21 runs; Flintoff, straight and fast, leaked just nine in his first eight overs. However, Dravid and Yuvraj Singh broke loose, adding a run-a-ball 62, and though England filched four wickets from the last four balls, their spirits were soon flagging again. Knight underestimated Kaif's agility and was run out in the second over of the reply, Marcus Trescothick mis-hooked, and as the ball swung under the lights, Michael Vaughan barely survived a mesmeric spell from Zaheer Khan. Nehra then made the key thrusts: in his third over, he induced a bottom-edge from Nasser Hussain, then trapped Alec Stewart with an inswinger; in his fourth, he had Vaughan caught behind with something equally unanswerable. The top six had made 62 between them, and only Flintoff, in his best all-round performance for England, prevented a massacre.

India v Sri Lanka
Super Sixes, at Johannesburg, March 10, 2003
India 292-6;
Sri Lanka 109 (J. Srinath 4-35, A. Nehra 4-35).
India won by 183 runs.
Tendulkar: 97

Wisden 2004

Jayasuriya arrived with a bad thumb and a bruised forearm; from the moment he inserted India on a decent pitch, he had a colossal headache as well. Sri Lanka's fast bowlers – Chaminda Vaas apart – were ill equipped for the task, leaving Tendulkar and Sehwag to put on 153, the third and highest century stand they had shared in ten innings opening together. Tendulkar met Vaas judiciously, Muttiah Muralitharan introspectively, and regally dismissed the rest from his presence. He fell just short of a hundred for the second time in ten days, but passed 500 runs for the second World Cup running. Sehwag played with a responsibility often lacking before his late blitz ended at long-on. India's 292 for six looked insurmountable and, by the fourth over of their reply, a misconceived Sri Lankan batting order had proved as much. Marvan Atapattu, Jehan Mubarak, a static and inexperienced No. 3, Mahela Jayawardene, hopelessly bereft of form, and de Silva all went for nought. When Jayasuriya scooped Javagal Srinath to Kaif at cover it told of his handicap. Kaif finished with four catches – a World Cup fielding record – but Srinath's four wickets deservedly won the match award and made all India's labours to tempt him out of retirement worthwhile. India's zest and skill had ensured their place in the semi-finals; Sri Lanka could still get there, but they began to wonder quite how.

India v Kenya
Semi-final, at Durban, March 20, 2003
India 270-4 (S. C. Ganguly 111*);
Kenya 179.
India won by 91 runs.
Tendulkar: 83; 2-28

Wisden 2004

The steel instilled into the Indian team and distilled by Ganguly, drop by steady drop, ensured there were no Disneyfied endings for Kenya. Captaining India for the 99th time in a one-day international, Ganguly re-emphasised his batting mastery against modest attacks to guide his team to an imposing if not unanswerable total, then sat back as his pace trio did the needful. India equalled their record for consecutive successes, set in 1985, with win No. 8. India began carefully enough but Ganguly was in no mood to accept dictation. After five runs had been squeezed from leg-spinner Collins Obuya's opening two overs, he darted out to launch a six off the first ball of his third, then repeated the message four balls later; the chastened Obuya lasted just six overs. Tendulkar seemed destined for a hundred until he pulled Tikolo to deep midwicket. But Ganguly matched Mark Waugh's 1996 feat of three centuries in a World Cup tournament, getting there with his fifth six.

India had made it to a World Cup final for the first time in 20 years. But Ricky Ponting's finest one-day innings coincided with Tendulkar's second single-digit score of the tournament, after a run of 36, 81, 152, 50, 98, 5, 97, 15 and 83. It all started to go wrong at the toss, when Sourav Ganguly decided to bowl. And there was no coming back after Australia reached 359 for two, with Ponting hitting a blistering 140 not out. It was yet another bittersweet end to a World Cup for Tendulkar, who had to watch the Australians celebrate on the podium as he waited to collect the Man of the Tournament trophy from Garry Sobers.

Australia v India
Final, at Johannesburg, March 23, 2003
Australia 359-2 (R. T. Ponting 140*);
India 234.
Australia won by 125 runs.
Tendulkar: 4

John Stern, *Wisden* 2004

Ricky Ponting played a captain's innings to deliver Australia their third title. His 140, the highest individual score in a World Cup final, and his leadership through the tournament completed his ascent from underachieving Tasmanian devil to cornerstone of Australian dominance.

Just like Nasser Hussain at Brisbane a few months earlier, Ganguly raised eyebrows by putting Australia in. He was acting from fear of Australia's bowlers rather than on aggressive intent: against any other opponents, he would surely have batted first. Yet it had been 71 matches and three years since Australia last failed to defend a total of 200 or more.

Ganguly was right to think that the pitch would offer movement and bounce, but his in-form seamers were now under pressure to perform. They buckled. The first over from Zaheer contained ten deliveries and 15 runs, and there was no coming back. Gilchrist and Hayden chanced their arms, as they do: after nine overs, Australia were 74 without loss. "Intent and intimidate – that has been our motto," said Ponting afterwards. The grammar was dubious; the effectiveness beyond question.

Ganguly turned to spin in the tenth over, and Harbhajan Singh did send back both openers. But Australia were not reined in for long. The partnership of 234 between Ponting and Damien Martyn was Australia's highest for any wicket in one-day internationals. So was their total. Martyn's performance was the more remarkable because he had missed the semi-final with a finger injury and was not expected to play. His batting was the perfect foil for Ponting – selfless, intelligent and perfectly tuned to the situation. Martyn actually reached his fifty first, despite a six-over handicap. Ponting was just warming up. He started slowly, his first 50 taking 74 balls to Martyn's 46, and containing a single four. Off his next 47 balls, he scored 90 runs and hit three more fours and eight sixes – the most in a World Cup innings, beating seven by Viv Richards and Ganguly – all on the leg side.

Australia's acceleration had been breathtaking: 109 off the last ten overs, 64 off the last five. Srinath conceded 87 runs, the most in a final.

The army of Indian supporters – many from the UK – had been bemused when Ganguly asked Australia to bat. By the interval, they had all but given up hope. The dream was shattered entirely when Tendulkar tried to pull McGrath's fifth ball and was caught by the bowler off a top edge. Sehwag, who was caught off a Lee no-ball on four, did his best to keep India in it with a bullish run-a-ball 82, including ten fours and three sixes. But he was run out by a direct hit from Darren Lehmann at deep mid-off, ending a promising stand of 88 with Dravid.

Rain had briefly threatened the unsatisfactory prospect of a replay the following day, with Australia's record-breaking performances consigned to history – so every sign of precipitation was greeted uproariously by India's fans. Knowing his side had to bowl 25 overs to ensure a result, Ponting brought on his spinners: there was a surreal period where Brad Hogg and Lehmann were being thrashed to all parts as Indian supporters cheered and the fielders, running to their positions to speed up the over-rate, got wet.

Then the umpires called for a drinks break. After drinks, McGrath and Andy Bichel returned, the lights came on, and the rain became heavy enough for the players to leave the field, with India on 103 for three. They returned 25 minutes later – no overs were deducted – and the formality of Australia's third World Cup (and 17th consecutive one-day victory) was completed under darkening skies to the sound of frequent thunderclaps.

2007 WORLD CUP

Of his six World Cups, 2007 was India's – and Tendulkar's – worst. Controversy behind the scenes did not help. Unhappy to be batting at No. 4, a move instigated by coach Greg Chappell, Tendulkar scored seven and nought against Bangladesh and Sri Lanka. And, for the first time since 1992, India did not make it past round one. Back home, angry fans attacked M. S. Dhoni's home in Ranchi, and questioned the players' commitment, while pundits predicted the end was nigh for Tendulkar. The BCCI machinery swung into action by resting "senior players", including Ganguly and Tendulkar, for India's tour of Bangladesh in May 2007, and clamping down on endorsements. Tendulkar later blamed Chappell for backroom politics, unprofessional behaviour and his zealous engagement with a sensationalist media – only to receive a show-cause notice from the BCCI for his troubles. Chappell resigned as India and Tendulkar looked to pick up the pieces.

2011 WORLD CUP

Tendulkar will, it turns out, live happily ever after, finishing his final World Cup with victory in his home town and a shoulder-high escort around the Wankhede from his team-mates. Though he made only 18 in the final against Sri Lanka, his 85 against Pakistan in the semi-final at Mohali – arguably the most high-pressure game of the tournament – was crucial. His tournament tally of 482, including centuries against England and – his 99th in all internationals – South Africa, was second only to Sri Lankan Tillekeratne Dilshan's 500 for Sri Lanka. Perhaps just as gratifyingly, he was finally part of an Indian team that did not rely only on him to marshal tricky run-chases.

India's campaign had begun with a win against Bangladesh, took in a thrilling tie with England in Bangalore, then went from strength to strength with victories over Ireland, the Netherlands, West Indies, Australia, Pakistan and Sri Lanka – the last four being the only other teams to have won the World Cup. There was just one defeat, against the South Africans in Nagpur, when Tendulkar's 101-ball 111 was followed by India's only collapse of the tournament.

So nervous was Tendulkar during India's pursuit of Sri Lanka's 274 in the final that he refused to watch the game from the players' balcony. Instead, he was praying in the dressing-room. Someone was obviously listening.

India v England
Group B, at Bangalore, February 27, 2011 (day/night)
India 338 (S. R. Tendulkar 120, T. T. Bresnan 5-48);
England 338-8 (A. J. Strauss 158).
Tied.
Tendulkar: 120

Wisden 2012

This was the match that had everything – except, astonishingly, a winner. Of the 23 previous ties in one-day internationals, only Napier in 2007-08, when New Zealand and England made 340 apiece, had produced more runs. Now, India and England were left with the same mixture of relief and regret, for the last hour contained the ebb and flow of a mini Test classic. Set 339, more than any team had ever scored batting second in a World Cup match, England were 280 for two after 42 overs when they took the batting powerplay. Zaheer promptly removed Ian Bell, who was suffering from cramp, to end a third-wicket stand of 170 with Andrew Strauss, who was trapped next ball by an unplayable yorker. England needed an unlikely 29 off two overs. With 14 needed off the last over, Ajmal Shahzad calmly hit the third ball for a straight six, then ran a bye and, when Graeme Swann took two off the fifth, England required two to win off the last ball. Swann could manage only a single to mid-off, and the atmosphere at the Chinnaswamy Stadium deflated like a bad soufflé. England had seemed out of it completely while Tendulkar was compiling a record fifth World Cup century and Anderson was conceding more runs than any England bowler in the competition's history. But India slipped from 305 for three in the 46th over, and were left to regret the short run signalled against Munaf Patel as India lost their final wicket attempting a second.

India v South Africa
Group B, at Jamtha, Nagpur, March 12, 2011 (day/night)
India 296 (S. R. Tendulkar 111, D. W. Steyn 5-50);
South Africa 300-7.
South Africa won by three wickets.
Tendulkar: 111

Wisden 2012

This was a match that ebbed and flowed to the last, enriched throughout by undercurrents of dazzling strokeplay, fabulous fielding and exceptional bowling. At one stage, with Tendulkar and Sehwag treating the world's best new-ball attack like schoolboys, a total of 400 seemed possible on a typical Nagpur shirtfront. Sehwag started the Indian innings with a boundary for the fifth match running and, although he eventually fell after 12 fours in 66 balls, Tendulkar's masterful 111 – his sixth World Cup hundred and 99th in all international cricket, reached in 92 deliveries – led India to 267 for one with more than ten overs to go. However, Morne Morkel removed Tendulkar, slicing high to point, before Dale Steyn embarked on a perfectly controlled spell of reverse swing, picking up five for four in 16 balls as India disastrously lost nine for 29. Hashim Amla and Jacques Kallis led an assured South African reply and, although Harbhajan Singh was rediscovering his zest, a magnificent 39-ball knock from A. B. de Villiers appeared to leave the visitors dead certs. India, though, refused to fade into the night. Cameos were cut short and, when Zaheer conceded only four from a high-class penultimate over, South Africa needed 13 off six balls. After lengthy deliberation, Dhoni tossed the ball to Nehra rather than Harbhajan. An inside-edged four and a swiped six from Robin Peterson later, the game was as good as over. Two balls after that and it finally was, leaving a capacity crowd to trudge home in contemplative silence, and Dhoni to vent his irritation at India's profligacy with the bat.

India v Australia
Quarter-final, at Ahmedabad, March 24, 2011 (day/night)
Australia 260-6 (R. T. Ponting 104);
India 261-5.
India won by five wickets.
Tendulkar: 53

Wisden 2012

A tense game that many thought would be the final was settled by the cool head of the in-form Yuvraj Singh after a bloody-minded hundred from Ponting had threatened to leave Australia only two wins away from a fourth successive World Cup triumph. The story of a baking-hot afternoon was Ponting's magnificent – and, it turned out, final – tantrum against the dying of the captaincy light. India bowled tidily, with Yuvraj again central to the plan, and fielded better than they had at any point in the tournament. But Ponting, grimly and gutsily placing substance before style, drew on all his experience to compile his 30th one-day international hundred – and fifth in World Cups – before a breezy 38 from 26 balls by David Hussey set India a target that Australia's bowlers seemed equipped to defend. Sehwag left early, but resolute fifties from Tendulkar – who moved past 18,000 one-day international runs – and Gautam Gambhir kept the game in the balance until an awful shot from Virat Kohli, who heaved a full toss to midwicket, ceded the initiative. When Dhoni departed, India still needed 74, but Suresh Raina, chosen ahead of Yusuf Pathan, eased nerves with a flurry of shots and, with Yuvraj's help, saw off a superb spell from Lee. In the end, with Shaun Tait losing his bearings, it was Australia who cracked. Yuvraj's bended-knee and swinging-bat celebrations echoed the thoughts of a raucous Motera crowd convinced the home side had passed the sternest test of all.

India v Pakistan
Semi-final, at Mohali, March 30, 2011 (day/night)
India 260-9 (Wahab Riaz 5-46);
Pakistan 231.
India won by 29 runs.
Tendulkar: 85

Dileep Premachandran, *Wisden* 2012

Not even a rare diplomatic tête-à-tête between the two countries' political leaders, sitting side by side beyond the boundary, could distract an intense crowd, including a small smattering from across the border, from the action within it. Like most matches between these bitter rivals, this could have been scripted in Bollywood, as jubilant heroes jostled for attention with cartoon-style villains. Sehwag started with a boundary barrage before Wahab Riaz swung one into his pads, but the action quickly centred on his opening partner Tendulkar. First he was reprieved on 23, after umpire Ian Gould initially upheld Saeed Ajmal's convincing shout for leg-before; to gasps from fans on both sides, Hawk-Eye ruled the ball was missing leg stump by the narrowest of margins. Next ball he was almost stumped, then, astonishingly, he was dropped four times – on 27, 45, 70 and 81, all of them catchable, three of them off Shahid Afridi – as Misbah-ul-Haq, Younis Khan and the Akmal brothers tried to outdo each other for comical ineptitude. Ajmal finally got Tendulkar 15 runs short of his 100th international hundred after Riaz, who finished with his first five-for in one-day internationals, had silenced India's middle order. But Umar Gul went AWOL, and Raina's nuggety 36 ensured Pakistan would have to chase more than five an over. They were in control until Mohammad Hafeez's daft attempt to paddle-sweep Patel from wide outside off stump ended with an edge through to the keeper. When Younis spooned Yuvraj Singh to cover, the mood around the ground changed to one of shrill celebration. India fielded almost maniacally, and with Misbah unaccountably leaving the big hitting until the cause was lost, they were comfortable winners for the fifth time out of five in World Cup games against Pakistan.

India v Sri Lanka
Final, at Mumbai, April 2, 2011 (day/night)
Sri Lanka 274-6 (D. P. M. D. Jayawardene 103*);
India 277-4.
India won by six wickets.
Tendulkar: 18

Simon Wilde, *Wisden* 2012

India, favourites with a battery of pundits and a billion supporters, made light of the expectation to win a seesaw encounter worthy of the occasion. Twice they lost control of the game: first towards the end of Sri Lanka's innings, when Jayawardene swept to a sublime century; then at the beginning of their own, as Lasith Malinga silenced a partisan crowd. But, led by an impressively cool innings from Dhoni, they ended up decisive winners, sparking mass celebrations on the streets of Mumbai, across India as a whole and throughout the nation's vast diaspora.

Their previous World Cup triumph, in 1983, had been a surprise. This time, anything but victory would have been a failure, and it was a measure of their progress under Gary Kirsten, their departing coach, that they took so much in their stride. By adding the scalp of Sri Lanka to those of Pakistan in the semi-finals, Australia in the quarters and West Indies in their final group match, they had beaten all the other World Cup winners.

India also became the first team to win a final on home soil, and the outcome was particularly sweet for Tendulkar, playing his sixth World Cup – equalling Javed Miandad's record – and surely his last. The dream scenario entailed a 100th international century to win the game in the city of his birth, but despite an unscripted failure for 18 he described the day as one of his most memorable in a career now spanning four decades. Both he and Kirsten were chaired around the outfield. As Kohli, who had just celebrated his first birthday when Tendulkar made his international debut in 1989, put it: "He has carried the burden of the nation for 21 years. It is time we carried him on our shoulders."

Plaudits also fell to Dhoni, who played a captain's innings on a par with Clive Lloyd's in the 1975 final and Ricky Ponting's in 2003, when five of the Indians playing here had finished on the losing side. Despite a quiet tournament with the bat, he boldly promoted himself to No. 5, partly to take on Muralitharan, partly to take on responsibility. And with his side 114 for three chasing 275, the game was in the balance: only two teams had won finals batting second, and neither had pursued as many. But Dhoni maintained his exceptional record as a finisher by slapping Sri Lanka into submission.

Well though India played, Sri Lanka appeared daunted. Previously, no side had made more than one change for a World Cup final; curiously, the Sri Lankans made four. Angelo Mathews had picked up a leg injury in the semi-final, but Ajantha Mendis and Rangana Herath, who boasted respective tournament economy-rates of 3.14 and 4.27, were left out, and Chamara Silva was also dropped.

One of those preferred, Suraj Randiv, had only just arrived in India after being summoned to replace the injured Mathews. Then, Kumar Sangakkara's call at the toss was not heard properly by Jeff Crowe, the referee who had presided over the bad-light farce in the final at Bridgetown four years earlier. Now, after some confusion, he ordered a retake. To Dhoni's irritation, Sangakkara – who seemed content for a second go – won and opted to bat. Zaheer got them away strongly with three successive maidens, followed by the wicket of the becalmed Upul Tharanga. Shanthakumaran Sreesanth, brought in as India's only change because Nehra had broken a finger in the semi-final, was less effective. Sri Lanka were still only two down at halfway, but Yuvraj's utilitarian slow left-armers were again vital as he removed Sangakkara for a well-crafted 48 and Thilan Samaraweera, lbw on review.

When Zaheer quickly accounted for Chamara Kapugedera, Sri Lanka were wobbling at 182 for five. While Nuwan Kulasekara provided the iron fist – hitting Zaheer for a huge six over midwicket – Jayawardene was all velvet glove. He scarcely deserved to become the first World Cup final centurion to finish on the losing side. With Tissara Perera taking 16 off the final four balls, Zaheer's last 13 deliveries cost 39, and Sri Lanka went into the break apparently holding the initiative. This was certainly the case once Malinga ripped out India's openers in a burst that stunned the stadium. Sehwag, who needlessly challenged his lbw verdict, was trapped on the back foot second ball, and Tendulkar, who had shaped well, was also beaten for pace as he attempted a big drive. But Sri Lanka's reshuffled pack was short of a second ace, and Gambhir – dropped on 30 by Kulasekara – and Kohli turned things round in a stand of 83. Muralitharan, entering in the 19th over, cut a forlorn figure and did not even complete his allocation after two overs cost 19. A fine return catch by Dilshan removed Kohli. But then came Dhoni.

WHEN SACHIN WEPT

Sambit Bal, *Wisden* 2012

As Sachin Tendulkar was hoisted on the shoulders of Virat Kohli and Suresh Raina – who were aged one and three when their boyhood hero first played for his country – the poignancy of the moment resonated across India. On a balmy April evening at Mumbai's Wankhede, Tendulkar wept, and a nation felt fulfilled, for while the noughties had belonged to India off the field, trophies remained the fans' only true currency. By 2010, a decade of sustained progress had earned the Test team the No. 1 spot. Now, 28 years after their first World Cup, the atmosphere in Tendulkar's home town seemed akin to cricket's second coming.

The contrast with 1983, when Kapil Dev's team had almost stumbled on World Cup glory, was instructive. Back then, fans watched the games on black-and-white television sets, often at the homes of their neighbours; owning a car was a big deal, even though there were only two models to choose from; and every large infrastructure project was funded by the World Bank. Even qualification for the semi-final that year felt like a triumph. From the final itself, they could have lived with the memory alone of Krishnamachari Srikkanth cover-driving Andy Roberts on bended knee. So the joy following the defeat of Clive Lloyd's

---

West Indians was heightened by an overwhelming sense of incredulity.

In 2011, in a results-driven, entrepreneurially charged, materially aspiring nation, winning the World Cup was not merely an expectation: it was seen as all but a right. The humiliation of 2007, when India were knocked out in the group stages, still rankled; there was a score to be settled with Australia for the drubbing in the 2003 final, and a perfect tournament record against Pakistan to be maintained; and then there was Tendulkar, who now had everything apart from a World Cup. Every day, every hour, every minute, India's players felt the demand of an expectant nation.

Mahendra Singh Dhoni, their otherwise unflappable captain, admitted there were times when he could not bear to look at some of his team-mates: some could not eat, others could not sleep, while Yuvraj Singh, who threw up regularly, said in the end they left it to God, which was not thought to be a reference to Tendulkar. They were fortunate enough to have Dhoni, who developed the knack of insulating himself from the outside world. He shielded his players from the media, attending most of the press conferences himself, and on the field dispensed his earthy calm. His sangfroid was well placed, for this was hardly a team of invincibles in the mould of the Australians of 2003 or 2007. Quite simply, without Dhoni's native intelligence, it is hard to see how India could have won.

Chapter 5

Leading Question:
The Captaincy Conundrum

N apoleon Bonaparte, strangely fond of anagrams, once said: "A leader is a dealer in hope." Sachin Tendulkar dealt mostly in a sense of hopelessness during his two stabs at the India captaincy, in 1996-97 and 1999-2000: his time in charge ranged from the merely unsuccessful to the very depths of despair. It is not a subplot that sits easily within his narrative.

Tendulkar struggled with several aspects of the job: man-management of players less talented than he was, frustration over selection politics, an inability to switch off once he left the field, and the debilitating pressure generated by the standards he set himself and his team.

"When I was not able to bowl an outswinger, he would shout from the slips, 'bahar dalo' [make it move away]," Javagal Srinath recalls. But Srinath could not. In the nets after the game, Tendulkar bowled a few outswingers and told Srinath: "Do it like this." There appeared to be little understanding that what came so naturally to him was the result of excruciating toil for his team-mate. "You could see him getting frustrated," said Srinath. "He wanted to win so badly."

Tendulkar hated losing even a game of table tennis on tour. If India placed an unreasonable burden of expectation on Tendulkar the batsman, Tendulkar the captain placed an even more exacting burden *on his team-mates. In his autobiography, he wrote of feeling devastated by defeat and ravaged by self-doubt. In 1997, he even contemplated walking away from cricket.*

His predecessor, Mohammad Azharuddin, was no great leader of men either, but Tendulkar had big shoes to fill nonetheless: Azhar had been India's most successful Test and limited-overs captain. For Tendulkar, a record of four wins and nine defeats in 25 Tests, and 23 wins and 43 losses in one-day internationals, felt unacceptable.

His first crack at captaincy began in August 1996 with a century in a limited-overs game against Sri Lanka, and a thrashing of a champion Australian Test team in the newly instituted Border–Gavaskar Trophy. But it ended a year later with his sacking – a phase in his career, Tendulkar admits, that rankles him even now.

Captaincy: Part One

Sri Lanka v India

Singer World Series, Game two, at R. Premadasa Stadium, Colombo

August 28, 1996 (day/night)

India 226-5 (S. R. Tendulkar 110);

Sri Lanka 230-1 (S. T. Jayasuriya 120).

Sri Lanka won by nine wickets.

Tendulkar: 110; 1-29

Trent Bouts, *Wisden* 1998

Tendulkar launched himself into captaincy with a century. But his 110, off 138 balls, was made to look pedestrian by Sanath Jayasuriya, who scored an unbeaten 120 off just 128. He saw Sri Lanka home with nine wickets and 5.4 overs to spare, but had to be carried from the field because of cramp. After Jayasuriya and Romesh Kaluwitharana had raised Sri Lanka's first-wicket record to 129, Aravinda de Silva scored a composed 49 not out.

India beat Zimbabwe in the qualifying stages, but losses to Sri Lanka and Australia meant they failed to make it to the final of the four-team tournament.

Playing Pakistan has always been a test of nerve, and India – though they and Tendulkar began well – were not up to the challenge in the first Sahara Cup, a five-match one-day series in Canada.

India v Pakistan

Sahara Cup, First one-day international, at Toronto, September 16, 1996

Pakistan 170-9;

India 173-2.

India won by eight wickets.

Tendulkar: 89*

R. Mohan, *Wisden* 1998

The series made a belated start, after rain prevented any play over the weekend. Atmosphere was distinctly lacking, with only 750 watching on the Monday. The match was reduced to 33 overs a side and the pitch was still damp. India's bowling was spot on after Saeed Anwar, with 46 from 34 balls, and Ijaz Ahmed had taken Pakistan to 80 for one; only tailender Saqlain Mushtaq lifted them past 150. Timing the ball was not easy, but Tendulkar gave impetus to India's chase with a run-a-ball 89, including nine fours and three sixes, and settled the issue by adding 65 in nine overs with Mohammad Azharuddin.

India lost the second game, won the third and lost the fourth. With the series level at 2–2, Pakistan won the decider. While his limited-overs captaincy hadn't enjoyed the most auspicious start, in his first Test as captain, 23-year-old Tendulkar led his team to victory against a Warne-less Australian side on a stereotypical Delhi dustbowl.

India v Australia

Border–Gavaskar Trophy, Only Test, at Delhi, October 10–13, 1996

Australia 182 and 234 (A. Kumble 5-41);

India 361 (N. R. Mongia 152) and **58-3;**

India won by seven wickets.

Tendulkar: 10 and 0

Mike Coward, *Wisden* 1998

Conspiracy theories were inevitable once the bone-dry, fractured and shifting pitch was revealed at this neglected and unprepossessing ground. Would such a substandard pitch have been presented had Shane Warne recovered from delicate finger surgery in time to play? Mark Taylor chose to bat on what could have been mistaken for a third-day strip, but suspicions about the pitch seemed to dominate Australian thinking.

In fact Australia were bowled out in 73 overs on the opening day, eight of their wickets falling to spin. Their opponents' makeshift opener, Nayan Mongia, constructed a memorable 152 and thus ensured that India's new captain, Tendulkar, would maintain the team's unbeaten record in home Test series since March 1987. Sourav Ganguly and Steve Waugh were the only other batsmen to manage half-centuries, which was testimony to the magnitude of Mongia's performance. Waugh batted for 273 minutes at his second attempt – nine minutes longer than the entire Australian first innings – and remained unconquered on 67 as Anil Kumble and Venkatesh Prasad ran through his team-mates.

Though he had no reason to recall the match as a batsman, Tendulkar revealed himself to be a thoughtful and aggressive captain. The Australians were subdued and haunted by the realisation they had failed Allan Border when competing for a trophy partly named in honour of their mate and mentor. But Tendulkar had the satisfaction of becoming the first Indian captain to beat Australia since his own mentor and the other cricketer commemorated by the trophy, Sunil Gavaskar, in 1980-81. There was some hope that India's victory over the generally acknowledged Test champions, completed with a day to spare, would lift the profile of Test cricket in a country obsessed with the shortened form of the game.

The one-off Test was followed by a triangular tournament featuring Australia and South Africa – two of the most competitive one-day sides at the time. Tendulkar seemed to relish the challenge of close contests as he experimented with innovative field-settings and part-time bowlers.

India v Australia

Titan Cup, Game three, at Bangalore, October 21, 1996 (day/night)

Australia 215-7 (M. A. Taylor 105);

India 216-8.

India won by two wickets.

Tendulkar: 1-45; 88

Greg Baum, *Wisden* 1998

Taylor at last made his maiden one-day century in his 98th match and, with Steve Waugh, established a sound position. But a late collapse left Australia to defend a modest 215. India were quickly in trouble as night fell and, when Tendulkar was eighth out at 164, defeat seemed inevitable. Then bowlers Javagal Srinath and Anil Kumble gave the tale a final twist with an unbroken match-winning stand of 52 in seven overs.

India v Australia

Titan Cup, Game nine, at Mohali, November 3, 1996 (day/night)

India 289-6;

Australia 284.

India won by five runs.

Tendulkar: 62

Greg Baum, *Wisden* 1998

India scraped through in the match to decide South Africa's opponents in the final. Sent in by Taylor, who wanted to avoid bowling with a ball affected by the evening dew, they had mocked him by rattling up 289, equalling their highest score against Australia. Tendulkar, Azharuddin and Rahul Dravid were murderous on a perfect pitch. But Taylor and the rejuvenated Michael Slater replied in kind. When Australia began the last ten overs needing 62 with six wickets in hand, it seemed they must win. Then a series of accidents left them to get six from the last over with one wicket standing. Tendulkar brought himself on and appealed for lbw first ball; he did not get it, but wicketkeeper Mongia ran out Brad Hogg as he tried to steal a leg-bye.

India v South Africa

Titan Cup, Final, at Mumbai, November 6, 1996 (day/night)

India 220-7;

South Africa 185 (A. Kumble 4-25).

India won by 35 runs.

Tendulkar: 67

Greg Baum, *Wisden* 1998

The toss was crucial. Tendulkar won it, and took advantage of the pitch while it was still good, leading the way for India with 67. But the scoring-rate slowed until one-time opener Ajay Jadeja arrived at No. 7 to thrash 43 not out from 42 balls, including successive sixes from off-spinner Pat Symcox. India's 220 was worthier than it looked, and Tendulkar increased the pressure by keeping the field up, forcing South Africa to try to hit over the top on a pitch that got ever slower. At 96 for seven, the game was lost.

Buoyed by his victory in the Titan Cup, Tendulkar looked to preserve India's impeccable record at home, against South Africa in a three-Test series.

India v South Africa
First Test, at Ahmedabad, November 20–23, 1996
India 223 and 190;
South Africa 244 and 105 (J. Srinath 6-21).
India won by 64 runs.
Tendulkar: 42 and 7

Colin Bryden, *Wisden* 1998

Devastating pace bowling by Javagal Srinath gave India victory on a poor pitch. Though it seemed best suited to the spinners, Srinath's fast, accurate inswingers and off-cutters brought him career-best figures of six for 21. South Africa crashed for 105 after being set a modest 170 to win.

It was obvious that batting would not be easy on a brown, dusty pitch, and by winning the toss Tendulkar gave India a substantial advantage. But there were frequent changes of fortune and several questionable umpiring decisions. India negotiated the first morning safely enough until Sanjay Manjrekar misread a top-spinner from the unorthodox Paul Adams. Thereafter, they struggled against accurate bowling and sharp fielding. Allan Donald was superb, but the two most critical blows were struck by Jonty Rhodes. He held a dazzling diving catch at midwicket to dismiss Tendulkar and then ran out Azharuddin with a direct hit from cover.

Having restricted India to 223, South Africa needed to bat sensibly. Instead, they slumped to 119 for seven. Fanie de Villiers showed the application needed over three hours: first with Symcox, then Donald, he established a 21-run lead.

Donald struck twice before India erased the modest deficit, and they were 38 for three when Tendulkar sliced a slower delivery from Brian McMillan to Rhodes – again – at backward point. Donald had Azharuddin brilliantly caught at second slip by McMillan, and, when Dravid was trapped by Symcox, India were just 70 ahead with five down. The 22-year-old debutant V. V. S. Laxman showed a cool head during a 56-run partnership with Kumble.

Needing 170, with nearly two days to get them, South Africa looked to their openers for a solid start before the spinners came on. Instead, Srinath took centre stage. His fifth delivery swung in to Andrew Hudson and umpire S. K. Bansal's fateful finger rose (replays suggested it would have missed leg stump). Daryll Cullinan edged the next, and South Africa were two down without a run on the board. With Hansie Cronje the only batsman to last long, his team seldom looked like reaching the target. From 96 for four, South Africa lost their last six for nine runs. Tendulkar said he could not recall a Test with so many twists and turns.

South Africa came back forcefully to square the series at Eden Gardens, on the back of match-winning performances from Gary Kirsten and the debutant Lance Klusener. With the series tied at 1–1, the pressure was back on Tendulkar.

India v South Africa
Third Test, at Kanpur, December 8–12, 1996
India 237 (P. R. Adams 6-55) and **400-7 dec.** (M. Azharuddin 163*);
South Africa 177 and **180**.
India won by 280 runs.
Tendulkar: 61 and 36

Colin Bryden, *Wisden* 1998

India maintained their unbeaten record at home for a tenth series with a crushing victory. They managed only 237 in the first innings, but South Africa struggled even more, allowing India, inspired by a breathtaking century from Azharuddin, to take complete control.

Woorkeri Raman shared a solid stand of 76 with Mongia before McMillan removed them both. Then, after tea, Sourav Ganguly's dismissal by Cronje sparked off a collapse against the unorthodox left-arm spin of Adams, who celebrated each of his six wickets with a cartwheel. Tendulkar made his first Test half-century as captain, batting grimly for more than three hours and striking only two fours, plus a six off Symcox, as he reached 50. He then seemed ready to step up a gear, hitting Adams for two fours in an over, only to sky him to mid-off.

South Africa batted poorly against tight and accurate bowling. Again, the middle and lower orders were disappointing, and they were all out 60 behind.

The early loss of Raman gave South Africa hope and, even after India fought their way to 192 for five, a collapse might have given the tourists a chance. Azharuddin ended such thoughts. He was in majestic form and found the ideal partner in the unflappable Dravid, with whom he added 165.

South Africa, 460 behind, needed to survive ten hours. But their first series defeat since losing to West Indies in April 1992 was effectively sealed at 29 for three on the fourth afternoon.

Tendulkar's next assignment was a return series in South Africa – his first tour as captain was made even more challenging by the fact that India played just one practice game before the First Test on a lively Durban track. Acclimatising to foreign conditions, never a strength of the Indian team in the 1990s, was complicated by the lack of experience in the batting unit – Dravid, Ganguly and Laxman had all made their Test debuts just earlier that year. Zonal politics meant Tendulkar's plea for a quality third seamer had been disregarded, leaving Javagal Srinath and Venkatesh Prasad to do the heavy lifting.

South Africa v India

First Test, at Durban, December 26–28, 1996

South Africa 235 (B. K. V. Prasad 5-60) and **259** (B. K. V. Prasad 5-93);
India 100 (A. A. Donald 5-40) and **66**.
South Africa won by 328 runs.
Tendulkar: 15 and 4

Dicky Rutnagur, *Wisden* 1998

Inspired bowling by Donald on a pitch the like of which most of the Indians had never seen before created a three-day finish. India's two innings required a mere 73.2 overs, with Donald claiming nine for 54. Their second innings, 66, fell nine short of the previous-lowest against South Africa – by Australia, on the same ground in 1949-50.

The pitch provided excessive bounce as well as movement off the seam. South Africa's own batsmen were discomfited and the match would have been shorter still if India had had a third seamer of quality to support Srinath and Prasad, who bowled magnificently for five in each innings, and held their catches. Adding to the pitch's perils, the sky was overcast at the start, encouraging swing, so it was inevitable that Tendulkar would ask South Africa to bat. India struck early, when Prasad bowled Kirsten through the gate, but then Hudson and Adam Bacher, impressively self-assured, batted until lunch.

Despite the clouds lifting, South Africa lost four wickets in the next session. McMillan initiated a recovery which Shaun Pollock and Richardson sustained against a tiring attack.

India's reply realised just 100 and lasted barely three hours, with Donald taking five for 40. He produced what he himself pronounced one of the most lethal balls he had ever bowled. It uprooted Tendulkar's off stump, and not only came back at him, but also beat him for pace. Four overs later, Azharuddin mishooked McMillan and, with Donald showing no mercy, the Indians surrendered an hour before tea.

South Africa's second innings featured the only three-figure partnership of the match, between Hudson and Bacher, who scored a distinguished maiden fifty.

Facing arrears of 394, India submitted meekly. Donald broke their spirit by dismissing Vikram Rathore and Ganguly in his first over. In his third, Raman missed a full toss, and the end was near when Tendulkar and Azharuddin fell to Pollock. Tendulkar was superbly caught in the gully by Kirsten, but Azharuddin gifted his wicket with a heave that would embarrass a No. 11.

Despite a scintillating 222-run partnership between Tendulkar and Azharuddin in the Second Test at Cape Town, including a masterful 169 from Tendulkar, India lost by 282 runs. But their batsmen were now more in tune with the conditions and the captain was hopeful India would put up a better show in the Third Test. The weather denied them any chance of victory, however, and Tendulkar felt the 2–0 scoreline did not represent just how close India had come to winning their first Test in South Africa. So disappointed was Tendulkar he admitted he "locked myself in the bathroom and just cried".

South Africa v India
Third Test, at Johannesburg, January 16–20, 1997
India 410 (R. Dravid 148) and **266;**
South Africa 321 (J. Srinath 5-104) and **228-8** (D. J. Cullinan 122*).
Drawn.
Tendulkar: 35 and 9

Dicky Rutnagur, *Wisden* 1998

With only honour and prize money to play for, India almost won. The weather, plus Cullinan's heroic unbeaten century and two-hour eighth-wicket stand with Klusener, saved the day for South Africa.

The pitch was not as lively as expected, and the Wanderers did not live up to its reputation for encouraging bowlers on the first morning – for the first time in the series, the new ball did India no harm. The openers survived 23 overs, though they scored only 25. The innings eventually acquired momentum through a fourth-wicket partnership of 145 between Dravid and Ganguly, after Tendulkar, who had promised something substantial, sliced at Cronje's outswinger. But that was the last wicket South Africa captured on the opening day.

Overnight rain cost the second morning and, within 20 minutes of resuming, Ganguly edged a ball slanted across him. Azharuddin tried to storm the bowling but left quickly, while Laxman was cut short by a fractured finger. Kumble and Srinath lent Dravid support until he finally holed out, having batted nine hours for 148.

South Africa faced only two balls that night before the light failed. Next morning, Srinath and Prasad bowled superbly; and half an hour after lunch South Africa were 147 for five, Srinath claiming three. The all-rounders turned the tide. McMillan dropped anchor while Pollock flayed the bowling; they put on 112. Then Klusener dug in, and India led by just 89.

They widened this to 355, thanks to their only worthwhile opening stand of the series, 90 from Rathore and Mongia, and a 108-run partnership between Dravid and Ganguly. Dravid missed his second century, but batted with more panache this time.

South Africa were 77 for five, still 278 behind, when a thunderstorm suddenly halted play. The resumption was unduly delayed, though that seemed irrelevant when two more wickets fell in nine overs. But then Klusener settled in to bat most responsibly with Cullinan, who played a magnificent innings of 122 not out. As the light dimmed, so did India's chances; it denied them the use of their quicker bowlers. With four overs remaining, play was called off.

The Standard Bank triangular series, also featuring South Africa and Zimbabwe, had each team playing the others three times. India could not get past South Africa in the qualifying games – and it was the same story in the final.

India v Zimbabwe

Standard Bank Series, Game nine, at Benoni, February 9, 1997

Zimbabwe 240-8;

India 241-4 (S. R. Tendulkar 104).

India won by six wickets.

Tendulkar: 104

R. Mohan, *Wisden* 1998

With Zimbabwe two points ahead going into the last group game, India had to overtake their 240 in 40.5 overs or less to slip past them into the final on net run-rate. Tendulkar returned to the top of the order and to his fluent best, scoring a chanceless 104, his 11th one-day international hundred, off 97 balls, with a six and eight fours. Even when he was out, India needed 83 from 80 balls. But Jadeja and Robin Singh completed the task in a spirited stand. Zimbabwe's captain, Alistair Campbell, had also regained his touch, scoring 86, but it was not to be enough.

The final in Durban had to be replayed after the first attempt was washed out. The tour ended where it had begun, with another disappointment for Tendulkar and India.

India v South Africa
Final, at Durban, February 13, 1997 (day/night)
South Africa 278-8;
India 234.
South Africa won by 17 runs
(India's target revised to 251 in 40 overs).
Tendulkar: 1-19; 45

R. Mohan, *Wisden* 1998

The pitch played better than on the previous day, and most of South Africa's top order contributed to getting sufficient runs on the board. Rain interrupted the match again, but there was time to set India a reduced target, which they pursued with gusto. Tendulkar smashed 45 off 33 balls, with a six and seven fours, and added 66 with Dravid at eight an over. Cronje had him caught off a well-disguised slower ball, but Dravid kept cranking up the rate, supported by Azharuddin. The chase only petered out when Azharuddin fell to a fine diving catch by Rhodes and Dravid drove to Kirsten on the midwicket boundary.

Tendulkar's next challenge was in the Caribbean for a five-Test series, one of only three he would play in a 24-year career. After a couple of draws on frustratingly slow tracks in Jamaica and Trinidad, the pitch at the Kensington Oval in Barbados was volatile, offering enough bounce to excite fast bowlers, yet with the occasional delivery staying low to keep the batsmen on guard. Tendulkar, already hamstrung without his main strike bowler, Javagal Srinath, was denied a third seamer yet again. Instead, Srinath's replacement on the tour was an off-spinner, Noel David. Tendulkar is believed to have asked "Noel who?" when informed of the selectors' decision, though this has never been confirmed. The best that can be said, given the haphazard nature of Indian cricket politics at the time, is that it rings true.

West Indies v India

Third Test, at Bridgetown, March 27–31, 1997

West Indies 298 (S. Chanderpaul 137; B. K. V. Prasad 5-82) and

140 (A. P. Kuruvilla 5-68);

India 319 and **81.**

West Indies won by 38 runs.

Tendulkar: 92 and 4

Tony Cozier, *Wisden* 1998

At the behest of the captains, frustrated by featherbeds, a pitch was prepared with more grass than usual at Kensington Oval. It was also dry and hard and the seven fast bowlers – all six-footers – were encouraged by its progressively uneven bounce and lateral movement. The pitch was widely criticised but produced an intense match and an unforgettable finale: India, requiring just 120 for their first victory in the West Indies since 1975-76, collapsed to their lowest total in the Caribbean amid bacchanalian celebrations.

India read the obvious signs. They brought in fast bowler Dodda Ganesh in place of spinner Sunil Joshi and chose to bowl. The three pace bowlers duly worked through the batting but could not dislodge Shivnarine Chanderpaul, who entered in the third over and remained unbeaten after nearly seven and a half hours, during which he struck 12 fours and offered no chance. His 137 followed a sequence of 13 scores between 50 and 82 in his previous 18 Tests. His relief was evident as he kissed the pitch.

Tendulkar was near his assertive best as he and Dravid built a commanding position by adding 170. Punishing short and wide bowling and taking advantage of attacking fields, Tendulkar unleashed his full repertoire to score a hooked six off Franklyn Rose and 14 fours. It took Sherwin Campbell's leaping catch at gully to dismiss him, for 92, off what television suggested was a no-ball by Ian Bishop; Rose rounded off the innings.

India led by a seemingly insignificant 21 but promptly dismissed Stuart Williams and Chanderpaul. Brian Lara counter-attacked boldly until falling, for the second time in the match, to a slip catch off Prasad, who took eight wickets in his most threatening performance of the tour. West Indies were only 86 ahead when last man Mervyn Dillon

Sweating it out: Tendulkar prepares to face Imran Khan, Wasim Akram and Waqar Younis in his first Test.

© Ben Radford/Getty Images

Where it all began: youngsters practise in Mumbai's Shivaji Park. Tendulkar spent hours here as a child honing his craft.

© Michael Steele/Getty Images

Flat cap, warm beer: Tendulkar toasts his arrival as Yorkshire's first overseas player with a pint of Tetley's.

© Thierry Saliou/Getty Images

Before the storm: as a shy-looking 16-year-old shortly before his Test debut in Karachi.

© Ben Radford/Getty Images

Teen spirit: Tendulkar walks off after saving India at Old Trafford in 1990 with his maiden Test hundred.

© Ben Radford/Getty Images

Tearful farewell: an emotional hundred against Kenya during the 1999 World Cup, following the death of his father.

© Craig Prentis/Getty Images

Leg theory: by cutting out the cover-drive on his way to 241 not out at Sydney in 2003-04, Tendulkar provides a masterclass in self-discipline. © William West/Getty Images

Healing power: celebrating with Yuvraj Singh after the win against England at Chennai in December 2008.
© Indranil Mukherjee/Getty Images

On the up: not for the only time in his career, Shane Warne gets the treatment – during the 1996 World Cup, in Mumbai.
© Shaun Botterill/Getty Images

Bittersweet: Tendulkar collects the Player of the Tournament award from Garry Sobers after India lost the 2003 World Cup final to Australia in Johannesburg.

© Patrick Eagar/Getty Images

High and mighty: Virat Kohli provides the seating after India clinch the 2011 World Cup. © Matthew Lewis/Getty Images

Child support: celebrating the World Cup win with his children, Sara and Arjun.

© Matthew Lewis/Getty Images

The morning after: cradling the World Cup in front of Mumbai's Gateway of India, in April 2011.

© STRDEL/Getty Images

Leg up: a characteristic pull shot, against England at Headingley in 2002, when India squared the Test series.

© Patrick Eagar/Getty Images

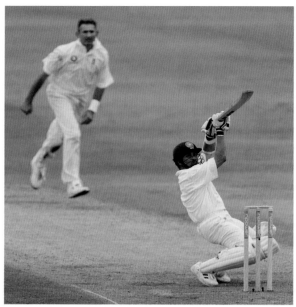

Pointing the way: Tendulkar ramps England's Andrew Caddick for another boundary on his way to 193 at Headingley in 2002.

© Laurence Griffiths/Getty Images

Picture perfect: Tendulkar practises his straight-drive ahead of the Wellington Test against New Zealand in April 2009.

© Dibyangshu Sarkar/Getty Images

Fine balance: driving through the off-side at The Oval in 2011 – his final Test in England.

© Gareth Copley/Getty Images

Trade secrets: during
Tendulkar's career,
Brian Lara was the only
batsman mentioned
in the same breath.

© Dibyangshu Sarkar/Getty Images

The fab four:
Tendulkar, Sourav
Ganguly, Rahul
Dravid and V. V. S.
Laxman in 2004.

© Indranil Mukherjee/Getty Images

On top of the world: the Indian team celebrate their ascent to No. 1 in the Test rankings following victory over Sri Lanka in Mumbai, in December 2009.

© Pal Pillai/Getty Images

First among equals: even in glittering company, Tendulkar could stand out – here against England at Ahmedabad in 2001-02.

© Laurence Griffiths/Getty Images

Happy snappy: Tendulkar relaxes after the win over Australia in Mohali in October 2008, when he broke Brian Lara's record for most Test runs. © Global Cricket Ventures/BCCI/Getty Images

Champagne moment: Tendulkar and teammates celebrate the Test series win at home over Australia in 2008-09. © Global Cricket Ventures/BCCI/Getty Images

Go India: a Tendulkar lookalike does his best to keep the batting gods happy during the 2011 World Cup. © Sam Panthaky/Getty Images

Super fan: Sudhir Kumar Chaudhary, Tendulkar's most devout worshipper, in familiar pose during a one-day international in 2015. © Hindustan Times/Getty Images

Omnipresent: early-morning joggers run past a sand sculpture of Tendulkar in Orissa around the time of his retirement. © STRDEL/Getty Images

Facing off: schoolchildren in Nagpur before Tendulkar's final Test.

Waxing, not waning: the Tendulkars admire Madame Tussaud's handiwork in Mumbai, shortly before it was unveiled at the London museum in 2009.

Rain doesn't stop play: practising inside the pavilion before a Test against New Zealand in Nagpur in 2010. © AFP/Getty Images

Smash hit: during a Mumbai Indians net session in 2012. © Hindustan Times/Getty Images

Sitting pretty: scoreboard operators at Gwalior take in Tendulkar's historic achievement. © Gallo Images/Getty Images

Paper boy: the headlines say it all after Tendulkar becomes the first player to make a double-century in a one-day international, against South Africa at Gwalior on February 24, 2010.

© STR/Getty Images

Reaching for the stars: at Centurion in December 2010, it's 50 Test hundreds.

© Gallo Images/Getty Images

HUNDRED 100

All smiles: Tendulkar
addresses the media after
completing his 100th
international hundred in
2012. © Hindustan Times/Getty Images

Family matters: with dad
Ramesh, mum Rajni and
older brother Ajit. Sachin
credits his father for all
he has achieved.

© Sportsworld, courtesy of the Clayton
Murzello Collection

Sibling revelry: with Ajit, his lifelong mentor. © Indranil Mukherjee/Getty Images

To sir, with love: Tendulkar's coach, Ramakant Achrekar, shares his pupil's pride after he became the first sportsman to receive the Bharat Ratna, India's highest civilian award. © AFP/Getty Images

Home comfort: Sachin's wife Anjali with their children. Sachin believes his marriage has been his "greatest partnership". © Noah Seelam/Getty Images

Image-conscious: fans photograph Tendulkar emerging from the Wankhede Stadium dressing-room to resume his final Test innings. © Atul Kamble/MiD-DAY Infomedia Ltd

Son of the soil: Tendulkar says his final goodbye to the wicket – his temple for 24 years.
© Atul Kamble/MiD-DAY Infomedia Ltd

joined Curtly Ambrose for the innings' highest partnership, 33. It seemed a merry irrelevance.

West Indies had never defended such a meagre target, but reminded themselves of their triumph here five years earlier, when South Africa, 122 for two at the start of the last day needing another 79, lost their last eight for 26. India, needing just 120, similarly capitulated next morning against irresistible fast bowling on a capricious pitch.

Rose undermined them with three wickets in an opening burst; Bishop and Ambrose completed the demolition. While Navjot Sidhu fended a flyer off his throat to slip and Dravid and Azharuddin succumbed to balls that came through at shin height, Tendulkar could not blame the pitch when he edged Bishop's outswinger low to the left of the solitary slip, Lara. The rest went quietly, amid the Barbadian excitement.

Tendulkar called this defeat in Barbados "a dark day in the history of Indian cricket and definitely the worst of my captaincy career". His team-mates' lack of application hurt him, and India were denied the chance to recover during the next two Tests in Antigua and Guyana because of fickle weather. The series ended in a 1–0 defeat.

In the limited-overs series that followed, India managed just one win in four games. After victory in the second one-day international in Trinidad, they were in a winning position in St Vincent when the batsmen squandered the advantage. A distraught Tendulkar had a meltdown in the dressing-room.

West Indies v India

Third one-day international, at Kingstown, April 30, 1997

West Indies 249-9;

India 231 (O. D. Gibson 4-61).

India lost by 18 runs.

Tendulkar: 1-13; 9

Tony Cozier, *Wisden* 1998

India were seemingly heading towards another victory while Ganguly and Dravid were comfortably adding 130 in 29 overs for the second wicket, but then collapsed to defeat: their last eight fell for 46 in nine overs thanks to a mixture of hysterical swiping and mindless running. On the best pitch of the tour, Stuart Williams made 76 in 110 balls, and his stand of 84 with Carl Hooper was the basis of a challenging West Indies total. Tendulkar's dismissal in the fifth over was an early setback for India but Ganguly and Dravid were in charge until panic set in.

A string of one-day tournaments followed the tour of the Caribbean, including the Independence Cup – featuring Pakistan, New Zealand and Sri Lanka – and the Asia Cup. India failed to qualify for the Independence Cup final, but did get to the final of the Asia Cup.

India v New Zealand
Independence Cup, Game three, at Bangalore, May 14, 1997 (day/night)
New Zealand 220-9;
India 221-2 (S. R. Tendulkar 117).
India won by eight wickets.
Tendulkar: 117

R. Mohan, *Wisden* 1998

Nathan Astle almost reached his second century in as many games, scoring 92 in 111 balls, with ten fours, but New Zealand slid from a promising 109 for one to an inadequate final total of 220, with four run-outs. That was due to poor running as much as brilliant fielding. India's batsmen found the New Zealand bowling no trouble at all. Tendulkar and Ganguly put on 169 in 32 overs, and Tendulkar continued to complete his 12th century in one-day internationals. He had made 117 from 136 balls, with 13 fours and two sixes, when he was bowled with his team needing only five to win.

India v Pakistan
Independence Cup, Game six, at Chennai, May 21, 1997 (day/night)
Pakistan 327-5 (Saeed Anwar 194);
India 292 (R. Dravid 107; Aaqib Javed 5-61).
Pakistan won by 35 runs.
Tendulkar: 2-61; 4

R. Mohan, *Wisden* 1998

Saeed Anwar broke the record for the highest individual innings in a one-day international by scoring 194, from 146 balls, with 22 fours and five sixes, three in succession in one over from Kumble, which went for 226664. He beat the previous record, Viv Richards's unbeaten 189 for West Indies against England at Old Trafford in 1984, by five, and might have reached a double-hundred had he not top-edged a sweep to be caught at fine leg in the 47th over. India were left a target of 328. They began on a poor note when Inzamam-ul-Haq took an athletic catch to dismiss Tendulkar, but Dravid sustained them with his maiden hundred in limited-overs internationals. They soon fell behind, however, after he pushed a catch to midwicket, one of five wickets for Aaqib Javed. Afterwards, Tendulkar said Anwar's innings was the best he had seen.

The Asia Cup was India's next limited-overs assignment. India and Sri Lanka qualified for the final, but Sri Lanka won by eight wickets to end India's attempt at bagging a fourth consecutive Asia Cup trophy.

Sri Lanka v India

Pepsi Asia Cup, Final, at R. Premadasa Stadium, Colombo, July 16, 1997 (day/night)

India 239-7;

Sri Lanka 240-2.

Sri Lanka won by eight wickets.

Tendulkar: 53

Sa'adi Thawfeeq, *Wisden* 1999

Jayasuriya and Atapattu ensured a one-sided final, wiping out more than half a target of 240 with an opening partnership of 137 off 109 balls. Sri Lanka won with more than 13 overs to spare, to regain the Asia Cup after 11 years. India fielded only three frontline bowlers, and paid dearly; Jayasuriya raced to 63 off 52 balls and Ranatunga finished the job with an unbeaten 62 off 67. Atapattu, meanwhile, played the anchor role to perfection. India's total revolved around their most experienced pair, Tendulkar and Azharuddin, who added 109. Azharuddin scored 81 but hit only one four and two sixes, while Tendulkar made 53 with two fours. A stunning Sri Lankan fielding display featured five marvellous outfield catches.

A three-Test series followed the Asia Cup in Sri Lanka. The matches resulted in a series of draws played on featherbeds, which allowed the batsmen a slew of records. That made it five drawn Tests out of five between India and Sri Lanka in 1997. Tendulkar took advantage to score three big hundreds.

Sri Lanka v India

First Test, at R. Premadasa Stadium, Colombo, August 2–6, 1997

India 537-8 dec. (N. S. Sidhu 111, S. R. Tendulkar 143, M. Azharuddin 126);

Sri Lanka 952-6 dec. (S. T. Jayasuriya 340, R. S. Mahanama 225, P. A. de Silva 126).

Drawn.

Tendulkar: 143

On the fifth and final morning, crowds gathered to see a Sri Lankan assault on the peak of Test cricket. Brian Lara's Test record of 375 was under threat from another left-hander, two months his junior: Sanath Jayasuriya. He began the day on 326, and confidently moved to 340 with three fours and two singles. Then an off-break from Rajesh Chauhan bounced a little more than he expected; Jayasuriya popped a simple catch to silly point to end his hopes of beating Lara. The disappointment was alleviated to some extent by Sri Lanka establishing two other world records. Jayasuriya and Roshan Mahanama put on 576, the highest partnership for any Test wicket and only one run short of the all-time first-class record; and Sri Lanka's total of 952 for six was the highest in Test history.

The liaison between Jayasuriya and Mahanama began at the start of the third day, when they added 283 runs together. They carried on throughout the fourth day, adding a further 265. The partnership eventually ended on the morning of the final day, when Mahanama went back to a leg-break from Kumble and was given out lbw for 225, his maiden double-hundred.

Losing Mahanama shook Jayasuriya's concentration; he left at the same score, 615, two balls later, having made 340, the fourth-highest innings in Test cricket after Lara's 375, Sobers's 365 not out and Len Hutton's 364. In a chanceless display of 799 minutes – the second-longest innings in first-class cricket, after Hanif Mohammad's 970 minutes batting for Pakistan against West Indies at Bridgetown in 1957-58 – Jayasuriya faced 578 balls and hit two sixes and 36 fours. He was also the first Sri Lankan to score a first-class triple-century. He was applauded by all the Indian fielders and received a standing ovation from the crowd.

It was a terrible toss to win. "We should have batted second," said Tendulkar. Even so, his team had dominated the first two days of the Test, piling up an apparently impressive 537 for eight – their highest total in Sri Lanka. After Sidhu had completed his eighth Test century on the opening day, Tendulkar and Azharuddin put on 221 in 242 minutes – a record for India's fourth wicket against Sri Lanka. They, too, scored hundreds.

This remarkable Test produced 1,489 runs for only 14 wickets, with both teams batting only once on a pitch to break bowlers' hearts.

In the second edition of the Sahara Cup in Toronto, India's 4–1 scoreline meant victory at last for Tendulkar in a one-day series – only the second of his captaincy career, following the Titan Cup the previous year. While it coincided with a dip in his personal form and the decision to drop himself down the order, India managed to seal victory as early as the third game, thanks to Sourav Ganguly. The Sahara Cup was followed by a one-day series in Pakistan. Once again, Tendulkar and India were struggling.

India v Pakistan

Sahara Friendship Cup, Third one-day international, at Toronto

September 18, 1997

India 182-6;

Pakistan 148 (S. C. Ganguly 5-16).

India won by 34 runs.

Tendulkar: 0

Tony Cozier, *Wisden* 1999

India made sure of the Cup with a resilient performance, and Ganguly won the match award for his bowling, after scoring only two. Having to bat first on a bowler-friendly pitch, India could raise only 182 for six – a strong recovery from 23 for three, when Tendulkar went for nought in the 12th over. Azharuddin charted a course through choppy waters, while Jadeja and Robin Singh, who hit 32 off 29 balls, provided late momentum. As Shahid Afridi smashed six fours in 44 off 38 balls, a Pakistan victory seemed assured. But complacency led to reckless strokes – all ten wickets fell to catches – and they were undone by Ganguly, who claimed five for 16.

Pakistan v India

Wills Challenge Series, Second one-day international, at Karachi, September 30, 1997

Pakistan 265-4;

India 266-6.

India won by four wickets.

Tendulkar: 21

Stone-throwing from the crowd interrupted Pakistan's innings four times, and perhaps cost them the match. When Ganguly became the fifth Indian fielder to be hit, Tendulkar told referee Ranjan Madugalle he could not risk his players any longer, and Madugalle agreed. Pakistan were halted in mid-over and their disappointed supporters murmured that, with Inzamam-ul-Haq unbeaten on 74, India might have faced a target much stiffer than 266 from 47 had he continued to hit out. Pakistan's initial momentum came from Afridi, who struck 72 in 56 balls. Ganguly was almost as forceful in reply. He hit 89 off

96 balls, with 11 fours. India then stumbled, losing four quick wickets, two to run-outs. But Robin Singh, with a run-a-ball 31, and Saba Karim fought back in a stand of 62. Off-spinner Saqlain Mushtaq suddenly went for 33 in three overs. Even then, Karim's dismissal might have ended India's challenge, but Chauhan hit a six in the final over to ensure victory.

India's loss in the third one-day international of the Wills Challenge Series meant they lost the one-day tournament 2–1 to Pakistan. A wretched Champions Trophy followed in Sharjah as India lost all three qualifying games against England, Pakistan and West Indies. Tendulkar, batting in the middle order this series, on instruction from the selectors, had scores of 91, 3 and 1.

India v West Indies
Akai-Singer Champions Trophy, Game six, at Sharjah, December 16, 1997
West Indies 229-6 (S. C. Williams 105*);
India 188 (C. L. Hooper 4-37).
West Indies won by 41 runs.
Tendulkar: 1

Mike Selvey, *Wisden* 1999

An unbeaten century from Williams, his first in limited-overs internationals, and fine all-round cricket from Hooper completed a miserable week for India. The sound of selectors' axes was soon heard in the subcontinent. Having gone against convention by putting West Indies in, Tendulkar saw Williams bat throughout the innings, hitting ten fours in 149 balls. India could still have qualified by winning in 45 overs. An opening stand of 87 between Ganguly and Sidhu put them well on the way. Instead, they were undone by the three spinners, and a death wish that saw first Tendulkar, who reached the crease this time in the 29th over, and then Azharuddin run out by Rawl Lewis. More than seven overs remained when Hooper bowled Prasad.

Tendulkar's first stint as captain ended when he was sacked after India drew a limited-overs series at home to Sri Lanka 1–1 in December 1997. "No one from the BCCI managed to call me or inform me… before someone from the media called to say I was no longer captain," wrote Tendulkar in his autobiography. "I felt extremely humiliated to hear this, but the manner in which the whole thing was handled strengthened my resolve to be a better cricketer in the years to come."

Captaincy: Part Two

Mohammad Azharuddin was reappointed captain until a woeful performance with the bat in the 1999 World Cup, and serious doubts over his fitness after shoulder surgery, persuaded the selectors to give Tendulkar another go. This time he was promised more say in selectorial matters.

But this stint wasn't much happier than the first: it lasted just 19 one-day internationals and eight Tests. After a 2–0 defeat in home Tests to South Africa in March 2000, Tendulkar resigned, never to return to the job – despite being offered the opportunity in 2007 following Rahul Dravid's resignation.

His second coming began with the Aiwa Cup in August 1999, a triangular tournament also featuring Australia and Sri Lanka. In spite of scoring its only century, Tendulkar had another unhappy series: India failed to make the final yet again, winning just one of four qualifying games. Next came a quadrangular in Singapore, where India did get to the final, only to be beaten by West Indies, despite Dravid's fighting century.

India v West Indies

Coca-Cola Challenge, Final, at Singapore, September 8, 1999

India 254-6 (R. Dravid 103*);

West Indies 255-6 (R. L. Powell 124).

West Indies won by four wickets.

Tendulkar: 0

Wisden 2001

The previous day's rain granted India only a brief stay of execution. After a shaky start, West Indies ran out deserved winners, 20-year-old Ricardo Powell concluding a successful tournament with a whirlwind 124, his first one-day international hundred. It was an astonishing performance, the more remarkable because West Indies, chasing 255, were struggling at 67 for four in the 17th over when he reached the crease. By the time he was out, top-edging a pull, he had hit nine fours and eight sixes in his 93 balls – and West Indies were only nine short of victory. He added 61 with Chanderpaul and 118 with Nehemiah Perry. Earlier, India had lost Tendulkar to the last ball of the first over, but were held together by Dravid, who batted with mounting confidence to finish unbeaten on 103.

Tendulkar had a spectacular run with the bat in the three-Test series against New Zealand at home, scoring 435 runs at an average over 100.

According to Wisden, *he "eschewed flamboyance and daredevilry to fulfil his responsibility as captain". Slow pitches meant, however, that he was unable to force results: India managed to win just one Test and draw two. The highlight was Tendulkar's first double-century; and victory in the Tests was followed by a win in the one-day series.*

India v New Zealand

First Test, at Mohali, October 10–14, 1999

India 83 (D. J. Nash 6-27) and **505-3 dec.** (R. Dravid 144, S. R. Tendulkar 126*);
New Zealand 215 (J. Srinath 6-45) and **251-7.**

Drawn.

Tendulkar: 18 and 126*

Dicky Rutnagur, *Wisden* 2001

Even though 20 wickets fell in less than a day and a half, the match remained unfinished, the principal reason being the steady decline in the pace of the pitch. At the start it contained sufficient moisture, partly from sweating under the covers, to make batting a trial, and New Zealand reaped a rich dividend from putting India in. Four wickets down for ten runs in six overs, they were all out for 83 in 27, equalling their second-lowest total at home. Dion Nash bowled outstandingly to capture six for 27, his best figures in Test cricket.

New Zealand also lost their openers quickly, recovered, then faltered again – and that despite a marked improvement in batting conditions on the second day. With Srinath probing away, a model of accuracy in line and length, the last six wickets added just 59 runs.

India's openers wiped off a deficit of 132, although Sadagoppan Ramesh, sometimes tentative against balls outside the off stump, could have been caught three times while making 73. Devang Gandhi, in a more sedate innings of 75, survived him for another 25 overs in partnership with Dravid, who batted on and on for a faultless 144 spread over seven hours.

Off the first ball Tendulkar received, bowled by Astle, he survived the first of several appeals for lbw. Out of the game for a month because of back trouble, he played within the limitations imposed by uncertain form, batting steadfastly for more than six and a half hours and completing his 20th Test hundred. When the time came for the offensive, he let first Dravid and then Ganguly head the charge.

India became the first Test side to follow being dismissed for under 100 with a second innings of more than 500. They led by 373 and had 135 overs in which to dismiss New Zealand. But while the ball turned, it turned slowly. Thanks mainly to Stephen Fleming, who batted almost five and a half hours, and was out to the last ball of the match, New Zealand survived.

India v New Zealand
Third Test, at Ahmedabad, October 29–November 2, 1999
India 583-7 dec. (S. Ramesh 110, S.R. Tendulkar 217, S. C. Ganguly 125) and **148-5 dec.;**
New Zealand 308 (A. Kumble 5-82) and **252-2.**
Drawn.
Tendulkar: 217 and 15

Dicky Rutnagur, *Wisden* 2001

Three of the four previous Tests played on the Motera ground had finished decisively, and more than once its pitches had been rated "poor". This time the pitch was so firm that it produced one of the most boring draws in recent memory.

With the dry atmosphere denying the bowlers any assistance from swing, it took New Zealand the best part of two sessions to exploit Ramesh's vulnerability around the off stump, in which time he compiled his second Test hundred. His wicket was their last success until halfway between lunch and tea on the second day when Ganguly, who made 125 (20 fours), failed to get sufficient carry on a lofted on-drive off Astle. By then, he and Tendulkar had added 281 – breaking the Indian fourth-wicket Test record they themselves had set at 256 against Sri Lanka two years earlier – and Tendulkar was well on his way to his first Test double-century and highest first-class score. Acquired steadily over eight and a quarter hours, he may have been slow by his own standards, but few loose balls among 343 escaped punishment. He hit 29 fours.

Yet, twice the Indian captain might have been out in the nineties late on the first day. Until then he had refrained from going for bouncers, but he was unable to resist the short one that Chris Cairns slipped him in his first over with the second new ball. Astle, running back from second slip, narrowly failed to complete what would have been a stunning catch off a top edge. A run later, there was not much daylight between the ball and Tendulkar's outside edge as he played a forcing shot at Nash.

Tendulkar was eventually out shortly after tea on the second day, magnificently held just off the ground at straightish midwicket by Nash from a full-blooded pull at Daniel Vettori. India declared at 583, their highest total against New Zealand.

The tourists lost Matt Horne in negotiating the remains of the day, and three more wickets fell on the third morning. A hardy stand of 70 between Fleming and Astle halted the collapse. New Zealand's innings lasted 55 minutes beyond lunch, which was long enough to persuade Tendulkar to rest his bowlers before mounting another assault.

India, 275 ahead, increased their lead to 423 with a rush of merry batting that brought up 100 in 93 minutes. Tendulkar declared with time for 13 overs that evening, but Horne and Gary Stead, who had come from New Zealand to replace the injured Craig McMillan, put on 131 in 55 overs before falling in the space of seven balls. These reverses proved to be a minor tremor: Craig Spearman and Fleming shut the door in India's face with an unbroken stand of 121.

After a cracking century in the second match of the limited-overs series against New Zealand, Tendulkar contributed almost nothing, with scores of one, two and nought. But India claimed the series 3–2.

India v New Zealand
Second one-day international, at Hyderabad, November 8, 1999
India 376-2 (R. Dravid 153, S. R. Tendulkar 186*);
New Zealand 202.
India won by 174 runs.
Tendulkar: 186*

Dicky Rutnagur, *Wisden* 2001

India hit back with a vengeance and a clutch of records. Their total was second at this level only to Sri Lanka's 398 for five against Kenya in the 1996 World Cup. Tendulkar and Dravid added 331 for the second wicket in 46 overs, an all-wicket record for any side in one-day internationals, beating Dravid's 318 with Ganguly in a World Cup game against Sri Lanka six months earlier. In that match Ganguly had made 183, the highest limited-overs score for India, but now Tendulkar surpassed him, batting throughout the innings for an unbeaten 186, then the fourth-highest score in any one-day international. It was his 24th century in such games, coming nine days after his 21st Test hundred, and he hit 20 fours and three sixes in 150 balls. Dravid partnered him with a run-a-ball 153, striking 15 fours and two sixes. New Zealand lost both openers in the first five overs and lasted only two-thirds of their batting allocation. But for Scott Styris, last out for 43 in only his second international, they would not have reached 200.

India departed for Australia after the series against New Zealand. While the Border–Gavaskar Trophy was a great outing for Tendulkar the batsman – he was Man of the Series with scores of 61, 0, 116, 52, 45 and 4 in three Tests – Tendulkar the captain was left frustrated and disappointed as India capitulated to a 3–0 defeat. "Apart from Sachin Tendulkar and Sourav Ganguly, India's batsmen could not come to terms with the pace and bounce of Australia's pitches," wrote Dicky Rutnagur in the 2001 Almanack. "Tendulkar, despite being the victim of dubious umpiring decisions in both innings of the First Test, averaged 46.33, scoring a splendid 116 in the Second and two half-centuries." India were outclassed not just in all three Tests, but in the Carlton & United limited-overs series that followed against Australia and Pakistan, losing seven games out of eight.

Australia v India

Border–Gavaskar Trophy, First Test, at Adelaide, December 10–14, 1999

Australia 441 (S. R. Waugh 150, R. T. Ponting 125) and **239-8 dec.;**

India 285 and **110** (D. W. Fleming 5-30).

Australia won by 285 runs.

Tendulkar: 61 and 0

Dicky Rutnagur, *Wisden* 2001

Losing their top four for 52 on the opening morning proved only a pinprick for Australia. Their batting had enough depth to overcome periodic slumps and, with Warne's powers restored, their bowling was not stretched in subduing opposition whose own batting strength was concentrated on three high-class performers.

With Tendulkar employing Ganguly after lunch, rather than one of his frontline bowlers, and keeping him on too long, Steve Waugh and Ricky Ponting were under little pressure as they prepared the ground for Australia's largest fifth-wicket partnership against India, 239. Audacious and versatile in his range of strokes, Ponting contributed 125. If more watchful, Waugh left nothing loose unpunished and had 17 fours in his 150. His innings gave him not only hundreds against the other eight Test-playing countries – the first to achieve this – but also 150 against all of them except New Zealand, and took him past 8,000 Test runs.

India, beginning their reply 40 minutes before tea, lost both openers for just nine. Ramesh was beaten by Greg Blewett's direct hit from long-off as he tried to complete a fourth. But Laxman batted with freedom, unlike his more experienced partner Dravid, as they put on 81 before he paid the penalty for square-cutting Glenn McGrath without getting on top of a high-bouncing ball. McGrath in that spell bowled eight overs for one run, and he and Warne, subtle and accurate, allowed Dravid and Tendulkar little licence. Dravid did not survive until stumps, caught at short leg off Warne; Tendulkar, weighed down by the crisis, managed only 12 off 69 balls.

He cast off his shackles the following morning. With Ganguly also at ease and free with his strokes. India added 92 in 22 overs before Tendulkar, having scored his last 49 off 64 balls, was adjudged caught at short leg off Warne. The videotape proved him unlucky. However, Warne's dismissal of Ganguly, 14 runs later, was a masterpiece. He drew the left-hander out to scotch the menace of a ball pitched into the rough outside his off stump, beat him with a googly and had him stumped. India were left with a deficit of 156.

As the pitch became uneven in bounce, India made Australia fight for runs by bowling with zest and discipline, and Waugh felt unable to declare until 25 minutes after tea on the fourth afternoon.

In the 26 overs remaining to the close, McGrath, Warne and Damien Fleming virtually settled the issue by reducing India to 76 for five, still 319 behind. Any hope of a significant revival had been extinguished when Tendulkar ducked to evade a short delivery from McGrath. The ball did not get up, he was struck on the shoulder, and umpire Daryl Harper deemed contact had been made in line with the stumps and within their height. Next morning, Fleming claimed four of the remaining wickets.

Australia v India
Second Test, at Melbourne, December 26–30, 1999
Australia 405 and 208-5 dec.;
India 238 (S. R. Tendulkar 116, B. Lee 5-47) and **195.**
Australia won by 180 runs.
Tendulkar: 116 and 52

Dicky Rutnagur, *Wisden* 2001

Australia's elation at winning this Test, and with it the series, was all the greater for the contribution of their new recruit, Brett Lee, who took seven wickets in the match, including five for 47 in the first innings.

India's fast bowlers were not disciplined enough to capitalise on first use of a bouncy pitch which, having sweated under the covers, also provided movement off the seam. Michael Slater was in splendid touch and, with Mark Waugh patient in the absence of form, Australia rallied from a poor start to share the honours of a rain-shortened first day.

There were further interruptions for rain on the second day. When Australia resumed at 332 for five on the third day, India's hopes of a win were already distant. By the close, the spectre of defeat was staring at them. The satisfaction of removing Ponting, the rapacious Adam Gilchrist – this pair had put on 144 for the sixth wicket, mostly the previous day – and Warne in the space of four runs all came to nothing once the tail wagged furiously. Lee, the debutant, spent 77 productive minutes in the middle with Fleming, adding 59.

This cameo helped ensure that Lee was free of stage fright when Waugh brought him on to bowl the sixth over of the Indian innings. He struck with only his fourth ball, bowling Ramesh off the inside edge, and later in the day was in line for a hat-trick, reverse-swinging a ball almost 59 overs old to dismiss Mannava Prasad and Ajit Agarkar. By then, the innings was a shambles, for all that Tendulkar remained unscathed, gathering runs with deft placements and assaults on the rare loose ball. He and the equally defiant Kumble saved the follow-on but, with only five overs left to the close, Tendulkar pulled a long-hop straight to square leg. He had made 116 out of a total of 212, with a straight six off Warne but only nine fours.

Next day, Waugh declared with a lead of 375 and a minimum of 126 overs remaining. Laxman again fell cheaply, and Ramesh batted for only one over on the final morning before retiring hurt, his left thumb broken the previous evening when he fended a bouncer from Lee on to his helmet. Warne's only wicket of the innings sealed India's doom, for it was Tendulkar. Absolutely composed hitherto in making 52, Tendulkar misread his old adversary's intentions, shouldered arms and was lbw.

Hrishikesh Kanitkar and Prasad held the Australians up, but Waugh again proved the adage that fortune favours a winning captain. Turning to his brother Mark's off-spin, he was rewarded with consecutive wickets. Kumble was able to prevent a hat-trick but not the defeat.

A tired Indian unit had three weeks to recover before a two-Test series against South Africa at home. This was the final nail in Tendulkar's captaincy coffin: India lost both Tests, which ended their sequence of 14 unbeaten home series stretching back to 1987. Tendulkar had announced before the series he would relinquish the captaincy immediately after the Tests, but any prospect of ending his second stint on a happy note was ruined when South Africa became the only country in the 1990s to win Test series in all three countries of the subcontinent (Bangladesh were yet to join the fold). "The timing of his resignation roused speculation that it was linked to the reinstatement of Mohammad Azharuddin and Nayan

Mongia – out of the side since Tendulkar's return as captain – and the coinciding appointment of Kapil Dev as coach," wrote Dicky Rutnagur in the 2001 Almanack. "In the unpleasant atmosphere that prevailed, India were vulnerable."

India v South Africa
First Test, at Mumbai, February 24–26, 2000
India 225 and 113;
South Africa 176 and 164-6.
South Africa won by four wickets.
Tendulkar: 97 and 8; 3-10 (1st inns)

Dicky Rutnagur, *Wisden* 2001

A pitch made to order could not mask India's shortcomings, but highlighting their weaknesses would not do justice to South Africa's achievement. From its appearance – the surface was not just shorn by the mower but also scraped with a wire brush – it was clear that the ball would turn wickedly, and South Africa were persuaded to include both left-arm spinners, Clive Eksteen and Nicky Boje, at the expense of the speed of Nantie Hayward. Instead it was Donald, Pollock and Jacques Kallis, backed up by Cronje, who determined the course of the match with skill and swing more than sheer pace.

Donald struck quickly to spoil Wasim Jaffer's debut, and vitally when he went through Dravid's gate. Pollock's slower ball, inviting Ganguly to his doom, had India 96 for four, of which an unbeaten 44 came from Tendulkar. The captain kept the innings breathing until, three runs short of his century, he half-heartedly glanced at Kallis and was taken low down by Mark Boucher. Batting responsibly, yet without being inhibited, he hit 12 fours, as well as two sixes off Eksteen; if his bat was passed on occasions, all credit to the bowlers, who harnessed the breeze that got up with the afternoon tide. A gallant last-wicket stand of 52 between Agarkar and newcomer Murali Kartik helped the total to minor respectability.

South Africa failed to build on the splendid start of 90 given to them by Kirsten and Herschelle Gibbs. Tendulkar, bowling a medley of off- and leg-spin, made the initial breakthrough, and took two more wickets in a later brief stint. Between these strikes, Kumble also made inroads and, although Klusener batted defiantly, all ten South African wickets fell for 86 more runs. India's lead of 49 was substantial, but generally woeful batting against Donald, Pollock and Cronje stretched it only to 162.

Kirsten, batting staunchly, and Gibbs, using his feet to attack the spinners, took South Africa almost a third of the way there. But it was the run-out of Cronje at 107, an agile piece of fielding by Jaffer at short leg, that triggered a collapse. Three more wickets went in the space of 21 runs, leaving South Africa 128 for six and turning the finish into a fierce test of nerves. Kartik, playing his first Test, could not rise to the challenge and the final runs came easily. Kallis, unbeaten for 129 balls, could reflect on a job well done, having kept one end stable when the innings was at its most turbulent.

Tendulkar's captaincy record

	Matches	Won	Lost	Drawn	Tied	No result	Win %
Tests	25	4	9	12	–	–	16.00
One-day internationals	73	23	43	–	1	6	35.07

Chapter 6

First Among Equals:
2001 to 2013

I t was the beginning of a new era, as the Indian cricketers attempted to put the ghosts of match-fixing behind them and start afresh. They faced a huge responsibility: to renew a disillusioned public's faith in the game.

Sourav Ganguly was just the leader they needed. He ushered in a new brand of cricket: more competitive, more confident and – overseas – more competent. In Tendulkar, Dravid, Laxman and Kumble, the general had just the army he needed. Tendulkar was now first among equals, no longer the lone star, one against 11, defying the odds, raging against the dying light of another defeat. He was now one of many match-winners. Proof that he finally felt relieved of the burden he had carried for nearly a decade came when he felt able to call the 2000-01 series against Australia "the greatest ever" – despite being little more than a bit-part player himself. Yes, his century in the Third Test at Chennai was crucial to India closing out the series, but this edition of the Border–Gavaskar Trophy belonged to three men: V. V. S. Laxman, Rahul Dravid and Harbhajan Singh.

There were many firsts to celebrate. India won a Test series in Pakistan for the first time ever, in England for the first time since 1986, and in New Zealand for the first time since 1967-68; there were overseas Test wins in Australia, South Africa, Sri Lanka and West Indies. They moved to No. 1 in the Test rankings, and won a World Cup. And while Tendulkar often played a significant part, others took up the slack.

But it wasn't all good news: as Tendulkar entered the second half of his career, his body bore many battle scars – a bad back, a crushed toe, a damaged elbow. There was surgery aplenty, and the constant threat of something career-ending. But he managed to weather many injury storms. And the series against Australia was just the beginning of India's golden era.

India lost the First Test in Mumbai, but came back in unbelievable fashion at Kolkata to win by 171 runs. The "281 Test" – as it came to be known, in honour of Laxman's second-innings fightback – instantly became the greatest of all India's Test wins. Horns locked at 1–1, India and Australia headed to Chennai, Tendulkar's favourite ground.

India v Australia

Border–Gavaskar Trophy, Third Test, at Chennai, March 18–22, 2001
Australia 391 (M. L. Hayden 203, Harbhajan Singh 7-133) and
264 (Harbhajan Singh 8-84);
India 501 (S. R. Tendulkar 126) and **155-8.**
India won by two wickets.
Tendulkar: 126 and 17

Dicky Rutnagur, *Wisden* 2002

Appropriately, the deciding Test of an enthralling series, marked by dramatic shifts of fortune, produced a grandstand finish. India, requiring 155 in the final innings, seemed to be heading for a comfortable win, only to encounter a brave, if unavailing, challenge from the Australian bowlers.

That Australia took any advantage from their continued luck with the toss was all down to opener Matthew Hayden, who was last out for 203. But support was confined to Justin Langer and the Waugh twins and Harbhajan collected the remaining six wickets for 26 in 9.4 overs.

India's reply, launched by Shiv Sunder Das and Sadagoppan Ramesh with a century partnership, also tapered away after the fall of the fifth wicket. The difference was that their collapse started with the total already at 453, which included four fifties and Tendulkar's superb century. He reached it with his second six off Colin Miller, and also hit 15 fours in his 126. Helped by Tendulkar's 169-run partnership with Dravid, the eventual lead was 110. Hayden and Michael Slater quickly chipped away at this before a diving catch by Zaheer Khan at deep midwicket dismissed Hayden. Mark Waugh then added 100 with Langer and Steve Waugh before Harbhajan had Steve caught next morning. This time India's off-spinner took the last six wickets for 15 in 17.1 overs to finish with a career-best eight for 84.

Australia seemed beaten as India reached the hundred mark with only two wickets down. Laxman and Tendulkar were in such firm control that victory looked a formality. However, Gillespie's dismissal of Tendulkar, caught by Mark Waugh at second slip off a ball of lethal speed and aim, was the signal for two more wickets in the next three overs.

After tea, with 20 runs wanted, Mark Waugh removed Laxman with an amazing midwicket catch that put the match wide open once more. When the seventh wicket fell at the same score, the balance was tipping Australia's way. Stand-in wicketkeeper Sameer Dighe and Zaheer tilted it back again and, with India nine short, Glenn McGrath – suffering from a stomach disorder and having to be sparingly used – was called on to make a final effort. Aided by Mark Waugh's fourth catch of the innings he prised out Zaheer, but it proved to be Australia's last throw. The two-wicket margin matched India's narrowest Test win, also against Australia, at Bombay in 1964-65.

Testing Times

Tendulkar got off to a good start in the series against South Africa, achieving yet another career milestone as he reached 7,000 runs in the First Test. But, on the final day of the drawn Second Test at Port Elizabeth, a huge controversy around him threatened to disrupt India's tour.

India v South Africa
First Test, at Bloemfontein, November 3–6, 2001
India 379 (S. R. Tendulkar 155, V. Sehwag 105) and 237 (S. M. Pollock 6-56);
South Africa 563 (H. H. Gibbs 107, L. Klusener 108, J. Srinath 5-140) and 54-1.
South Africa won by nine wickets.
Tendulkar: 155 and 15

Dicky Rutnagur, *Wisden* 2003

Though the margin of victory did not flatter South Africa, it did understate the strength of India's opposition. For the first three days of this Test, the cricket was combative and, for the most part, spectacular.

The pitch, relaid not many months earlier, was liberally grassed. It was not fast but initially provided bounce and lateral movement. Shaun

Pollock's decision to bowl earned good returns in the short term. However, South Africa's advance was halted by the awesome mastery with which Tendulkar scored his 26th Test hundred, and his partnership of 220 with Virender Sehwag, who made a flawless century in his maiden Test innings.

Tendulkar became comfortably the youngest player to score 7,000 Test runs, at 28 years 193 days in his 85th Test, beating David Gower (who was 31). The range and power of his shots took him to his hundred in only 114 balls when, to his immense annoyance, he got himself caught off a short delivery – he had hit 23 fours and a six. Watching ball after ball hit the middle of Tendulkar's bat can only have been reassuring for Sehwag, but his composure and the manner in which he shaped his own innings, 105 in 173 balls, including 19 fours, testified to a sound temperament.

South Africa's reply began early on the second day and ended six overs after tea on the third. Their eventual 563 was founded on a third consecutive century-opening stand between Herschelle Gibbs and Gary Kirsten.

With four wickets left, South Africa were still two runs behind. From that point, however, they took decisive control, thanks to Lance Klusener and Mark Boucher, to set up a formidable lead of 184.

India cleared 96 for just one wicket by the end of the third day. But on the fourth there came a sudden and sharp decline. Nine wickets went down for 129 runs and Pollock earned a Test haul of ten for the first time. Chasing 54, South Africa settled the argument by tea.

WHEN INDIA TOOK TO THE STREETS

Dicky Rutnagur, *Wisden* 2003

This tour made history of a thoroughly undesirable sort. The final Test, to be played at Centurion from November 23, was stripped of its official status by the International Cricket Council when India refused to play under the supervision of Mike Denness, the appointed referee. Denness had imposed penalties on six Indian players he had found in breach of the ICC Code of Conduct during the Second Test. The list included the captain, Sourav Ganguly, and the people's favourite, Sachin Tendulkar.

When the ICC rejected India's demand for Denness to be replaced, the Indian board threatened to cut short the tour, a drastic action which could have left their South African counterparts facing swingeing financial penalties for not fulfilling commitments to sponsors and broadcasters. This factor, as much as government pressure, persuaded the South African board to agree that the teams should go ahead with an unofficial Test.

At the eye of the storm was the allegation against Tendulkar that he had brought the game into disrepute through "interference with the match ball, thus changing its condition". This statement could only mean that Tendulkar had tampered with the ball and, by implication, he was a cheat. At first, Denness refused to comment on his verdicts or penalties, but he later issued a vague explanation of the Tendulkar case: it suggested he had not tampered with the ball, but had failed to observe the technicality of asking the umpires to supervise removal of mud from it. Denness added that there had been no complaint from the umpires; he had acted on his own initiative after scrutiny of video footage. Tendulkar, who hitherto had an unblemished disciplinary record, was fined 75 per cent of his match fee, with a suspended ban for one Test. The Indian public were outraged at the slight against the character of their idol.

There were street protests in towns and cities throughout the country, and scenes of uproar even in parliament. It did not escape notice that Denness had overlooked a highly aggressive appeal by the South African captain, Shaun Pollock; the omission reinforced the general view held in the subcontinent that ICC referees are racially biased. Therefore, BCCI president Jagmohan Dalmiya had to take a stand – not that he needed much provocation to adopt a bellicose posture.

Controversy followed Tendulkar back home in the series against England after India won the First Test at Mohali and drew the Second at Ahmedabad.

India v England
Third Test, at Bangalore, December 19–23, 2001
England 336 and 33-0;
India 238.
Drawn.
Tendulkar: 90

David Hopps, *Wisden* 2003

Dank weather which had more in common with Manchester than Bangalore initially encouraged England to think that they could still pull off a victory to tie the series. But the overcast skies – floodlights were in use throughout – increasingly bore unseasonal rain. As a hard-fought series petered out, the depression clung not just over the Bay of Bengal but also over the England dressing-room.

A chief source of that depression was the criticism of their negative bowling tactics against Tendulkar, apparent throughout the series, but here employed more bloody-mindedly than ever. The unedifying spectacle of Andrew Flintoff and, in particular, Ashley Giles aiming outside Tendulkar's leg stump left both Nasser Hussain and Duncan Fletcher unrepentant and, in Hussain's case, resentful that an inexperienced team's attempts to compete in alien conditions had not been given unreserved support.

Tendulkar is a special talent, and the need to curb him encouraged extreme tactics. First Flintoff conjured up memories of Bodyline by banging the ball in short from round the wicket. Then Giles deliberately landed his slow left-armers a foot outside leg stump, where the wicketkeeper, Foster, stood in readiness. On the third morning, 90 per cent of Giles's balls pitched outside leg, and Tendulkar padded away more than half. But even if Hussain felt he could justify his methods, the umpires had the power to rule these persistent negative deliveries as wides; in the broader interests of the game, they should have done.

It was the buccaneering leg-side blows of his partner and acolyte, Sehwag, that finally tempted Tendulkar into indiscretion, shortly after he passed 1,000 Test runs in the calendar year. When he charged at Giles to be stumped for the first time in his 89-Test career, England were convinced their suffocating tactics had been successful. But Tendulkar had made 90, and, if he required four and a half hours, then the lost time was to England's disadvantage. They, after all, were chasing the game.

Hussain had won the toss again, but the chief talking point on the first day was the controversy when Michael Vaughan became the seventh batsman in Test cricket to be dismissed for handling the ball. Vaughan was batting with more authority than at any time in his Test career when, on 64, he missed a sweep at the off-spinner Sarandeep Singh. As the ball became tangled beneath him, he first smothered it, then brushed it away from his crease, a lapse that would be condemned in a club match.

BODYLINE PART TWO?

David Hopps, *Wisden* 2003

Nasser Hussain went too far in his attempts to smother India's star batsman, Sachin Tendulkar. First, he instructed his bowlers to aim wide of off stump, to a seven–two or even eight–one field; then, when Tendulkar still made runs, Hussain told Giles (left-arm over) and Flintoff (right-arm round) to aim outside leg. The tactics had a touch of Douglas Jardine about them, as another England captain, Mike Brearley, remarked – saying that he felt "a deep uneasiness". To oppose these ploys was to goad Hussain into employing them all the more. The debate about the handling of Tendulkar was valid: although his scoring-rate slowed to 49 per 100 balls, he still made more runs at a far higher average than anyone else on either side. Like Mike Atherton before him, Hussain did not lack a stubborn streak.

Tendulkar's performance was central to India's first Test win in the Caribbean in over two decades.

West Indies v India

Second Test, at Port-of-Spain, April 19–23, 2002

India 339 (S. R. Tendulkar 117) and **218;**

West Indies 245 and **275.**

India won by 37 runs.

Tendulkar: 117 and 0

Tony Cozier, *Wisden* 2003

True to form, the Queen's Park Oval staged another nail-biter. As against South Africa a year earlier, the West Indians carried high hopes of victory into the last day. Then, they had needed another 200, with nine wickets left; this time, they were 131 for two, needing 182 more, with Brian Lara and Carl Hooper together. Again, they fell short; India completed their third Test victory in the Caribbean at the same venue as their earlier two, in 1970-71 and 1975-76.

They had laid the groundwork on the first day, scoring 262 for four after Hooper chose to bowl. Following a difficult start – on six, he survived a confident claim for a catch at the wicket off Adam Sanford – Tendulkar settled to build his 29th Test hundred, which put him level with Don Bradman, though he had taken 93 Tests to Bradman's 52. Only Sunil Gavaskar, with 34, had more. It was a resolute rather than commanding innings; Dravid looked the more assertive in a partnership of 124. Tendulkar added only four on the second morning before Cameron Cuffy ended his six-hour stay, prompting a decline in which the last six wickets went down for 63. Laxman remained unbeaten on 69.

West Indies were making a strong response at 179 for three, then three wickets fell for one run inside ten balls. Hooper resisted stoutly for three hours, but had little gainful support next morning as India gained a lead of 94. They were ebbing again at 56 for four, when Sanford dismissed Tendulkar fourth ball for nought, but Ganguly and Laxman batted through to the close and an hour into the fourth day, adding 149 to restore the balance.

West Indies needed 313 to win, a tall but not overwhelming order. They lost Stuart Williams early and Chris Gayle retired with cramp, but Ramnaresh Sarwan and Lara looked set to see out the day. They had added 57 when Sarwan dabbed a straight ball from Harbhajan to slip.

The stage was set for Lara to convert his overnight 40 into a first Test hundred on his home ground, in front of a crowd of 10,000. He spent an uncertain hour adding seven, before Nehra's fourth ball of the day induced a catch to first slip. Hooper pulled to midwicket in Nehra's next over, and the Indians whooped with joy.

At 237, West Indies needed 76, and Shivnarine Chanderpaul could find no one to help him get more than halfway. He was still there nine overs later, when last man Cuffy was caught at gully to give India their first Test win in the Caribbean since 1975-76, when they made 406 for four, the highest fourth-innings total to win a Test.

NOT LOVED BY EVERYONE

Rahul Bhattacharya, *Wisden Asia Cricket*, May 2002

The Relator is da man. Thirty years ago he wrote a song about Gavaskaa and calypsoed his way into Indian folklore almost like Gavaskar had into the West Indian. But, Relator don't like Tendulkar. "He is a bit snobbish, to me. Gavaskaa can reach you from even off the field. Tendulkaa, he's right up there, you don't reach him. He's out, walking to the pavilion, he doesn't look left, he doesn't look right. He's telling the umpires to go and fix the boards, we don't dig that here. Sunil is the man everyone can touch. A people's person. You never thought about that, eh? Well it's true."

And so, in the shade of the Concrete Stand, the Relator found it important to make an extempore calypso to explain it all. Around him, men were drinking rum, women were chatting, and, out in the open, Lara was batting. They all had one ear on the Relator.

Now you come to the Relataa
And you questioned me about Gavaskaa,
You even want the Relataa,
To sing about Tendulkaa,
But Mr Gentleman I will tell you plain,
I'm not singing about Indian cricketers again,
I don't want you to say that Relator pass,
But Tendulkaa is not in Gavaskaa class...

India in England in 2002, having lost the First Test at Lord's and drawn the Second at Nottingham, had their work cut out. Coming back from 1–0 down had never been their strength...

England v India
Third Test, at Leeds, August 22–26, 2002
India 628-8 dec (R. Dravid 148, S. R. Tendulkar 193, S. C. Ganguly 128);
England 273 and **309**.
India won by an innings and 46 runs.
Tendulkar: 193

Tanya Aldred, *Wisden* 2003

England can usually rely on Headingley for home comforts. So it was a nasty shock that this year the old girl turned against them, embracing instead India – out-of-form, contract-disputing India. It was they who were invited to Geoffrey Boycott's pre-match curry buffet, and it was they who breathed in the dank Leeds air, looked up at the furious age-old leaden skies, mastered the demons in the pitch, and served up a win by an innings – something they hadn't achieved overseas since routing a Packer-scarred Australia at Sydney in 1977-78.

It was a magnificent performance, built on a sublime first-day century by Dravid which Hussain graciously described as one of the finest he had seen. With that in the vaults, Tendulkar and Ganguly had the licence to play, and play they did – Tendulkar smoothing his way to his highest Test score against England, and Ganguly producing a knockabout hundred that would have been at home in a seaside cabaret. It was the first time all three had made a century in the same innings. Tendulkar passed David Gower to go seventh on the all-time Test runs list. The really unexpected part of the tale was that this excellent batting was matched by wise, wily bowling from an attack much mocked even at home.

For England it was a big step backwards. Seemingly weary from the start, they were outfoxed on the opening day by the Indians, who Boycottishly refused to play at any balls they did not have to.

The game had started slowly after Ganguly, fearlessly going against all Headingley precedent by picking two spinners, won the toss and batted. Sehwag gloved a catch in the seventh over; Dravid and Sanjay Bangar settled back and worked to rule – the first 50 came up ten minutes before lunch, to much foot-shuffling in the crowd. Dravid was immaculate from the start; Bangar was an admirable sidekick, but his demise was greeted with excitement as the crowd prepared for Tendulkar, Yorkshire's prodigal son, who despite his year here as a 19-year-old had never made a first-class century at Headingley. Now, in his 99th Test, as visitors quaffed champagne in the hospitality box Yorkshire had named after him, he did it, overtaking Don Bradman's total of 29 Test hundreds as he stroked the ball round the ground. But the highlight of the match was not the moment of his longed-for century; it was the silly session late on Friday afternoon when, as the skies darkened, he and Ganguly saw four lights on the scoreboard, disdained them, and ran amok, scoring 96 off the first 11 overs of the third new ball. Together they added 249, an Indian fourth-wicket record against England.

India's total was their highest against England when Ganguly declared. England began brightly, as if not missing Marcus Trescothick at all. Vaughan again dashed on to the attack, but after he drove loosely at the skinny Ajit Agarkar, England stalled. All the main batsmen bar Flintoff got a start, but nobody came close to the big hundred the situation demanded. India had batted for two days before losing their fifth wicket; England managed less than four hours.

England's follow-on wasn't necessarily doomed, but India were showing intensity in the field. Vaughan couldn't help for once, Mark Butcher lost patience after a solid start and John Crawley completed a double failure, so it was left to the old sweats, Hussain and Alec Stewart.

They came together in rich late-afternoon sunshine on Sunday and by the close Hussain had 90, Stewart had 40 and England had a chance. Hussain went on to his hundred the next morning but fell soon afterwards, and with him went England's hopes of going to The Oval with a lead still in their pockets. Kumble and Harbhajan twirled and fizzed and showed that spin could be a weapon anywhere in the right hands.

BACK TO PAKISTAN

There had rarely been more at stake in a cricket series when India crossed the border in 2004 for the first time since Tendulkar's international debut in 1989; he was the only player from that series still playing. Rather than degenerating into another edition of war minus the shooting, the Indian cricketers found their way into Pakistani hearts – despite the results. India won the one-dayers 3–2 and the Tests 2–1. But there were many tense moments as a media-manufactured controversy involving Tendulkar erupted during the First Test at Multan.

Pakistan v India
Second one-day international, at Rawalpindi, March 16, 2004 (day/night)
Pakistan 329-6;
India 317 (S. R. Tendulkar 141).
Pakistan won by 12 runs.
Tendulkar: 141

Rahul Bhattacharya, *Wisden* 2005

Once again the hunters fell tantalisingly short in a high-scoring thriller, with India just failing after needing 16 off the last two overs. On a pitch that he said became progressively slower, Tendulkar scored a superb century, India's first in a one-day international in Pakistan, and became the first player to reach 13,000 one-day runs. But his dismissal, sweeping to deep mid-wicket in the 39th over, galvanised the bowling; seven overs later India slumped to 284 for eight when Shoaib Akhtar fired out two in two. The valiant hitting of Lakshmipathy Balaji and debutant Ramesh Powar won the heart of Pakistan's president, Pervez Musharraf, who took tea with the Indians next day. It also kept India in the game until the penultimate over, when Mohammad Sami theatrically defeated last man Ashish Nehra's uncalculated swipe.

Pakistan v India
First Test, at Multan, March 28–April 1, 2004
India 675-5 dec (V. Sehwag 309, S. R. Tendulkar 194*);
Pakistan 407 and **216** (Yousuf Youhana 112, A. Kumble 6-72).
India won by an innings and 52 runs.
Tendulkar: 194*; 2-36

Rahul Bhattacharya, *Wisden* 2005

From about 10 a.m. on March 28, a regular thud, rather than the roars associated with cricket in the subcontinent, began to emerge from the Multan Cricket Stadium, a modern ground situated on farmland 45 minutes out of town. The stadium was virtually desolate, and the thumps, from Sehwag's bat, were to resound for a day and a half as he constructed India's first triple-century in Test cricket. It laid the foundation of a historic victory, India's first in Pakistan in 21 Tests spread over 49 years. It was also, briefly, their most substantial win in a largely wretched 72 years of Tests away from home.

Sehwag's 309, and his partnership of 336, an Indian third-wicket record, with Tendulkar, who crafted a meticulous century, carried India to their third-highest total, and second-highest away: 675 for five declared.

Sehwag's glitzy epic was not without luck. Nonetheless, it was an innings of sustained and versatile violence. He thrashed six sixes and 39 fours in 375 balls; he went from 99 to 105 with a glided six over third man off Shoaib Akhtar, and from 295 to 301 with a roundhouse blast over wide long-on off Saqlain Mushtaq.

Yet despite the continued flowering of the batting, India's real success, as Dravid, acting-captain for the injured Ganguly, explained, was in taking 20 wickets on a grassless, crack-free, crumble-proof surface. To do it virtually in four days (Pakistan's last wicket fell 12 balls into the final day) amid Multan's infamous combination of heat and dust was doubly creditable.

Two bowlers stood out. Leg-spinner Kumble took seven wickets out of 13 on the pivotal fourth day, making it 32 from his last four Tests, all abroad. Left-arm seamer Irfan Pathan not only bagged six wickets in the match but bowled 17 maidens in 49 overs. It was Pathan, too, who surprised Abdul Razzaq with a bouncer as soon as he took guard on the fourth morning at 364 for six: the dismissal provided India with just the push they needed to press for the follow-on.

Pakistan's hopes of saving the match diminished with every thrust from Kumble the following day. The final nail was Inzamam-ul-Haq's second-innings run-out by a brilliant hit from Yuvraj Singh, swooping at midwicket to leave Pakistan 44 for three – 224 short of making India bat again.

AN UNTIMELY DECLARATION

Rahul Bhattacharya, *Wisden* 2005

Strangely, the biggest of the game's controversies – dwarfing the umpiring and Pakistan's request for a shaved pitch – came from the victorious camp. Dravid stunned observers by declaring when Yuvraj fell an hour before the second-day close. Nothing sensational – except that Tendulkar was 194 not out. Tendulkar did not take the field that evening, claiming a sprained ankle; at a press conference, he made clear his disappointment and surprise.

Back home, some believed Tendulkar had been robbed; others thought his comments were selfish, and demonstrated an obsession with personal milestones. (As it was, the innings put him one ahead of Steve Waugh's 32 Test hundreds, and one behind Sunil Gavaskar's record of 34.) Many in the first group aimed their vitriol at Ganguly, who had no official role as he sat out the game with a back injury, but was seen on television gesturing impatiently.

In fact, Tendulkar had played the perfect innings for his team, a discreet, chanceless companion to Sehwag's theatricals. His pacing was perfect too, each fifty coming quicker than the last, and the final 40 at almost a run a ball. But because he was operating without obvious risk, he seemed not to be pushing on. And Dravid probably erred not in his timing, but in failing to communicate with Tendulkar. The two had an honest discussion next morning to clear the air, which would have been beyond some faction-ridden Indian teams of the past.

MORE RECORDS

Under "injuries" in the index to Tendulkar's autobiography are the following: ankle, back, elbow, finger, groin, hamstring, hand, shoulder and toe. The elbow was the worst of the lot. Forced to sit out the 2004 Champions

Trophy in England, he had no choice but to miss the first two Tests of the 2004-05 series against Australia as well. India lost the First and Third Tests, but came back to win the Fourth in Mumbai. Tendulkar, on a constant diet of painkillers, continued to play. His double-century against Bangladesh was his last major innings before he finally underwent elbow surgery.

Bangladesh v India

First Test, at Dhaka, December 10–13, 2004

Bangladesh 184 (I. K. Pathan 5-45) and **202** (I. K. Pathan 6-51);

India 526 (S.R. Tendulkar 248*).

India won by an innings and 140 runs

Tendulkar: 248*

Amit Varma, *Wisden* 2005

That India would win, and easily, was never in doubt. Two of their greatest ever – Tendulkar and Kumble – were chasing records and hungry to do well, perhaps against the weakest opposition of their long and distinguished careers. And when India put Bangladesh in on a Bangabandhu Stadium pitch with a bit of bounce in it, one sensed Kumble would be among the wickets. But even he had to wait, as Pathan immediately hit his stride. Before the batsmen could come to terms with what was swerving at them, they were 50 for five.

But Mohammad Ashraful looked a cut above his team-mates. With the gutsy Mohammad Rafique, he pushed the score from 106 for seven to 171, before Kumble claimed his slice of history, trapping Rafique in front with a typical fizzing slider to give him his 435th Test wicket – one more than Kapil Dev, India's previous record-holder, but in 40 fewer Tests. Bangladesh had clawed their way back to some extent, but 184 all out on the first day was never going to be enough. Sure enough, the second day was a roaring Indian bat-fest. The fall of seven wickets did not stop them from racking up 348, with Tendulkar drawing level with Sunil Gavaskar as Test cricket's most prolific centurion. An unbeaten 159, his 34th hundred, was not the toughest test of his career, yet he was dropped three times – two of them sitters – before he reached 50. For Tendulkar, who had been battling a painful tennis elbow for at least four months, the century was reconfirmation that a day would come when strength would return to his left arm, and with it the range of strokes.

On the third day, India romped to 526. Tendulkar's final contribution was a Test-best 248 not out, from 379 balls and including

35 fours in nine hours 12 minutes. "Forget about the record, forget the double-hundred, the very fact that I could bat this long was a relief and joy," he said.

Five months after his surgery, Tendulkar returned to Test cricket to set another record...

India v Sri Lanka

Second Test, at Delhi, December 10–14, 2005

India 290 (S. R. Tendulkar 109, M. Muralitharan 7-100) and **375-6 dec.**;

Sri Lanka 230 (A. Kumble 6-72) and **247**.

India won by 188 runs.

Tendulkar: 109

R. Kaushik, *Wisden* 2006

Fortunes swung dramatically before finally settling decisively in India's favour in a Test that will be remembered as the one that saw Sachin Tendulkar keep his appointment with destiny. Tendulkar reaffirmed his status as probably the finest batsman of his generation by passing Sunil Gavaskar to become the record-holder for the most Test centuries.

Tendulkar's 35th hundred, in his 125th match – the same number that Gavaskar played to score his 34 hundreds – was the highlight of a game that had more twists and turns than a Grand Prix circuit. It was an innings that, in contrast to his recent approach, mushroomed from the circumspect to the awe-inspiring. The first half of his only Test hundred of 2005 was a lesson in the art of innings-building, but his second fifty passed in a flash, filled with deft strokes. It was a fitting innings with which to break the record, a knock that by his own admission made him "truly emotional", and it was met with equal relief and elation by a doting nation when he turned Chaminda Vaas to fine leg for the vital single in the gloaming at 4.45 p.m., the last ball before bad light ended play for the day.

It was just one of a number of impressive performances in a match in which India's collective strength and Sri Lanka's inability to maintain concentration made the difference. In what Sri Lanka's coach Tom Moody called 45 minutes of madness, they were spun to their doom by Kumble, enjoying his return to a ground where he had taken 38 wickets in four previous Tests, including all ten in an innings against Pakistan in 1998-99.

Tendulkar and Kumble were not the only Indian heroes. With Sehwag out with a throat infection, Dravid asked Pathan to open in the second innings to build quickly on the lead of 60. Without resorting to slogging, Pathan made a rapid-fire 93. Dravid applied himself for 53, then Yuvraj Singh and M. S. Dhoni tore into the bowling.

Dravid declared shortly after lunch on the fourth day, setting an unlikely target of 436. Marvan Atapattu and Mahela Jayawardene again provided most of the resistance, but for the second time in three days Sri Lanka collapsed after tea.

TENDULKAR BOOED

Shoulder surgery followed less than a year after Tendulkar's elbow operation, and shortly after England managed to draw a three-match series with a surprise win in the Third Test at Mumbai. Signs that Tendulkar's status was changing from the man-who-could-no-wrong were clear when he was booed from the cheap seats. "The tour highlighted a new phenomenon – the emergence of high-class cricketers from families of modest means outside the major cities that had traditionally produced the sport's stars," wrote Simon Wilde in Wisden. *"Dhoni's feats in one-day cricket had quickly turned him into a nationwide star and a very wealthy young man. Startlingly, he walked to the wicket to bigger cheers than were accorded to the struggling hero, Tendulkar, who was booed by some during the Test in Mumbai, his home city. He was hampered by shoulder trouble, which put him out of the one-dayers, but England reinforced the impression gained during India's previous series against Pakistan that he was growing uneasy with the short-pitched ball."*

NINETIES IN THE NOUGHTIES

Although Tendulkar struck a rich vein of form in 2007, a one-day century proved elusive after the series against West Indies in January. However, thanks to his 90-plus scores in the Future Cup and at home against Pakistan, India won the two series. Unfortunately, Tendulkar couldn't see India over the line in the NatWest Trophy against England – they lost the series 4–3.

India v South Africa
Future Cup, Second one-day international, at Belfast, June 29, 2007
South Africa 226-6;
India 227-4.
India won by six wickets.
Tendulkar: 93

Julian Guyer, *Wisden* 2008

During a thrilling innings which navigated the path between the sublime and the reckless in a manner reminiscent of Brian Lara, Tendulkar became the first batsman to pass 15,000 runs in one-day internationals – a mark he reached when he passed 50 with the aid of a single and four overthrows – as India levelled the series. Chasing 227, Tendulkar and Ganguly shared a first-wicket stand of 134. Tendulkar hooked Makhaya Ntini dismissively for four, square-cut Charl Langeveldt with something akin to disdain, and pulled Andre Nel, world cricket's answer to the pantomime villain, commandingly for six. Thandi Tshabalala's off-spin was driven for six and four off successive balls, but he did finally dismiss Tendulkar, cutting on to his stumps, out in the nineties for the second match running.

India v England
Natwest Trophy, Second one-day international, at Bristol, August 24, 2007 (day/night)
India 329-7 (A. Flintoff 5-56);
England 320-8.
India won by nine runs.
Tendulkar: 99

Richard Hobson, *Wisden* 2008

Short boundaries conspired with a flat pitch to produce an imbalance between bat and ball – not that any of the 16,000 crowd were complaining, after 11 sixes and 73 fours. Flu-like symptoms failed to restrict Tendulkar and Dravid any more than a one-dimensional bowling attack: India's 329 for seven was their highest total against England. The decision to omit Monty Panesar in favour of yet another seamer in Chris Tremlett backfired, and the target could have been greater still had umpire Ian Gould not adjudicated that Tendulkar had gloved Flintoff's bouncer on 99. Replays suggested the ball deflected via the arm-guard. It fell, instead, to Dravid to give the late impetus, with 92 from 63 balls. India did at least give England a chance, squandering five chances in the first 19 overs alone. But the spin of Powar and Piyush Chawla did for the middle order.

India v England
Natwest Trophy, Sixth one-day international, at The Oval, September 5, 2007
England 316-6 (O. A. Shah 107*);
India 317-8.
India won by two wickets.
Tendulkar: 94

Richard Hobson, *Wisden* 2008

A game that brought 50-over cricket into considerable repute was eventually won with successive fours by Robin Uthappa off Stuart Broad. When England were 137 for five in the 31st over, it was impossible to imagine the drama ahead. Owais Shah recovered from Kevin Pietersen's run-out to accelerate from 50 to a maiden international century in 29 balls. Yet he, too, was trumped when Dimitri Mascarenhas forced the innings' last five balls, from Yuvraj Singh, for successive sixes between long-on and deep midwicket. Undaunted, Tendulkar responded with a brilliance based on timing rather than power, before cramp took a hold. He needed help to climb the dressing-room steps after falling in the nineties for the fourth time in nine one-day innings. Roused by a spat with Broad, Ganguly had helped him put on 150 in 23 overs, but wickets fell steadily, leaving India 42 short after 46 overs. They took a total of 28 off the 47th and 49th from James Anderson to leave ten needed from the last.

India v Pakistan

Fourth one-day international, at Gwalior, November 15, 2007 (day/night)

Pakistan 255-6;

India 260-4.

India won by six wickets.

Tendulkar: 97

Anand Vasu, *Wisden* 2008

On another pitch not suited to strokemaking, Tendulkar mastered the art of the limited-overs ninety with a sublime innings that left watchers wondering why the cricketing gods seemed intent on denying him his 42nd one-day hundred. Pakistan's batsmen were again hamstrung by an overcautious approach, and although Mohammad Yousuf made 99 and Younis Khan passed 50, they consumed 193 balls between them. The target did not look unduly demanding, and once Tendulkar read the pace of the pitch it proved to be woefully inadequate. He set the pace, and despite his now-routine departure in the nineties – his sixth such dismissal of 2007 – Yuvraj and Dhoni applied the finishing touches and sealed the series 3–1.

BOLLYLINE GRABS THE HEADLINES

Tendulkar continued his good form into 2008. After India lost the First Test of the Border-Gavaskar Trophy in Melbourne, the action shifted to

Sydney. A century from Tendulkar gave India a real chance of squaring the series, but a charge of racism against Harbhajan Singh – by Australian player Andrew Symonds – and terrible umpiring overshadowed his brilliance and prevented any chance of a win.

Australia v India

Border–Gavaskar Trophy, Second Test, at Sydney, January 2–6, 2008

Australia 463 (A. Symonds 162*) and **401-7 dec.** (M. L. Hayden 123);
India 532 (V. V. S. Laxman 109, S. R. Tendulkar 154*, B. Lee 5-119) and **210**.

Australia won by 122 runs.

Tendulkar: 154* and 12

Geoffrey Dean, *Wisden* 2008

On a melodramatic final day in front of a smallish crowd of just under 11,000, Australia won with just nine minutes of the last hour remaining, when occasional slow left-armer Michael Clarke took three wickets in five balls, helping his side equal the world record of 16 consecutive Test victories which they themselves set in 2001. However, they would never have done so but for a series of umpiring blunders. Most of these went against India, who were so incensed that their board successfully asked the ICC to remove Steve Bucknor from the next Test at Perth.

Australia's victory was overshadowed by the row that erupted over the allegation that Harbhajan Singh had racially abused Andrew Symonds, the only non-white player in the Australian side. The original decision of referee Mike Procter to suspend Harbhajan for three Tests angered the Indians, and there was talk of the tour being called off if his appeal was unsuccessful. In the end, wiser counsel prevailed.

The match had begun so well for India: they reduced Australia to 134 for six in good conditions for batting. There was some first-day life in the pitch, which gave the Indian pace attack, weakened by the loss of Zaheer Khan with an injured heel, some early encouragement. Phil Jaques was the victim of extra bounce, cutting injudiciously in the third over, and then R. P. Singh swung the ball away from the left-handers from an ideal line to give Tendulkar three sharp catches at first slip. Harbhajan chipped in with a brace of lbws – Ponting was given out by Mark Benson despite getting an inside edge, while Clarke padded up to a straight one. Benson's error was his second involving Ponting: when 17, he should have been given out caught behind down the leg side off Ganguly.

A much worse decision – a howler that had a major influence on the match's outcome – came from Bucknor after Australia had rallied to 193 for six. Symonds, then 30, got what he later admitted was a thick outside edge when he tried to force Ishant Sharma off the back foot.

Bucknor failed to spot it. By the time the excellent partnership between Symonds and Brad Hogg was finally broken, they had put on 173 in 36 overs, a record for the seventh wicket in any Test at Sydney.

Capitalising on his good fortune, Symonds cantered to his second Test hundred. In all 329 runs were burgled by the last four wickets.

On a pitch that had flattened out, India batted outstandingly. Dravid, with another painstaking innings, and Laxman laid an ideal platform, putting on 175 for the second wicket. Laxman, driving elegantly through extra cover and on-driving wristily, raced to fifty in 43 balls before consolidating to complete his third hundred in successive Tests at the SCG.

For all Laxman's brilliance, though, Tendulkar's 38th Test century – also his third at the SCG, where he averages 221.33 – was a masterclass, virtually without flaw. Unlike Laxman, he gave no chances in 429 minutes at the crease. Wary of big off-side shots, he preferred the leg. That he hit as few as 14 fours (and a six off Hogg) and as many as 66 singles was largely because Ponting stationed permanent boundary sweepers square on both sides of the wicket in an attempt to restrict him. Content to let Ganguly outscore him at first, Tendulkar was left with the tail after Brett Lee filleted the lower middle order during a top-class spell with the second new ball.

Harbhajan came in, and Tendulkar – who had 69 at the time – had no qualms in allowing him the strike, which brought out the best in the tailender. Harbhajan responded with his first Test fifty against Australia. They put on 129, a record for India's eighth wicket against Australia.

All this ought to have made the game safe for India, who appeared the only possible winners at the start of the fourth day. More bad umpiring decisions, however, allowed Australia to prosper in their second innings. Mike Hussey appeared to have been trapped in front by Kumble when 22, and he should also have been given out caught behind off Singh when 45. He went on to his eighth Test century, before accelerating to allow Ponting to declare 332 ahead, with a minimum of 72 overs to bowl India out.

Until Dravid was fourth out, to the first ball of the 34th over, it did not look as if Ponting had left himself enough time. A concerted appeal for a caught-behind, led theatrically by Adam Gilchrist, was upheld by Bucknor despite the fact that Symonds's off-break had only brushed the front pad, with the bat hidden behind it. India still had a good chance of saving the match, for even though the pitch was offering turn and bounce, Hogg was ineffective and Ponting was obliged to employ his part-time spinners Symonds and Clarke. To lose six wickets to them was carelessness, at best. Ponting admitted that the introduction of Clarke was "a last roll of the dice". Clarke responded with three wickets in his second over, two of them caught at slip, to complete the victory that gave Australia a 2–0 lead in the series and maintained their hold on the Border–Gavaskar Trophy.

ANOTHER FIRST FOR INDIA

India came back strongly in the Third Test at the WACA, becoming the first subcontinental team to win in Perth. A draw in the Fourth, at Adelaide, meant a 2–1 defeat for India, but after all the bitterness in Sydney, their performances in the last two Tests helped restore their confidence and fired them up for the one-day competition to follow. India gave Sri Lanka – the third team in the triangular series – absolutely no chance, as they advanced to the best-of-three finals. Ponting, who had claimed that Australia would settle the matter in the first two, had to eat humble pie, as Tendulkar had different ideas. His match-winning performances in the finals led India to their first limited-overs series win in Australia in 23 years.

Australia v India

Commonwealth Bank Series, First Final, at Sydney, March 2, 2008 (day/night)

Australia 239-8;

India 242-4 (S. R. Tendulkar 117*).

India won by six wickets.

Tendulkar: 117*

Malcolm Conn, *Wisden* 2009

The incomparable Sachin Tendulkar came good when it mattered most. In 38 one-day internationals in Australia, he had never scored a century – and in 11 one-day internationals against Australia in Sydney, India had never won. Now, though, one thing led to another: Tendulkar hit a glorious hundred, victory came, and India switched from rank underdogs to competition favourites in a few short hours. Batting with a resolve not previously seen in the tournament, Tendulkar compiled a wonderfully weighted, unbeaten 117. He added 123 for the fourth wicket with Rohit Sharma to guide India to an emphatic six-wicket win.

Australia v India

Commonwealth Bank Series, Second Final, at Brisbane, March 4, 2008 (day/night)

India 258-9;

Australia 249 (P. Kumar 4-46).

India won by nine runs.

Tendulkar: 91

Malcolm Conn, *Wisden* 2009

When India won the second final, they pulled off one of their greatest one-day triumphs since winning the 1983 World Cup. In their sixth appearance in Australia's triangular tournament, they were at last victorious. Once again Tendulkar was instrumental, scoring 91 from 121 balls while his team-mates could manage no more than cameos. He seemed to be heading for a second successive hundred when, moments after playing a reverse sweep (a rare, if not unprecedented shot for him), Tendulkar chipped to midwicket. In reply, Australia again faltered at the start of their innings and lurched to 32 for three – ultimately they were flattered by the margin of defeat.

Breaking Lara's Record

Australia travelled to India later that year to play four Tests. Ponting's attempts to win a Test series in India failed yet again as India won the rubber 2–0. It was a happy send-off for Sourav Ganguly, who had announced at the start of the series that it would be his last. Tendulkar scored a century in the Fourth Test at Nagpur – Ganguly's last – but it was his partnership with Ganguly in the Second Test that laid the foundation for an Indian win. And another Tendulkar milestone.

India v Australia

Border–Gavaskar Trophy, Second Test, at Mohali, October 17–21, 2008
India 469 (S. C. Ganguly 102) and **314-3 dec.** (G. Gambhir 104);
Australia 268 (A. Mishra 5-71) and **195.**
India won by 320 runs.
Tendulkar: 88 and 10*

Mike Coward, *Wisden* 2009

From the outset India signalled their intention to question the mighty reputation of the visitors on a glorious batting surface which mysteriously evolved into something like a goat track when Australia batted. Such was the ease of India's batting against an attack seriously depleted by the absence of the injured Stuart Clark that local pundits accused the top order of squandering a priceless opportunity to amass 600 or more. As it happened, 469 was more than enough to seize control of the proceedings and condemn the Australians to their heaviest defeat against India in terms of runs – and India's biggest victory.

Tendulkar and Ganguly made the most of the benign conditions to reach significant milestones. The pyrotechnics which greeted Tendulkar becoming Test cricket's highest run-scorer – he passed Brian Lara's mark of 11,953 with a glide for three off the debutant Peter Siddle that took him to 16, and later reached 12,000 with a single off Cameron White to go to 61 – were a loud, prolonged and spectacular precursor to the great Diwali festival of light throughout the country 11 days later. Tendulkar fell just 12 runs short of his 40th Test hundred.

That these splendid achievements were not witnessed by many more spectators was very disappointing; officials were rightly embarrassed by the small number of patrons at a venue which offers little protection from the elements and suffers from suffocating security. Had a few intrepid visitors from Australia not been joined by uniformed schoolchildren who had been brought in by bus, scarcely a soul would have witnessed one of Indian cricket's finest hours.

Despite the profligacy of the Indian batsmen on the first day, Australia were never in the match – Hayden again out third ball to the irresistible Zaheer, and Clarke again falling in the last over of the day.

By stumps on the third day India led by 301 with all their second-innings wickets intact. They extended the stand to 182 next day before Dhoni, who marshalled his forces skilfully in only his second Test as captain, put the Australians to the sword with a telling 68. Australia were set an unlikely target of 516.

In what was termed "Mad Monday", Australia lost five wickets for nine runs. It was Zaheer who ensured Australia would be defeated by lunch on the final day, when he took three wickets in four balls.

LORD OF ALL THINGS

India arrived in New Zealand with great hopes of being able to win their first-ever limited-overs series there. The mission was accomplished when India won 3–1. Tendulkar carried his imperious form into the five-day arena, as India piled on the misery for New Zealand with a 1–0 win in the Test series, their first in 41 years.

New Zealand v India
Third one-day international, at Christchurch, March 8, 2009 (day/night)
India 392-4 (S. R. Tendulkar 163 ret. hurt);
New Zealand 334 (J. D. Ryder 105).
India won by 58 runs.
Tendulkar: 163 ret. hurt

Anand Vasu, *Wisden* 2010

While Tendulkar gave a masterclass in innings construction, building his first one-day international hundred in New Zealand in perfect blocks, Yuvraj finished with strokes of such power and brutality that the home side did well eventually to respond in kind. Tendulkar's 163 (his 43rd and, at the time, second-highest one-day hundred) included straight-driving of the utmost quality, but what caught the eye was his innovation – inside-out hits over cover, and paddle-sweeps off the faster bowlers – before he retired at the end of the 45th over with an injured stomach muscle. India's 392 was easily the highest total in any one-day international in New Zealand.

New Zealand v India
First Test, at Hamilton, March 18–21, 2009
New Zealand 279 and **279** (Harbhajan Singh 6-63);
India 520 (S. R. Tendulkar 160) and **39-0.**
India won by ten wickets.
Tendulkar: 160 and DNB

Don Cameron, *Wisden* 2010

India were quick off the blocks in the Test series, cruising to a comfortable victory at Seddon Park. Six of their side – Dravid, Harbhajan, Laxman, Sehwag, Tendulkar and Zaheer – had lost here in 2002-03, when an extravagantly lively pitch allowed an aggregate of only 507 runs for 36 wickets, but this time India had a steely backbone.

The bland pitch had a hint of early moisture, but presented no obvious help to the bowlers or danger to the batsmen. However, Dhoni looked beyond that – at a New Zealand batting line-up that started with Martin Guptill in his first Test and Tim McIntosh in his third. The Indian captain sensed that there might be enough in the pitch to cause some early mischief, and let his four-man bowling attack loose when he won the toss.

It was the first masterstroke that led to India's four-day win. Ishant Sharma had the speed and lift, Zaheer the subtle movement in the air and off the pitch. Zaheer had Guptill caught in his fourth over, and Daniel Flynn (for a duck) in his fifth. Then Sharma struck, removing McIntosh, bowling Ross Taylor, and having James Franklin caught behind; next Munaf Patel had Brendon McCullum caught at second slip. The New Zealanders ate a tasteless lunch at 61 for six.

Fortunately for them, Jesse Ryder and Daniel Vettori added 101 between lunch and tea, and afterwards Vettori raced to his third Test century. The stand was worth 186 when at last a Vettori edge found Dhoni's gloves.

The last four wickets had lifted the score from 60 to an almost-respectable 279. India set out to profit from the inoffensive pitch. Sehwag wasted an opportunity, but Gambhir and Dravid produced a pleasant flow of runs that took India to 108 for one at lunch. They rather lost their way in the afternoon: Gambhir was undone by Chris Martin, and Dravid bowled by one of the few tricks the ball performed all day. Even Tendulkar seemed slightly out of sorts, his strokes out of harmony with the gentle pace of the pitch. At 13 he sent a weird swish toward midwicket, but Flynn could not latch on to a difficult catch.

Between lunch and tea India managed only 89, ending the session still 82 behind, but afterwards Tendulkar, who had been pecking away for runs like a farmyard fowl, changed to the soaring eagle that is Sachin at his sublime best. By stumps he had surged to 70, with a range of sumptuous shots, and on the third morning he was simply magnificent as he threaded stroke after stroke through the gaps, often to the fence. His eventual 160, which contained 26 fours from 260 balls, was the perfect counterpoint of classic charm to his brutal 163 in the one-dayer at Christchurch 12 days previously. This was his 42nd Test century, his fourth against New Zealand.

New Zealand's bowling was limp, conceding a deficit of 241, and by the end of the third day the batting was looking none too healthy either, at 75 for three. Only Flynn offered serious fourth-day resistance as Harbhajan's probing spin proved too much for the rest. At 199 for eight the bowlers relaxed a little, allowing McCullum to hit 11 fours in a quickfire 84 before India completed their first Test win in New Zealand for 33 years.

THE TENDULKAR OF OLD

Later that year, India played a seven-match limited-overs series against Australia at home. For one brief evening, Tendulkar showed us a glimpse of his 25-year-old self as he rampaged to 175 in a manic run-chase. But, like the Tendulkar of the 1990s, he couldn't prevent India from ending up on the losing side. And India eventually lost the series, tied at 2–2 until this game, 4–2.

India v Australia

Fifth one-day international, at Hyderabad, November 5, 2009 (day/night)

Australia 350-4 (S. E. Marsh 112);

India 347 (S. R. Tendulkar 175).

Australia won by three runs.

Tendulkar: 175

Daniel Brettig, *Wisden* 2010

One of the most bewitching limited-overs matches yet played saw Australian composure win out despite the majesty of Tendulkar. It was clear after only a few overs that the pitch was of the highest quality for batting, as Shane Watson struck crisply through the line to get Australia off to a powerful start. Shaun Marsh was more reserved, but gathered momentum as he went on. Late hammer blows by White (who hit five sixes from just 33 balls) and Mike Hussey took Australia as far as 350, a total India had never successfully chased. Knowing the required rate did not allow for a moment's hesitation, and again losing Sehwag after a start of unfulfilled promise, Tendulkar – who passed 17,000 runs in one-day internationals early on – took it upon himself to scale the mountain. Taking an approach reminiscent of his younger self, he was audacious in the manner of Sharjah 1998 (when he scored 80, 143 and 134 in successive matches against Australia in the Coca-Cola Cup), and for some time the Siddle-less attack had no answer. Suresh Raina provided the support to take India within sight, and the last three overs began with just 19 required and four wickets left. It was a slower ball, from the debutant Clint McKay, that Tendulkar scooped fatefully to short fine leg. A chaotically panicked end followed, as Australia salvaged a meritorious victory at the last gasp. But memories of Tendulkar's effort will live longer than those of the result. His superb innings, which occupied 141 balls and contained 19 fours and four sixes, was his 45th one-day hundred – and the 12th that failed to secure victory.

On Top Of The World

In December 2009, India climbed to the top of the ICC Test rankings for the first time, after a 2–0 win against Sri Lanka at home. Tendulkar was ecstatic: he went on record to say it was among the best Indian teams he had played in. With a view to preserving India's No. 1 spot, the BCCI hurriedly organised Test tours at home against South Africa and Australia. If 2009 proved fruitful for Tendulkar and India, 2010 was even better: he scored a double-century against Australia at home, and followed it up with his 50th Test hundred, on India's tour of South Africa later in the year.

"Sachin Tendulkar's bat appeared to widen the closer he inched towards his 40th year, and here it proved virtually impassable," wrote Daniel Brettig. "The Australians escaped relatively lightly at Mohali by dismissing him for 98 and 38, but in Bangalore, Tendulkar would respond by delivering the series to his homeland by compiling 214 and an unbeaten 53 to collect the winning runs. He gave scarcely a chance in either innings." Tendulkar continued to be among the runs the following year in the 2011 World Cup. But the big runs seemed to elude him in the second half of 2011 – while touring England and Australia – as it took him over a year to get from 99 international centuries to a 100.

India v Australia

Border–Gavaskar Trophy, Second Test, at Bangalore, October 9–13, 2010
Australia 478 (M. J. North 128) and **223**;
India 495 (S. R. Tendulkar 214, M. Vijay 139) and **207-3**.
India won by seven wickets.
Tendulkar: 214 and 53*

Daniel Brettig, *Wisden* 2011

Until an hour before lunch on the final day, the Second Test matched the First for quality and fluctuations. It did not quite carry through to the same kind of desperate conclusion, because India were finally able to shake a tenacious Australia.

The debutant Cheteshwar Pujara, in concert with fellow batting aspirant Murali Vijay, effectively won the game for India with a partnership of 72 that was brief but ferocious, resulting in a 2–0 series scoreline for the triumphant hosts.

For the second time in the series Australia had the advantage of batting first, and for the second time they went close to surrendering it with some inattentive batting. Shane Watson and Simon Katich were untroubled despite noticeable new-ball swing under overcast skies, and put on 99 before Katich cut at Harbhajan and was taken at slip. Ponting was again in decent touch, reaching the outskirts of a century only to squander it by missing a straight ball from the part-time spin of Raina.

Marcus North needed a score to make his place safe for the Ashes series. Taking a confident stride forward and timing the ball sweetly down the ground, he showed the array of his talents with help from the doughty Tim Paine, and their concentration took Australia towards 478.

Early incisions were made by the Australian attack when India batted. Sehwag swatted to deep square and Dravid again edged a ball slanted towards the cordon, but they were to prove the last wickets for more than six hours. Tendulkar, who passed 14,000 Test runs with a four off Nathan Hauritz through the covers, found a sprightly ally in Vijay, and together they made the touring attack look very pedestrian. In the case of Hauritz the batsmen's contempt was plain, and Tendulkar swung him for six on 93 and 99 with all the assurance of a man who knew precisely what his quarry was doing, or not doing, with the SG ball.

Vijay had a more torrid time against Australia's debutant, the gangling seamer Peter George from Adelaide, but held firm for a maiden Test hundred as he and Tendulkar added 308. Mitchell Johnson broke the stand by coaxing an edge from Vijay, and in the same over conjured a shooter from nowhere to defeat the unfortunate Pujara, who had sat padded up awaiting his chance through 90.3 overs, the longest wait for any Test debutant.

Tendulkar went on and on, converting his 49th Test hundred into his sixth double on the fourth morning, and taking India seemingly beyond the point of danger, before he was out to George, who found some old-ball swing to get an inside edge on to the stumps. George admitted to some shock at the identity of his first wicket, but it was the 19th time Tendulkar had been dismissed by a debutant. The unexpected success brought another twist, as five wickets went down for nine runs in eight overs.

For all Tendulkar's dominance, India led by only 17. Zaheer and Shanthakumaran Sreesanth (replacing the injured Ishant Sharma) summoned treacherous amounts of reverse on the fourth evening, and Ponting was lbw to limit his contribution to that of a masterpiece in miniature. The tail offered only nuisance value, and a target of 207 required plenty of early wickets to become defendable.

The Australians had one when Paine moved sharply to his right to claim an edge from Sehwag, and were surprised when Pujara was promoted ahead of Dravid at No.3. Wrongly sensing an easy wicket, they bowled like gamblers rather than misers, allowing Pujara and Vijay to capitalise nervelessly. Vijay played inside Watson to be lbw, and Pujara did the same to be bowled by Hauritz, but the remaining runs were gleaned, fittingly, by Tendulkar. All this was watched and cheered across five days at the Chinnaswamy Stadium by one of the largest and most buoyant Test crowds witnessed in India this century, a pointed lesson about the importance of wise venue choices for the continued health of Test cricket.

South Africa v India

First Test, at Centurion, December 16–20, 2010

India 136 (M. Morkel 5-20) and **459** (S. R. Tendulkar 111*);
South Africa 620-4 dec (H. M. Amla 140, J. H. Kallis 201*, A.B. de Villiers 129).

South Africa won by an innings and 25 runs.

Tendulkar: 36 and 111*

Neil Manthorp, *Wisden* 2011

India enjoyed the considerable consolation of Sachin Tendulkar's 50th Test century, but were otherwise wretched and were duly thrashed.

On a pitch offering decent but not lavish assistance to the seamers, the tourists were flung instantly on to the back foot – literally and metaphorically – by a single shot of the utmost stupidity, played by Sehwag before he had scored.

Tendulkar briefly but beautifully counter-attacked until a Dale Steyn delivery swung too fast and too late for him, but it was Steyn's new-ball partner, Morne Morkel, who enjoyed the greater success, with a career-best five for 20.

Exactly as forecast, the second day dawned hot and sunny. India really did have the worst of conditions with bat and ball, but it still wasn't enough to excuse their ineptitude in either discipline. Graeme Smith and Alviro Petersen were measured and assured during their century opening partnership. But their scoring-rate of four an over was made to look pedestrian by the carnage which followed.

Hashim Amla initially set the tone during a third-wicket stand of 230 with Jacques Kallis, but soon found that his more illustrious partner was not only keeping up but outscoring him. Kallis, meanwhile, was on a mission. His 130-ball century was the fastest of the 38 in his Test career, and he maintained almost the same pace in slaying the albatross around his neck, the much talked-about lack of a double-century.

The irony of the innings itself, however, was that it was completely overshadowed as a spectacle – by Kallis's own admission – by what was happening at the other end, where A. B. de Villiers was shattering the record for the fastest Test century by a South African. There could be no arguing with the precision and viciousness with which he handled the bowlers in reaching 100 from just 75 deliveries.

India's second innings was much better than their first. Gambhir fought hard and Sehwag belatedly showed that he was capable of tempering his aggression, making 63. Dravid was typically stoic, then Dhoni added 172 with the imperious Tendulkar, whose milestone 50th Test century received the attention and adulation it deserved despite all the other records which had preceded it in this match. Necessity determined what it was: an innings full of skill and discipline rarely seen before against Steyn and Morkel. Such was the effect of his technique that Steyn admitted that he had "given up trying to get him out once he'd reached about 40. I was just attacking the other guy".

THE LEADING CRICKETER IN THE WORLD, 2010

Ramachandra Guha, *Wisden* 2011

From the middle of October to the middle of December 2010, the Republic of India was beset by a series of corruption scandals – money illegally made on contracts for the Commonwealth Games, on housing projects in Mumbai and mining schemes in Karnataka, on the allocation of scarce airwaves for mobile-phone companies. The amount stolen by politicians (of all parties) ran into hundreds of billions of rupees. The scandals dominated the headlines for weeks until they were temporarily set aside to make way for Sachin Tendulkar's 50th Test hundred. This was met with relief, but also with wonder and admiration – indeed, it revived calls for the batsman to be awarded the Bharat Ratna, India's highest honour, previously reserved for politicians, scientists and musicians.

For Tendulkar to be viewed as a balm for the nation's (mostly self-inflicted) wounds was not new. As long ago as 1998, the Bombay poet C. P. Surendran wrote: "Batsmen walk out into the middle alone. Not Tendulkar. Every time Tendulkar walks to the crease, a whole nation, tatters and all, marches with him to the battle arena. A pauper people pleading for relief, remission from the lifelong anxiety of being Indian, by joining in spirit their visored saviour."

Over the next decade, the social anxieties of Indians abated. Economic liberalisation created a class of successful entrepreneurs, who in turn generated a growing middle class. Hindu–Muslim riots became less frequent. Meanwhile, Rahul Dravid, Sourav Ganguly, V. V. S. Laxman and Virender Sehwag arrived to take some of the burden of making runs (and relieving fans) off Tendulkar. It became possible once more to appreciate him in purely cricketing terms, rather than as the Saviour of the Nation.

Viewed thus, there appear to have been three distinct stages in Tendulkar's career as an international cricketer. For a full decade following his debut as a 16-year-old in 1989, he was a purely attacking batsman. Coming in at (say) ten for two, he would seek not to stabilise an innings but to wrest the game away from the opposition. This he did frequently, and in dazzling fashion, through slashing square cuts and pulls, and drives past the bowler and wide of mid-on. There was no shot he would not play, no form of bowling that in any way intimidated or even contained him. Then Tendulkar began to slow down. He now ducked the short ball (previously he would have hooked it), and played spin bowlers from the crease. The back-foot force through cover that was his trademark became scarce. He still scored runs regularly, but mostly through the on side, via dabs, sweeps, drives and the occasional pull.

We now know that this transformation in Tendulkar's game was due to a sore elbow. But while it lasted it appeared to be permanent; I even wrote at the time that "the genius has become a grafter". (My embarrassment at recalling this is tempered by the fact that some other writers were even more dismissive.) On the advice of a Mumbai doctor, he rested his left hand completely – he would not even, I am told, lift a coffee mug with it. The treatment worked, for as his elbow healed he recovered his fluency. The hook shot and the lofted drive were used sparingly, but his mastery of the off side was once more revealed in all its splendour.

It is commonplace to juxtapose Tendulkar with Don Bradman, but a more relevant comparison might be with the great Surrey and England opening batsman Jack Hobbs. There was a pre-war and a post-war Hobbs, and there has been a pre-tennis elbow and post-tennis elbow Tendulkar. Like Hobbs, in his late thirties he no longer so wholly dominates the bowling, but he is still pleasing to watch, and remains the batsman whose wicket (Sehwag, Dravid, Laxman notwithstanding) the opposition prizes most highly.

Young Sachin enjoyed several truly fabulous years, but 2010 was the *annus mirabilis* of the Late Tendulkar. Last year he scored more Test runs (1,562, at an average of 78) than anybody else. In February he scored the first double-century in one-day internationals; in December, he became the first man to score 50 Test hundreds, both landmarks achieved against the best pace attack in world cricket, South Africa. I was privileged to watch, live, a magnificent double-hundred he made against Australia at Bangalore, marked by cuts, drives, pulls, hooks and even two colossal sixes into the stands.

As he has grown older, Tendulkar has taken several measures to prolong his career. He does not play any Twenty20 internationals, bowls rarely, and fields mostly at mid-on, a position Sir Robert Menzies once called "the last refuge of mankind", but in this case a measure intended to preserve his fingers from damage (when younger he fielded very effectively in the slips).

Hanif Mohammad once said of Garfield Sobers that he "had been sent by God to Earth to play cricket". It is not only Indians who think that way about Tendulkar. Like Hobbs, he is equally admired by fans and players, by team-mate and adversary alike. His off-field conduct has been exemplary (with one trifling exception – when he asked for a tariff waiver on the import of a fancy foreign car). Australians venerate him; they do not even sledge him.

What might mean even more to him is the frank adoration and love of his team-mates. Indian cricket was long marked by personal rivalries and parochial jealousies; if that seems now to be behind us, this is the handiwork of a generation of gifted and selfless cricketers, among them Dravid, Laxman, Ganguly and Anil Kumble, but perhaps Tendulkar most. One image captures it all. A cake was being cut to mark victory in a hard-fought one-day series in Pakistan several years ago. The first piece was offered to the player of the tournament, Yuvraj Singh, who immediately turned the plate towards his hero and said, "*Pehle Sachin bhai ko*": the first one is for our elder brother, Sachin.

South Africa v India

Third Test, at Cape Town, January 2–6, 2011

South Africa 362 (J. H. Kallis 161) and **341** (J. H. Kallis 109, Harbhajan Singh 7-120);

India 364 (S. R. Tendulkar 146, D. W. Steyn 5-75) and **166-3.**

Drawn.

Tendulkar: 146 and 14*

Anand Vasu, *Wisden* 2011

After the stunning reversal at Durban, India piped up, renewing hopes of breaking their jinx by winning their first Test series in South Africa. At picturesque Newlands, neither team could force the issue in the end, leaving the series tied at 1–1.

For India, the result was acceptable on one level, as it was the first time they had come to South Africa and not lost. But Dhoni conceded that it was also a golden opportunity missed, as the core members of this team – Tendulkar, Dravid, Laxman and Zaheer – were unlikely to be around for the next such tour.

When the game began, with Dhoni winning the toss for a change and deciding to bowl, India were presented with their first challenge. In overcast conditions, and with grey clouds hanging around for most of the first day, their fast bowlers needed to lift themselves and pile the pressure on, but they were found wanting.

After the opening batsmen were dealt with fairly swiftly, Amla came at the Indians, attacking with fluency. When South Africa ended the first day with 232 for four they had done more than enough to negate the disadvantage of losing the toss.

The second day dawned bright and sunny, and the pitch temporarily quickened. Sreesanth asked many questions, but none was difficult enough to trip Kallis up. He overcame the opposition and the pitch to collect his 39th Test hundred – his 161 bound the innings together, pushing the total to a healthy 362.

India needed to show similar resolution to stay in touch, but what followed was the now-familiar top-order wobble, with Sehwag falling to yet another poor stroke and Dravid running himself out to make it 28 for two. Gambhir and Tendulkar were asked to repair the damage, and it was only a generous slice of luck and some dogged determination that helped them move towards safety, ending the day with 142 for two. Gambhir was dropped twice, and Tendulkar was put down at second slip by de Villiers: each time the unfortunate bowler was Lonwabo Tsotsobe.

The third-day contest was reduced largely to the match-up between Tendulkar and Steyn, whose sustained, high-quality swing bowling at great pace was a feature of the series. Getting the ball to move from lines that did not allow the batsmen the luxury of shouldering arms, Steyn induced so much playing and missing that he was very unlucky not to end with more wickets in the series than he did (21). But Tendulkar, taking a leaf out of Kallis's book, refused to be perturbed by several close shaves, and negotiated each ball on merit. His 51st century lifted the total towards 364, aided by a stand of 176 with Gambhir and a late flourish from Harbhajan. India led by two, and the match was reduced to a second-innings shoot-out.

Harbhajan pegged South Africa back to 64 for four to raise hopes of an unlikely Indian win. But, once again, Kallis towered above all around him. At 130 for six, when Mark Boucher joined Kallis, India were within one wicket of the tail and clear favourites. But the quick bowlers bowled into Boucher's pads and he raced to a half-century, adding 103 with Kallis, whose 109 made him the first South African to score two centuries in a Test twice. It was his 40th Test hundred, putting him ahead of Ricky Ponting and behind only Tendulkar. India were left with 90 overs to survive for the draw, as they were never likely to score quickly enough to reach their target of 340.

On the final day, Gambhir survived for more than four and a half hours for 64, while Tendulkar was uncharacteristically restrained in making 14 from 91 balls. When the captains shook hands little more than an hour into the final session, India had reached 166 for three at a shade above two an over.

WAITING FOR THE HUNDREDTH
Lawrence Booth, *Wisden India*, 2013

Sometimes, as a cricket writer, you are lucky enough to be in the right place at the right time. The stars – celestial and terrestrial – align, and all seems right with the world. In July 2011, when Sachin Tendulkar stood as tall as nature allows and punched Chris Tremlett through the covers on the Saturday of the Lord's Test, the world could hardly seem righter.

The Lord's buzz can be exaggerated, as if tradition automatically begets frisson. Just occasionally the place can be cold, damp and empty, though you rarely hear about it. But that day Lord's was magical. St John's Wood was in one of its hazy moods, and both sets of fans – plus those who turn up to drink, dine and be seen – were in good spirits.

More to the point, so was Tendulkar. He tucked James Anderson off his pads, then stroked Tremlett on the up through extra cover, thus providing us with a legitimate excuse – one we rarely need – to lapse into eulogy. Truly, the scene was set.

It goes without saying that Tendulkar did not reach three figures. Edging Stuart Broad to Graeme Swann in the slips, he fell just the 66 short, and so set the tone for a curious summer in which the expected waltz to a 100th international century would become a *danse macabre*. By the end, he was provoking sympathy and – among those who apparently believe Tendulkar exists only to boost their own self-esteem – even a touch of rancour.

Victorian circuses used to draw crowds with unusual attractions: the hairy lady, say, or the elephant man. Now, from north to south London, via Nottingham and Birmingham, we were treated to the sight of a run machine forced to recalibrate its own mortality – and all because of a blessed number. Roll up, roll up and see the 100th bead on the abacus refuse to budge! For students of psychology – and accountants at the England and Wales Cricket Board – this was gold dust and nectar. And for the man himself? Well, it was all a little undignified.

What became clear as the series developed was that, in sport, hope rarely defers to bitter experience. Tendulkar, let's not forget, scores a Test century roughly once every six innings. And while that may have suggested, at the start of a four-match series, that he would inevitably tick off the hundred at some point against England, it still meant he had only a 16 per cent chance of doing so in any given innings. (Apologies for the maths: it was that kind of summer.) The way England's seamers were bowling, you could have knocked off a few more percentage points too.

Anderson was especially skilful, dragging Tendulkar across his stumps with his outswinger, then zipping it back in to trap him leg-before in the second innings at Lord's. He got him again in the second innings at Trent Bridge. In between, Broad had him fending into the slips. The technical experts who have followed Tendulkar all over the world for more than two decades recharged their laptops.

In fact, Tendulkar wasn't playing all that badly. Among the Indian batsmen, only Rahul Dravid was coping. Tendulkar kept tantalising us, then getting out. It wasn't that the script kept being torn up, because the script existed, on red alert, in a hundred newspaper offices around the world, and all the editors needed to do was transfer the pre-written paeans to the page. Still, there was something especially cruel about the way Tendulkar fell at Edgbaston, run out at the non-striker's end via Swann's fingertips after playing like a genius to reach 40.

For English cricket followers, Tendulkar will always be synonymous with Old Trafford, where he saved a Test in 1990 at the age of 17 and walked off – innocent and barely bumfluffed – to bemused applause from ancient-looking players sporting a variety of facial hair. But Old Trafford wasn't on the rota this time, and instead Tendulkar headed in hope to The Oval for the fourth and final Test.

The Oval performs a particular function. Traditionally the final Test of the summer, it is where last-ditch bids are made for a spot on a winter tour, and the Ashes urn is regained or retained. It emits finality – Don Bradman's second-ball duck, and eternal average of 99.94, is the most infamous example.

Now, as India followed on – Tendulkar had made 23 in the first innings – the mood changed. Few sportsmen have the aura to transcend the narrative all by themselves. But Tendulkar's quest for that century had developed a mischievous momentum of its own. Fate appeared to be with him: on the fourth evening, England failed to appeal for a stumping that would have ended his innings on 34. Next day, in the company of nightwatchman Amit Mishra, he was making good headway.

When he moved into the eighties, I left the press box to sit by the crowd and soak in the atmosphere. You would not have guessed India were trailing 0–3. It was as if nothing that had gone before mattered. Tendulkar's pursuit of a nice round number of round numbers, however, most certainly did.

Enter Tim Bresnan, one of England's unsung heroes. Was his shout a fraction high? Or even leg-sidish? Umpire Rod Tucker thought not – and Tendulkar was gone, for 91. Bradman had left to a disbelieving, almost reverent, gasp, but crowds are more partisan now: English fans instinctively cheered even while Indians looked on in mute incredulity.

Throughout the summer, Tendulkar had been applauded to the crease – then applauded all the way back again. This time, there was a sadness that went beyond the missed landmark. English crowds suspected they would not see him bat in a Test again. Had they enjoyed him as thoroughly as they would have liked throughout the summer? Only to an extent. Greatness sets itself high standards. Statistics can be dry and unforgiving. Tendulkar fell short on both counts. But, really, we shouldn't hold it against him.

FINALLY, THE HUNDREDTH

A phenomenal achievement aside, there was no denying that the long drawn-out quest for the milestone left Tendulkar fans feeling just a bit jaded. The media blitz that followed the achievement earned scathing criticism from certain quarters. "For a man who, through his long career, has been a model of unassertive poise, the crassness of the publicity blitz and his own odd complicity, is startling," wrote Mukul Kesavan on ESPN Cricinfo. "It cheapens a great cricketing legacy, like a tinsel garland on a solid gold icon." Perhaps history will be kinder to Tendulkar's remarkable achievement.

Bangladesh v India

Asia Cup, Game four, at Mirpur, March 16, 2012 (day/night)

India 289-5 (S. R. Tendulkar 114);

Bangladesh 293-5.

Bangladesh won by five wickets.

Tendulkar: 114

Mohammad Isam, *Wisden* 2013

Under the Dhaka sun, Tendulkar reached his much-hyped oasis after a drought lasting a year (and four days). Such was a nation's collective sense of relief and release, it seemed almost incidental that his 100th international hundred came in a match India would contrive to lose. The search for this statistical nirvana – and the ballyhoo which had accompanied almost every innings since the 99th, against South Africa during the 2011 World Cup – slowed Tendulkar down late on and, with the Bangladeshi bowlers keeping the big hitters quiet at the end, India's final total was imposing rather than impossible. Between the 31st and 40th overs, they managed only 49 runs, with Tendulkar moving from 78 to 95 before finally reaching his milestone off the fourth ball of the 44th over; in all he faced 147 deliveries. Bangladesh, by contrast, collected 73 in that ten-over block, which put them in the box seat, and they completed their mammoth chase – their largest to beat a higher-ranked side – in the final over.

Teamwork has rarely been Bangladesh's forte but, on a night that should have belonged exclusively to Tendulkar, they ganged up to steal at least some of the headlines.

Milestone done and dusted, Tendulkar played with the freedom of a man who had just escaped from prison. Little was anyone to know, least of all Tendulkar himself, that the game after his 100th hundred would be his one-day swansong. He announced his retirement from limited-overs cricket more than eight months after the Asia Cup game against Pakistan through a press release distributed by the BCCI; apparently, the board and the selectors had made it clear they would no longer pick him. It was an anticlimactic end to what had been the greatest of one-day careers. But Tendulkar read the signs, and made sure to stage-manage his exit from Test cricket more carefully.

India v Pakistan
Asia Cup, Game five, at Mirpur, March 18, 2012 (day/night)
Pakistan 329-6 (Nasir Jamshed 112, Mohammad Hafeez 105);
India 330-4 (V. Kohli 183).
India won by six wickets.
Tendulkar: 52

Mohammad Isam, *Wisden* 2013

Kohli's fourth century at the Shere Bangla Stadium, an innings of 183 laden with 22 fours and a delightful six over long-off, kept India afloat.

He faced the third ball of the innings, after Gambhir fell to off-spinner Mohammad Hafeez, but combined well with Tendulkar, batting without the millstone of that 100th hundred for the first time in more than a year. Their stand was worth 133, before Kohli broke loose in concert with Rohit Sharma, adding 172 in 26 overs. Two overs later, India surpassed the 326 they had made against England on a heady day at Lord's in July 2002 to complete their highest successful one-day run-chase.

THE LONG AND WINDING ROAD

Steven Lynch, *Wisden* 2013

Sachin Tendulkar's 100th international hundred was – rather surprisingly – his first against Bangladesh in one-day internationals. His highest score in 11 previous games against them had been 82 not out, in July 2004. But he had made up for it in Tests, with five centuries in seven matches, including his career-best 248 not out at Dhaka in December 2004. Overall, 20 of Tendulkar's 100 international centuries had come at Australia's expense, 17 against Sri Lanka, South Africa 12, England and New Zealand nine, Zimbabwe eight, Pakistan and West Indies seven, Bangladesh six, Kenya four and Namibia one. Fifty-three came in Indian victories (20 in Tests and 33 in one-day internationals), 25 in defeats (11 in Tests, 14 in one-day internationals), 20 in draws (all in Tests), one in a tie (against England in the 2011 World Cup at Bangalore), and one in a no-result (a rain-affected one-dayer against England at Chester-le-Street in 2002).

Chapter 7

Praise From the Pros:
How Others Viewed Him

O n January 1, 2008, Sachin Tendulkar made a special visit through a little door, tucked behind the members' pavilion, at his favourite non-Indian venue. He stepped into the Sydney Cricket Ground's museum, and waited patiently in front of a glass case; the key was procured, the case unlocked. Out came Sir Donald Bradman's bat, all 2lb 2oz of it – a thing of beauty and a weapon of mass destruction. It was a memory Tendulkar would not forget. He spent a few moments examining the bat, carefully checking the grip, absorbing every grain, familiarising himself with each millimetre of its leather-stained, careworn blade. He took stance and played a few shots – cricket's version of Mark Knopfler strumming Chuck Berry's guitar. Then came the admission: "I could never play with such a light bat." Tendulkar's bat weighed over 3lbs for a long time before he switched to a lighter bat in the last decade of his career.

His pilgrimage to the SCG came almost ten years after he and Shane Warne had been invited to meet Bradman on his 90th birthday at his home in leafy, suburban Adelaide. Tendulkar, nicknamed "Bonzer" by Bradman, is a private man, and most details of the meeting remain a secret – though Tendulkar does recount in his autobiography a discussion about defensive field-settings and run-scoring in the modern era. When Warne and Tendulkar asked Bradman what he would have averaged in modern-day cricket, he said: "Around 70." Tendulkar expressed surprise and wondered "if he was sure it would be so much lower than his famous career average of 99.94". Bradman replied: "Well, 70 isn't bad for a 90-year-old!"

Bradman had already been responsible for the greatest compliment Tendulkar ever received, describing in a 1996 interview the moment he told his wife, Jessie, that Tendulkar reminded him of himself. Tendulkar, never one to let things go to his head, has only spoken of this comparison in terms of being humbled and honoured.

Once Bradman has said you bat like him, the danger is it's all downhill from there. But the perspectives of Tendulkar's peers which follow in this chapter – both team-mates and opponents – suggest otherwise.

AUSTRALIA'S FAVOURITE   Mike Coward, *Wisden India*, 2014

Only two men are the focus of a television presentation screening on a loop in the extensive Bradman Gallery which is the holy heart of the Bradman Museum and International Cricket Hall of Fame at Bowral in New South Wales. No sooner has an 82-year-old Sir Donald Bradman concluded a revelatory interview, than a 31-year-old Sachin Tendulkar appears speaking about his extraordinary life that so often is associated with the game's peerless batsman.

There is nothing jarring about the transition. Indeed, in the eyes of the overwhelming majority, this is how it should be. Born 65 years apart on disparate continents, the game's greatest batsmen are together. That it is known Bradman would not have objected to Tendulkar sharing his stage will help to put the self-effacing Indian maestro's mind at rest. That the Don once called his wife Lady Jessie to come to the television and watch Tendulkar at the crease has become a part of the rich lore of the game. In a rare television interview in 1996, Bradman said: "I asked my wife to come and look at him. Now, I never saw myself play, but I feel that this fellow is playing much the same as I used to play. She looked at him and said: 'Yes, there is a similarity.' I can't explain in detail. To me it's his compactness, his technique, his stroke production. It all seemed to gel as far as I was concerned. That was how I felt."

And bear in mind Lady Jessie was the only person in the world who could question or contradict the Don. And she didn't on this occasion.

Neil Harvey, the sole survivor of Bradman's "Invincibles" team to England in 1948, rarely speaks well of the contemporary cricketer, but he has no quarrel with the proposition that Tendulkar evokes powerful memories of Bradman in full cry.

Tendulkar, like Viv Richards and others before him, has been flattered and embarrassed in equal measure at any comparison with the grand master who averaged 99.94 in 52 Test matches over 20 years. At the same time there is a certain privilege in being directly associated with the Don. "Wow, the Black Bradman. I can take that," said Richards so memorably.

Tendulkar, who confessed to reacting like a star-struck schoolboy when he visited Adelaide to be with Bradman on his 90th birthday in 1998, has never quite known how to react to the heady comparison. "All I can say is I'm very happy and extremely delighted that Sir Don himself talked about my batting style," is his humble default position.

While the news of Tendulkar's retirement did not surprise his legion of Australian devotees it certainly subdued them and, for those of a certain age, revived memories of the mournfulness that descended on the cricket community in 1948 when Bradman bade farewell. Tendulkar, like Bradman, is a universal cricketer and irreplaceable.

Godless they may largely be but Australia's cricket watchers have had a special relationship with India's diminutive living deity since, at the age of 18 in 1992, he became the youngest scorer of a Test hundred in Australia. Of course, passionate crowds have a tendency to take to their hearts the young, gifted, instantly likeable and seemingly innocent, and Tendulkar was embraced with a vigour not seen since the elegant David Gower first toured for England at the age of 21 during the World Series Cricket revolution in 1978-79.

Australians have watched in awe as Tendulkar's exemplary technique, single-mindedness, fierce determination and naked ambition enabled him to prosper as the pre-eminent batsman of the contemporary game. As Brian Lara so graciously observed: "Sachin is a genius; I'm a mere mortal."

Not even his phenomenal success against Australian teams led by Allan Border, Mark Taylor, Steve Waugh, Adam Gilchrist, Ricky Ponting and Michael Clarke tempered their affection for Tendulkar. To a man the crowds stood every time he went to the wicket in 2007-08, convinced it would be the last time they would see him in Australia. When he returned four years later, approaching his 39th birthday, they rose to him again, and deeply felt his disappointment at such an unfulfilling last hurrah. While Tendulkar has always kept the tightest of reins on his emotions – save for the nod to the heavens to his much beloved father, Ramesh – he could not have been unmoved by the outpouring of affection in his honour.

In 39 Test matches in 12 Indo–Australian series – five in Australia – he amassed 3,630 runs at 55.00 with 11 centuries. He was even forgiven his mastery of Shane Warne, and a peculiar and alienating diffidence – even remoteness – when saddled with the captaincy in 1999-2000.

Such has been the endearment over 22 years that there have been rumblings in tourism and political circles of a statue of Tendulkar being considered, to complement the imposing Bradman sculpture which stands between the International Cricket Hall of Fame and the Bradman Oval pavilion.

A quarter of a century ago there were similarly reverent rumours in Kolkata that a statue of Bradman was to be commissioned by Jyoti Basu's government and placed near the shrines to Mahatma Gandhi and Sir Rabindranath Tagore in the vicinity of Fort William. The blueprints were set aside when Sir Donald declined invitations to attend the World Cup final at Eden Gardens in 1987. Yet the country's obsession with the master who never batted in India and only once stood on her soil – at Dum Dum Airport in 1953 – never waned.

Even if nothing more is heard of a bronze in his honour, Australia's warm attachment to Tendulkar will not diminish. Indeed, it is difficult to envisage a time when his name and his deeds will not be inextricably linked to the Don, as the television presentation on the loop at Bowral so emphatically affirms.

While it is not always recognised, a comparative study can extend well beyond their height – at 5ft 4in, Tendulkar was 2¾in shorter than Bradman – to take in technique, compactness, and stroke production.

Both men are renowned for their humility, decency and strict adherence to the traditional virtues and values of the game, a deep love for the Sydney Cricket Ground and its glorious and historic Members and Ladies pavilions, and an abiding appreciation of music, which helped them both negotiate life in the public gaze.

Tendulkar, named by his brothers Nitin and Ajit and sister Savita after popular Bollywood music director Sachin Dev Burman, amassed 785 runs at a phenomenal average of 157 at the SCG, which he considers his favourite ground outside the Chidambaram Stadium in Chennai. On his last visit to Sydney he was feted as the first overseas sportsman awarded honorary life membership of the SCG.

And while Bradman always railed against any notion that in any sense he was a professional cricketer, he was, like Tendulkar, a savvy businessman with an innate understanding of the marketing power of his image. But while Bradman lived an essentially modest middle-class existence in the two-storey brick home he had built in the leafy eastern suburbs of Adelaide in 1935, Tendulkar became the wealthiest player in the annals of the game and, to the amusement of Australians, a member – a financial one, no doubt – of the Middle Income Group Club in Bandra East.

That the Border–Gavaskar Trophy has attained such significance and produced some of the most competitive and memorable Test cricket of the past 20 years has in large part been due to Tendulkar's greatness and resilience. He was the Indian captain when the trophy was instituted in 1996 and, following the retirements of Rahul Dravid and Ricky Ponting, was the only surviving member of the inaugural match at the Feroz Shah Kotla ground in Delhi. Unquestionably, his universal popularity helped raise the profile of Indian cricket in Australia and better educate the game's avid followers and casual observers about the Indian diaspora. Like his admirers everywhere, Australians have marvelled at his discipline, limitless energy and remarkable endurance. His passion for the game has never faltered and they loved him openly for it.

Only in 2004-05, when stricken with a cursed tennis-elbow injury, did he feel his body could fail him. Thankfully, his wife Anjali told him to gird his loins, be grateful to the Almighty for granting him 15 years without major injury, and remain positive.

While Tendulkar has always jealously guarded the intimate details of his conversation with Bradman in 1998, in all probability discussion would have turned to living with the heavy burden of celebrity. As he grew older Bradman became increasingly resistant to any intrusion into his private life, and railed against the impertinence of a forever burgeoning and demanding media. As an old man he became reclusive, and such disturbances angered him and at times impacted on his health. It is to be earnestly hoped that Tendulkar has read extensively about the Don and is familiar with the sadness of his private life and the extent of the weight he bore in the public arena. There is much for him to learn now his playing days are over.

Too often Bradman's humanity was obscured by the public's perception of a sense of infallibility and invulnerability and an obsessive pursuit of perfection. He was primarily measured in cold, hard statistics. It was left to Lady Jessie to provide him with warmth.

Bradman spent the first 40 years of his life making certain of his immortality, and spent the rest of it trying to live with the uniqueness of his mortality. This is the challenge before Tendulkar now. For his sake and that of his wife Anjali, and children Arjun and Sara, he must not remain a prisoner of his fame.

Somehow India and Indians must pledge to provide him with the rarest and most precious of gifts in all Bharat – space and room to breathe.

From Steve Waugh to Allan Donald, even Tendulkar's fiercest rivals have generously acknowledged his virtuosity. Waugh, like Ponting, believed Tendulkar was right up there after Bradman; Donald said he never bowled to a better batsman, and Shane Warne ranked the world's best batsmen thus: 1. Tendulkar, 2. Daylight, 3. Lara. A long-time rival and friend, Lara himself once said: "When I speak about cricket, I will speak about Tendulkar. Just like you mention Muhammad Ali when you mention boxing and Michael Jordan when it comes to basketball." From the time he impressed England bowler Angus Fraser as a 17-year-old centurion until his retirement at the age of 40 – when Virat Kohli was playing just his 20th Test – Tendulkar evolved from prodigious talent to dressing-room mentor and batting coach. Here, his peers share their memories.

THE SUMMER OF 1990	Angus Fraser, *Wisden India*, 2014

As years go by more and more people will claim they played a vital role in Sachin Tendulkar becoming the cricketing great he is. Some will embellish technical tips they supposedly gave to the "Little Master", others will claim a quiet word in his ear at the right time led to his impeccable record off the field.

Few, however, have done more to get Tendulkar's career moving forward than myself. For I was the lumbering fast bowler that he pushed effortlessly through mid-off for three on an overcast August afternoon at Old Trafford in 1990. The runs took Tendulkar to his first international hundred.

He was 17 at the time, but nobody in the England team thought a great deal about his performance. Yes, it was a remarkable innings for a boy of his age, but my team-mates and I were more concerned about winning a Test series than assessing the potential of a teenager from Mumbai. Conversation on his batting would have been short, as Mohammad Azharuddin was the batsman causing mayhem. Not one of that England team would have dreamt that Tendulkar would reach three figures in international cricket on 99 further occasions.

As I sit in my office at Lord's writing this piece, and having watched highlights of the innings Tendulkar played at Old Trafford on YouTube several times, I can now reflect on what it was like to play against him and what it was that made him such a master. Like many other cricketers, I feel proud to have had the chance to play and pit my wits against one of the greatest players the game has ever seen. I feel proud that I dismissed him on a couple of occasions too. I am also pretty chuffed he thought I was a decent bowler.

It would be fair to say Tendulkar's greatness has grown on me since 1990, and it is not by chance that a signed completed scorecard of the Old Trafford Test proudly hangs on a wall of my home in north-west London. So, even then, he must have been doing something right.

Watching Tendulkar bat has been a joy for the past 20-odd years. Like Brian Lara, he is a player who caused you to be late for meetings and dinners. When they were at the crease you always wanted to watch another over.

There continue to be many batsmen with wonderful career records, but for most of them there is something missing. These players amass rather than compile, they beat the ball rather than caress it, and they possess brutality rather than charm. And it is the way Tendulkar scored his runs that has made him so special. The cuts, clips, front- and back-foot drives, all played with grace, control and elegance, were there at Manchester in 1990. The difference now is that they are almost ingrained in my mind. I don't have to go to YouTube to recall him clipping a good-length ball through the leg side for four. All I need to is lean back in my seat and close my eyes.

The wonderful strokeplay would be wasted without a strong, resilient and brilliant mind. No player in the history of cricket has had to cope with the pressure, intrusion and expectation Tendulkar has. Watching India come to terms with Tendulkarless cricket will be fascinating. The fact he has remained a humble, respectful and grounded man is almost as big an achievement as scoring more than 34,000 international runs. Tendulkar has been able to achieve this by being emotionally consistent. He seems to have an inner peace, a mental zone he goes to where he can cut off all the distractions and nonsense that his daily life must contain. I have never seen him rattled at the crease or away from the field. To be able to compartmentalise your emotions is a rare, remarkable and hugely advantageous talent.

Added to this is a relentless, unquenchable desire to master the craft of batting and score runs. There is huge pride too, and nowhere did I see this more than on India's 2007 tour of England. On that tour Tendulkar was completely out of form. For the first time he looked vulnerable. England's fast bowlers – James Anderson, Chris Tremlett and Ryan Sidebottom – sensed this and went after him. During the series Tendulkar was struck around the body on numerous occasions. It was not pretty. Many experts were stating that his eyes and reactions had gone. Apparently, the end of a glittering career was nigh.

In the series Tendulkar displayed characteristics rarely witnessed, namely guts and bravery. What we ultimately saw was how highly he valued his wicket. Lesser characters would have questioned whether they needed this aggro at this stage of their career. Not Tendulkar. He fought and fought and fought. By the end of the series I realised there was even more to this man than I originally thought.

The greatest sentiment, an emotion that remains today, is his love of batting and the game. Why else would he still be playing at 40? An example of this came at the end of a Test against Australia in 2010. Tendulkar scored a brilliant double-hundred in India's first innings, but it was scoring the match-winning runs that gave him the most pleasure. When he swept Nathan Hauritz for two to win the game the moment was greeted by an ecstatic roar from Tendulkar, followed by a look of complete fulfilment.

Comparisons between Tendulkar and Lara, the two truly great batsmen of my generation, are inevitable. I found Lara the harder to bowl to because there were days when you just couldn't bowl at the man. Lara, on most occasions, was more likely to give you a chance. You had to get Tendulkar out. He played most balls on merit. Tendulkar's greatness comes from his consistency and longevity. Many players are capable of producing the occasional moment of brilliance, but very few have been able to sustain a level of performance that is truly outstanding for a lengthy period of time.

It is more than 65 years since Sir Donald Bradman last batted for Australia, but his name in cricket remains as strong as ever. I am convinced the feats of Tendulkar will be remembered in the same way in 65 years' time. It is hard to believe any cricketer will compile as many international hundreds or collect as many runs as he ends up with.

Many of the biggest names in cricket have done an enormous amount to promote cricket, but nobody in the history of the game has done more to present the game of cricket as it should be played. Cricket may have produced greater players, but Sachin Tendulkar is the biggest name the game has ever seen.

NEVER LOST HIS HUNGER   Rahul Dravid, *Wisden Asia Cricket*, September 2002

Four innings on India's tour of West Indies in 2002 were all it took to start a national debate on Sachin Tendulkar: 0, 0, 8 and 0 is a sequence of numbers I don't need to explain, but they were discussed with more alarm than the annual budget. This, if nothing else, is a reflection of the expectations Sachin has had to face over the last 13 years and close to 100 Tests. Rising petrol prices and increased railways fares are unfortunate; but Sachin failing in four innings? Crisis!

As all this happened around him, Sachin remained calm and confident, almost casual, and you couldn't help wondering how, considering he is continuously badgered and besieged wherever he goes. Therein lies Sachin's great strength. He's able to ignore all the hype that surrounds him and focus completely on the job at hand.

I asked him about these expectations that pursue him, about the pressure of knowing that most people at the ground are there to watch him play. How does he live up to the extremely high standards he sets for himself – standards by which just four failures at the crease are viewed as a national tragedy?

He says that while he's aware of the expectations, he doesn't let them play on his mind once he crosses the white line. "I don't put any additional pressure on myself. I have a certain amount of pressure to perform, but I don't think of others' expectations when I'm batting." This is a reflection of a great athlete's ability to compartmentalise his thoughts and stay focused on the things that matter while batting. After all, they say the only pressure that exists is the one you put on yourself.

Failures or hiccups in form, however marginal, often affect top-class sportspeople, some more than others. I therefore wondered, during this brief period when Sachin didn't get the runs expected of him, and the other few times he'd had a run of low scores, did it ever bother him? "Not really," he replied. "I trust myself to be able to solve the problems that confront me." Trust is the key word here. All great sportsmen trust themselves (their ability to perform, to play the right shot) in times of stress and difficulty, and it's not just a false, outward bravado but a powerful feeling deep down – a quiet confidence that separates them from the rest.

Something that stands out when you spend enough time with Sachin is his almost childlike enthusiasm for the game and competition, even after more than a decade at the top. He loves playing cricket and scoring runs, and that love has not diminished. He'll be the first to be involved in any game of ball cricket that starts in the dressing-room during rain-breaks, and while he competes ferociously, he enjoys it too. Almost as if winning is very important, but more important is actually playing.

He's always playing little games with people at the nets when he's bowling, and he'll take great pleasure in setting fields and getting you out. Lots of great athletes tend to lose their love for the game after many years at the top, and wonder if facing the pressure is really worth it, but with Sachin the hunger still remains strong. Which is not good news for those around the world.

You can almost divide Sachin's career into two parts – his first 4,000 runs, and from then onwards. His second 4,000 have come much quicker, but people who watched him from the start say he was more exciting in the early part of his career. This may be so, but I think it is a silent maturity and ability that he has been able to learn to score a lot more runs even if it has meant restricting himself at times.

His 201 not out against Zimbabwe in 2000 was a great example. We were playing at Nagpur on a good, flat wicket, and he just set himself to get a big score. He didn't slog a single ball in the entire innings, even though he could easily have stepped out and hit their spinners out of the park. But he realised that it was a great chance for a big score and he didn't want to miss out.

Another innings that comes to mind was the one against Australia at Chennai in 2001, when we chased a first-innings score of 391. As soon as Sachin came out to bat, you could see that the Australians wanted to test his patience. By not giving him any runs early on, they hoped he would go after them and get himself out in the process. But Sachin quickly analysed the situation, and was willing to bide his time and be patient. Even though he didn't dominate initially, you felt he was in control. As if every defensive shot was measured and calculated, knowing that his time would soon come. It did, and he went on to score a crucial 126 which helped us win that game and the series.

The real victory for him that day was not when he started to dominate, but early on when he evaluated what was happening and played accordingly. When you have all that ability and talent, and can add an understanding of situations and a hunger to them, as he has done in the latter part of his career, you become a truly great player. The younger Sachin may have been more fun to watch, but I know who I'd want in my team.

I've been lucky to spend a fair bit of time with Sachin in the middle and have really enjoyed batting with him. You're in the best seat in the house if he goes on to play a great innings. Sachin always seems very relaxed when he's batting, and he'll come out with thoughts and suggestions if he notices something. It could be a technical tip or just a thought on how he feels the state of the game is at the moment and how we should react. What's good about these conversations is that they're never one-sided. He's more than willing to get your point of view, and will often ask you if you think he's doing anything wrong. He'll often ask you to remind him to stay focused if he feels he's getting carried away. I, and many of the other guys, have benefitted from having him at the other end, because he can drive the bowlers and fielders to distraction.

Watching Sachin in the nets has been an education in itself. He'll always come to practice with a plan for what he's trying to achieve. There is nothing frivolous about him in the nets: on the field he may be the master, but here he's the student, always learning. He works on particular shots, either defensive or attacking, depending on the conditions and bowlers he is likely to encounter. The time at practice is always well spent, which shows his constant desire to improve and raise the bar.

I've asked him a few times about his thought processes before he faces a delivery. He talks of "being blank". What that means is stilling your thoughts and just letting your instincts take over. As anyone who has been in "the zone" will tell you, it's a time when you just react to what's coming at you, without letting doubt and fear cloud your mind. It's a lot easier said than done, though – sometimes the simplest things are the hardest to accomplish.

There is no doubt that Sachin's consistency and success over the years have been due to his freakish ability and diligence at the nets. But having played with him for a while now, I think the primary factor has been his mental strength – his focus, determination, confidence, perseverance and discipline. All of which remain as strong as ever as he reaches his 100th Test and closes in on two other significant numbers: 34 (Test centuries) and 11,174 (runs). No doubt, once he reaches these milestones another debate of some sort will begin. It will not matter to him. As he has always done through the years, he will quietly go about his art with grace and dignity.

Rahul Dravid played 146 Tests and 245 one-day internationals with Tendulkar.

THE BEST I'VE BOWLED TO   Allan Donald, *Wisden Asia Cricket*, September 2002

I had been watching Sachin Tendulkar on and off before we [South Africa] were readmitted in 1991. People were always talking about him so I was aware of what we were going to come up against, and I remember Craig McDermott telling us that he was going to be the best in the world.

Our first engagement was in 1991, in Calcutta, in front of 90,000 people. He made 62. And it was blatantly clear then that he was going to be a player to remember. Before I played against him I was always looking forward to having a crack. Then I realised just what I was up against. When someone like Tendulkar walks to the crease, you have to know what you are going to do. You can't just run up and bowl. You have to have planned your attack, your line, a week in advance.

Everything about him is just so exceptional. He is wonderful technically and he has everything – class, speed, all the shots – and he is cool under pressure. Cricketers always talk about his amazing balance, even the Aussies. I've seen tapes of Sunil Gavaskar, and if you split the screen between him and Tendulkar, they look virtually identical. I have never seen a man with such immaculate balance – it is freakish.

People go to a Test match just to watch Tendulkar. I, for one, would rather watch him than bowl against him. Actually, I'm glad I'll never have to bowl to him in a Test match again, though I've been quite successful against him. He is No. 1 in my book – the best player I have ever had the privilege of bowling to. There's Steve Waugh and there's Brian Lara, who was wonderful in 1995, but Tendulkar is a class above, consistently special.

Your margin for error against him really is marginal. If you get him on a flat track, when he is, say, 50 not out off 24 balls, then you know that you have a very long day ahead and the situation can be very, very demoralising. The best knock I can remember him playing was at Newlands in 1997, when he was just unstoppable. We only got him thanks to a blinding catch by Adam Bacher off a hook shot, otherwise he would have gone on and on.

Under Hansie Cronje we studied hard for a Tendulkar weakness. We thought he might be vulnerable, especially early in his innings, to the ball that is bowled from wide of the crease, coming back in off a good length. He might then be bowled through the gate, or be lbw, especially on English wickets. We also tried peppering him with short balls – not many top-class batters like that – but it didn't really seem to bother him. The one thing that might rattle him is being restricted. He loves scoring, and scoring quickly, and if he is frustrated, sometimes he goes out and looks for the big shot.

I don't think he really gets rattled by sledging. Glenn McGrath tried it and Tendulkar just kept running at him and hitting him back over his head for four. I think that, like Steve Waugh, sledging just makes him more focused: I don't think it is a good idea to have a word.

The ball I bowled to him in Durban in 1996 was the best ball I have bowled to any cricketer. I think he hit the first two balls after lunch for four, then I came from wide of the crease and the ball really went a long way to bowl him. I don't think I've ever celebrated like that – you save those for the big ones. We had discussed how to bowl to him, and I knew what I was trying to do, but I never expected it to go so far off the seam to knock out the off stump. It was a great sight. That series was billed as the Donald–Tendulkar battle, but he got his own back at Cape Town with one of the best knocks I've ever seen.

Tendulkar is already a legend so I'm not sure how he'll be remembered – what comes after legend? He is still young and if he plays till he is 35 who knows what he'll achieve. He's the best in the world, one of the most magnificent players there's ever been. He's also a nice guy, a soft-hearted bloke who gives 110% and just loves playing cricket.

South African fast bowler Allan Donald played against Tendulkar in 11 Tests and 26 one-day internationals, and dismissed him ten times in all. He was speaking to Tanya Aldred.

ALWAYS A STEP AHEAD   V. V. S. Laxman, *Wisden India*, 2014

I am sure I am not in a minority when I say that, growing up, I was a huge fan of Sachin Tendulkar. Even though Sachin is older than me by just a couple of years, he was always a hero, for obvious reasons. So you can imagine my excitement when I got to play for India alongside him. I was in awe of him for a really long time in spite of the fact that we shared the same dressing-room, though Sachin did everything possible to ensure that I was relaxed and treated him as just another team-mate. As if that were possible!

I have been fortunate enough to be associated in several meaningful partnerships with Sachin, especially in Test cricket. I am not a great one for statistics, so I did a quick search and found out that we were involved in nine century stands and 19 half-century partnerships in 73 innings. Together, we added 3,523 runs at 51.05. These are good numbers, agreed, but numbers can't do justice to the joy and enjoyment I derived while batting with Sachin.

I will be merely stating the obvious when I say that Sachin is the best player in the world, therefore when you are batting with him, you have the best seat in the ground from where to watch him at work. And while Sachin at the crease was a sight for sore eyes, what appealed to me was to see how well he prepared for each and every game. Be it a first-class game or a Test match, his approach seldom varied, his routines before the match remained the same.

It's always a great learning experience when you watch someone prepare so meticulously and so hard, then go out and execute the plans, put the preparations into practice and achieve the desired results. Because you have seen the preparation from close quarters, you have an idea of what he is anticipating in the match. But it's one thing to have plans in place, quite another to be able to pull them off time after time. That is what distinguishes Sachin from the rest.

Sachin has always been one step ahead of the bowler. I am not exaggerating when I say that he could read a bowler's thought process well in advance. He either picks up cues from the way a bowler runs in or from other aspects of his body language. Occasionally, that led to his downfall but, more often than not, it brought him tremendous success because it helped him get into good positions a fraction of a second early.

This ability to pick up cues is a combination of an in-built sixth sense and the experience of having played so many matches over a relatively short period of time. When you are playing the same opposition or squaring up to the same bowler fairly regularly, you can make out how a bowler reacts to a particular shot or a particular situation. With Sachin, it used to happen even in the nets, which he approached with the same commitment and intensity as he would a match. He would play a particular shot against the bowler, then tell the guy next to him, "Wait and watch, this is where he is going to bowl the next ball." And nine times out of ten, he would be spot on, which is why he gets into position that bit earlier than the rest and, therefore, has more time to play his shots.

Sachin is extremely intense and involved when he is batting. Everyone has a different approach during the course of a partnership. Sachin loves to chat between overs. He would discuss bowlers, he would analyse the situation, but he would never tell you how to approach your innings. Even on the field, he is full of suggestions and ideas, but he always leaves it to the player or the captain to make the final decision, which alone makes him such a great asset to have.

My first big partnership with Sachin was in the match interrupted by a sandstorm against Australia in Sharjah in 1998, when we had to reach a particular score to make it to the final. You could see from his eyes that he wasn't going to take a backward step. He was in the zone – all focus and concentration. During that stand of 104, he once screamed at me because I turned down a single. He was very upset but, after the match, he came over and apologised for having a go at me. It showed not just the desire and hunger of the man, but also his greatness in that he was willing to apologise even to a youngster.

Our most memorable association was when we put on 353 against Australia in Sydney in early 2004. Sachin had been batting well in that series but he wasn't getting the runs. There were a couple of freakish dismissals, and at least one bad decision. He sat down before the Sydney Test, analysed his game and figured out that one of the reasons for his downfall was the cover-drive early in his innings. Sachin chose to cut out the cover-drive from his armoury for that match, and went on to make an unbeaten 241. During our entire partnership, I was amazed to see his mental strength and control.

A lot of players go into a match determined to avoid certain strokes but once they are set and timing the ball, they start to play their natural game. But here was a person who, even after reaching his double-hundred, refrained from playing the cover-drive even to part-timers such as Simon Katich. It showed how much control he had over his mind, how much discipline there is to his cricket. I was batting quite fluently during that partnership, but not once did Sachin try to catch up or match my strokeplay. He stuck to his game plan, not allowing his ego to cloud his thinking.

Sachin is also extremely aware of the strengths and weaknesses of his batting partner. He knew I was not the quickest between the wickets, so when we batted together he would tell me that we would only go for comfortable singles even though he is a very quick runner and an excellent judge of a run. Sachin likes to take a lot of quick singles early on, while I relied a lot on hitting boundaries at the start of my innings. Having that kind of communication and understanding between us was the reason why I always enjoyed batting with him.

I consider it a great privilege to have shared some wonderful moments with Sachin as a batting partner. The runs, the statistics, the averages – they are just a bonus. I will cherish those memories for life.

V. V. S. Laxman played 134 Tests for India, 120 of them alongside Tendulkar.

THE GOD OF SMALL THINGS   Aakash Chopra, *Wisden* 2014

I was only 12 when Sachin Tendulkar first represented India and left a nation instantly mesmerised. I remember watching him dance down the track to hit Abdul Qadir for three towering sixes, and must have tried to do the same innumerable times, if only in my imagination. While I was still learning how to stand properly at the crease, Tendulkar was earning standing ovations around the globe; while I was still learning how to use my feet to get to the pitch of the ball, Tendulkar was taking giant strides. The more I played the game, the more I admired him, for it was only through playing that one truly understood the scale of what he was doing.

By the end of the 1990s, it was as if he had ceased to be just a player, and now symbolised excellence. It was around this time that I started nurturing the dream of playing for India myself. And yet playing for India and playing alongside Tendulkar seemed two separate things. Playing for India would mean countless hours of toil, something I was prepared for. But nothing had prepared me for sitting in the dressing-room next to my idol.

I was a bundle of nerves when I walked into the conference hall of Ahmedabad's plush Taj hotel for my first India team meeting in October 2003. I had attended many team meetings before, but had little idea of how this one would unfold – and even less idea of how I would react to my first encounter with Tendulkar. Fifteen minutes in, I worried our chat wouldn't go beyond the customary exchange of greetings: words were failing me already.

Our coach, John Wright, divided the team into batsmen and bowlers to discuss the forthcoming Test against New Zealand. I'm glad he did, for that's when Tendulkar and I were introduced properly. I had played a couple of warm-up games against the tourists, so questions were thrown in my direction about how their bowlers were shaping up. To my utter surprise and pleasure, Tendulkar was the most inquisitive. How was Daryl Tuffey bowling? Had Daniel Vettori bowled his arm-ball? He wanted to know everything.

He had played these bowlers many times – and successfully. What need was there for a batsman of his capability to ask such questions of a rookie like me? But he did. And the reason became clear. He wanted to allow me to break the ice, to interact with him, to know him better. I suspect he realised that, as with most Indian debutants, I was overawed, and that this wasn't likely to change unless he made a special effort. I can't thank him enough for the gesture. A couple of days later, confident from our last interaction, I called his room seeking an audience. Once again, he was happy to oblige. Until then, I'd been to the hotel rooms of many senior and junior cricketers, and had found most of them like any boy's room, strewn with dirty laundry, shoes, cricket gear, laptop and iPod. Tendulkar's was different: meticulous and organised, like his batting.

Gods' idols were on the bedside table, bats neatly arranged in one corner, bed linen without any creases, dirty linen nowhere. He ordered a cup of coffee for us both, and chatted freely, as if we'd known each other for years. I asked him about his preparation and game plans, and he began to share details. What I saw of Tendulkar in the days that followed left an indelible mark. He was always first to the team bus, because he didn't like rushing. He would plan most of his innings by making mental notes for the bowlers he was likely to face – a habit that meant he wouldn't sleep properly for a fortnight before India's game against Pakistan in the 2003 World Cup. It was during our chat that I realised preparation for every battle was as crucial to success at the top as natural ability. Knowing the opposition is important, but so is knowing your own game. Those 40 minutes I spent with him changed the way I looked at Tendulkar – the player and the man – forever.

We batted first in the Test, and I made 42. As I walked back to the pavilion, the stadium erupted. Almost everyone in the stands was on their feet. So this was what it was like to play for your country! I was disappointed to have missed a fifty, but that feeling evaporated as I soaked up the ovation. The noise continued even after I was seated in the dressing-room – which was when I realised, to my embarrassment, that the applause might not have been for me. Needless to say, it had been for the man walking out to bat, not the man walking into the pavilion. Only then did I begin to wonder what it must be like to be Sachin Tendulkar, carrying the burden of so many hopes. And yet he behaved with the utmost humility. In that moment, my respect for him rose several notches.

The real measure of the man lay in the fact that even the most senior members of the team showered him with respect. "I want to protect him. Tendulkar must not come out to bat to play a few balls in the fading light against the raging Aussies – he is our best hope to win the game." Those words, spoken by another great man, Rahul Dravid, to

Nayan Mongia during the First Test at Mumbai during the famous 2000-01 series, still ring in my ears. The beauty of the relationship between Tendulkar and the other senior players was their mutual respect; no one behaved like a superstar. All of them encouraged an atmosphere of comfort, in which even a junior could happily pull a prank.

As I spent more time in the dressing-room, I gained a closer look at Tendulkar's quest for excellence. Every net session had a purpose, leading to a discussion about what he was doing right or wrong. And he was quite happy getting feedback from the newcomers, including me. Each time he asked me something, I would remind him that it should be the other way around. But he would have none of it, constantly prodding me for my view. Sachin would ask me about his stance, head position, backlift and downswing. And it wasn't just me: he would ask the net bowlers whether they could see him stepping out, or premeditating his strokes. Greatness isn't just what you know, but what you don't – and the effort you make to bridge that gap. Tendulkar mastered that art.

His gift was to appear in control. And that was so different from how I, or my colleagues, functioned. He didn't always need to score a truckload of runs to spread calm. Sometimes, he just needed to do what felt beyond the rest of us, and put bat to ball. Here was a man who not only timed his moves so well that he looked programmed by computer but, with a twirl of the bat, made the ball kiss the sweet spot.

Criticism is inevitable, and so it was for him. If you've spent your life in the middle, with every move scanned by the peering eyes of a billion people, you are bound to be judged. But he endured all censure without resentment. It was as if greatness went hand in hand with humility. That may have been the greatest lesson of all.

Aakash Chopra played ten Tests between 2003 and 2004, but batted with Tendulkar for only 26 balls.

MY GREATEST IDOL   Virat Kohli, *Wisden India*, 2014

I was just over a year old when Sachin Tendulkar made his Test debut. As a child growing up in the 1990s, my first memory of him is watching him play in the 1996 World Cup. The way he dominated the bowlers was simply brilliant, and that's when I decided to make him my idol.

When playing cricket as kids, we all pretend to be a particular player. I always wanted to be Sachin. I wanted to bat like him, so I tried to copy the shots he played and hit sixes the way he used to hit them. He was the one player that always made me think: "I want to bat like him."

I still remember the first time I met him. I was part of the Under-19 team that was to tour New Zealand in early 2007. The team was in Mumbai in January when Lalchand Rajput, our coach, asked Sachin if he'd like to have a word with us and tell us about the conditions we could expect in New Zealand, since he had played a lot of cricket there.

As soon as we saw Sachin enter the stadium, we got goosebumps, since none of us had met him before that. He walked towards the area where we were practising, and he spoke to us about the conditions. I just stood there looking at him. I didn't even blink my eyes because I couldn't quite believe it. It was something truly special.

After that, it was another two years before I had a one-on-one interaction with him, because I didn't have the guts to go up to him and talk to him. We finally spoke during the Champions Trophy in South Africa in 2009. That was the first chat I had with him about technique and my batting. He advised me to make some adjustments. He pointed out areas in which I could improve, and he actually wanted to help me out. I remember thinking that was a really good gesture on his part.

When I was making it into the national team, there were so many shots that Sachin hit which made me think, "Wow, I wish I could play that shot." He used to hit a lot of off-drives and straight-drives, and I don't think anyone at that point in time was able to hit fast bowlers the way he did. He would hit those shots that went straight over the bowlers' heads. That was something amazing, I was totally blown away watching those strokes. The straight-drive is something special.

Sharing a dressing-room with Sachin has been a huge learning experience for me. One of the things I've learned is to have total dedication and passion for the sport. Sachin has always been a great professional. He understands what it means to be on the field, he never compromises on professionalism. His work ethic and hard work are amazing, and a lesson for everyone. It's certainly something I picked up while playing alongside him.

I had the honour of having a few partnerships with him over the last few years. The one that has stayed in my mind is the one that we had against Pakistan in the 2012 Asia Cup. That was something really special because the match was a big one for us. That innings is special for me because I got 183, but to have a century partnership with Sachin – 133 in 19.1 overs – in the last one-dayer he ever played made it even more memorable. To watch him bat the way he did was amazing. It was an honour. The way he motivated me during that innings completed that experience for me.

After the World Cup final in 2011, I was part of a group that carried him around the ground. He had been carrying the country on his shoulders for 21 years, and I felt it was time that some of us carried him. Sachin has done so much for cricket, and we all knew it was a special win for him. He's always carried such a burden, all the time, so it was the most fitting thing that we could have done for him. I'm glad I had the opportunity to do something like that.

When I walked out to bat after Sachin lost his wicket in the final, the crowd at the Wankhede Stadium was completely silent. It was definitely one of the most nervous moments in my career. The memory of it will always stay with me, because it was such an important match for all of us. I could sense that everyone had lost a bit of hope when Sachin got out. I couldn't believe that I was going to bat after him, and knowing that it was probably his last chance to win the World Cup, I was pretty nervous.

Later that year, I was selected in the Test side to play West Indies, and I scored fifties in both innings in the third and final match of the series. This was a very important game for me because I was then selected in the squad for the subsequent tour of Australia. I was pretty nervous, so I decided to speak to Sachin about it. When I told him what I felt, he told me not to think too much about it, that it was important to just back myself and play my game. He told me I should stick to my strengths and not try to do something completely different. That was one chat I will always remember. Later on, in Perth, I remember I was batting on 69 going into lunch. He walked past me and told me to get a big one. I was the last wicket to fall after having scored 75, but that is something that has stayed with me and has motivated me always.

Virat Kohli was born a year before Tendulkar's Test debut in 1989. He played 17 Tests and 31 one-day internationals with Tendulkar.

Chapter 8

In His Own Words

It is a strange paradox. The man who dreamt of playing cricket for India since he was ten; of walking into a packed stadium to exhibit his craftsmanship; of publicly sharing his struggle against a swinging ball, or one that spins like a top from the rough outside leg stump; of being pushed to his limit in a run-chase; of trading punches under floodlights; of raising his bat and looking up to the skies after he scores a century, as the crowd roars "Sachin, Sachin"... And yet, this man, he hates the spotlight.

We are familiar with the scene, and can play it in slow-motion in our heads, over and over: Tendulkar strides to the wicket, the crowd rises to its feet, the helmet – with his beloved tricolour – and gloves are already on; he looks up to allow his eyes to adjust to the light, exchanges a quick word with the non-striker, hitches up his box, bends the knee, takes guard. And, at that moment, he blocks everything else out.

It seems incongruous, but it makes perfect sense. How do you take it all in, yet block it all out? How do you say "'Sachin, Sachin' will reverberate in my ears till my last breath..." – as he did in his farewell speech – but systematically shut yourself away from a public that has hounded you since you were 16, demanded a hundred each game, fallen to your feet in worship, taken selfies with you, touched you, stared at you, built temples dedicated to you, and called you God?

There is an explanation. His dream was never about adulation, fame or money: it was simply about a love of a game. When he is now asked about his son, Arjun, following in his footsteps, all he says is that cricket has *to find its way into Arjun's heart. He has to fall in love with the game. All else is irrelevant.*

Our problem is whether we can ever treat Tendulkar like a normal human being. His problem is that to know what is normal is all he's ever wanted. Not that he's ungrateful for all he has achieved and acquired. But he did not play the game for any of the trappings. He played it because it is him. As Peter Roebuck wrote, "Tendulkar's body seems to move in unison with the game, as if it flows through him, informing every muscle of its duties."

Sachin Tendulkar has always been a shy man. This you sense right from his first televised interview as a 16-year-old. The interview, done by Tom Alter for a documentary called Moods and Moments, *took place around the time he was a possibility for India's 1989 tour of West Indies (he didn't make the cut because the selectors were worried about a 16-year-old being scarred for life by Malcolm Marshall and Curtly Ambrose). Sample this excerpt:*

I think you must be getting tired now of people asking you questions and of giving interviews...
No, this is just the start...

If you get selected to go to the West Indies, will you be happy about that or do you think you want to wait a few years?
No, of course I'll be happy.

You don't think you're too young? So many people are saying that Marshall is so fast and Ambrose is so fast and you'll have trouble facing them. What do you think?
I don't think I will have any trouble to face Marshall.

You prefer facing fast bowling?
Yeah.

What is the reason for that?
I like to play fast bowlers because the ball comes straight on the bat...

Kapil Dev bowled to you at the CCI [Brabourne Stadium] nets – his outswing and inswing... you didn't have a problem with that?
No, I didn't have a problem.

That's it, interview over. A Tendulkar interview has almost always been more about getting one, rather than what he has to say. But there are rare occasions when he has been candid: on captaincy, selection issues, the criticism of his evolution from destroyer to run machine, how the art of batting has changed over the course of his career, and about the controversial declaration when he was on 194 in Multan against Pakistan. This interview with Sambit Bal is one of them.

A RIDE WITH SACHIN   Sambit Bal, *Wisden Asia Cricket*, October 2004

Sachin, this is your 15th year in the game. For many that's an entire career. How much do you think cricket has changed in your lifetime?
Definitely, the game has changed. I would say one-day cricket has changed more than Tests. When I started playing in 1989, 260 used to be a winning score, now it is just an average score. When we played in Pakistan this year, the first four innings in the ODIs had scores of above 300; it was amazing. There were near-300 scores in the last two matches too. Players know that you have to set a big target, and that has probably changed the way Test cricket is played because the same approach has spread.

The idea of opening the innings has changed. Matthew Hayden, Virender Sehwag, Chris Gayle, Herschelle Gibbs, they all defy convention.
Yes, you can say it is a different sort of batting technique. Earlier you saw off the new ball and then let bowlers watch you for the rest of the day. But now batsmen are prepared to take more risks and they feel that if you can unsettle the bowler in the second over, then why not?

Do you think the days of the defensive opener are behind us?
I wouldn't say so. There's Mark Richardson who is an old-fashioned opener, who likes to leave everything outside the off stump. And there's Aakash Chopra who is a very sound and solid opener. And then you have Sehwag, Hayden, Gibbs, the guys who play big shots from ball one.

Would you say that this has something do with the depletion of fast-bowling stock? For the best part of your career, you played some great quick bowlers. Wasim Akram, Waqar Younis, Allan Donald, Shaun Pollock, Curtly Ambrose, Courtney Walsh, Glenn McGrath at his peak. Now, most of them are gone.
McGrath and Pollock are still around, and there's Jason Gillespie. Pollock and McGrath may have lost a bit of pace but they are still great with the new ball. And there are some good bowlers who could go on to become great. Harmison bowls at 90mph, Flintoff bowls consistently at 86, 87, and England have Jones also. Australia have Lee and Kasprowicz,

there are Shoaib and Sami in Pakistan, we have Zaheer, Nehra and Irfan. In six or seven years, you'll be calling these guys great. Maybe not all of them, but three out of ten.

But would you agree that compared to the first ten years of your career, the last five have been dominated by batsmen and that the conditions have been somewhat favourable to batting? Pitches have flattened out. Even in Australia, the ball doesn't fly off as it used to.
Perth was quick this time too. But we didn't play a Test there. The other pitches were not too quick.

Even in England, you mainly get good batting wickets.
Lord's and The Oval, yes. But Headingley did quite a bit and Nottingham too wasn't a easy pitch.

In general would it be fair to say that batting has become slightly easier?
I wouldn't say so. There is another way of looking at it. On helpful tracks you get more scoring opportunities because captains set attacking fields. On flat surfaces, the bowling sides try to dry up the runs, so it's a different kind of challenge. When we played Australia here, I remember Steve Waugh posting a deep point in Chennai when I had scored only two runs. Colin Miller was bowling to a seven-two field. Nasser Hussain did that too. Matthew Hoggard was bowling two feet outside the off stump to a seven-two field and then Flintoff and Ashley Giles bowled to similar fields on the leg side. On flat surfaces, bowlers have to find a way of making it difficult for you.

Watching cricket these days it is obvious how the dynamics have changed. Bowling sides are often trying to choke batsmen out rather than bowling them out.
Another reason for that is batsmen are willing to play more strokes, forcing defensive fields. If you leave balls outside the off stump all day, the captain will say, "Why do I need a fielder in the deep?"

But as a batsman, scoring runs in conditions helpful to bowlers must give you greater satisfaction.
Any batsman would like to score runs when there is more help for bowlers. It is satisfying to score runs on seaming tracks, quick tracks and turning tracks. A great spinner can be unplayable on a turner.

That 136 against Pakistan at Chennai was on a turner.
Yes, and Saqlain bowled really well throughout that series.

And that century at Perth on your first tour to Australia was special.
Yeah. It was the last Test and the ball really zipped through. An innings like that is surely satisfying.

You don't get too many pitches like that any more.
The Headingley wicket in 2002 was quite juicy.

On the second day too?
Yes. I would say it was a dangerous pitch. The bounce was inconsistent throughout. I remember getting hit a couple of times in the ribs on the first evening and I came out wearing a chest-guard, which I normally don't wear, and an elbow guard. And then I got hit on my elbow by a ball that kicked up from a good length giving me no time to react. Hussain got hit on the elbow too.

There were suggestions after India's tour of New Zealand in 2002-03, where the pitches were quite difficult, that the defensive techniques of batsmen these days might not be as sound.
I will say one thing: the pitches on that tour were something I have never experienced before. Even while batting in the third innings, they hadn't dried out; the spikes were going in comfortably. The bowlers just had to land it on a decent length and then the pitch did the rest. Even the net wickets were terrible. Parthiv Patel was a handful on them; I remember facing him and I really had to apply myself. In the end it was down to who won the toss.

Coming to you personally, everyone says that your batting has changed.
When you play for a long time, it is natural. Changes are going to take place and you always try and make changes to become a better player. The basic idea is to cut down on the risky shots and try and be as consistent as possible

But does all this talk about your game affect you? You normally keep your feelings to yourself, but during the Asia Cup you came out quite strongly against people who were saying you had stopped enjoying your batting.
I thought too much was being said about it and unfortunately guys who have played cricket themselves were making too many rude statements. Someone who has played should definitely understand that there are things like team meetings and team plans. It's not all about what my natural game is, but about executing a team plan. I should be doing what the team wants me to and not what someone sitting 85 yards away

in the commentators' box feels. You can't be talking about what the country should be doing and then focus on an individual. There is no question that it is a team game, and it is the responsibility of all 11 individuals to execute a team plan on any given day.

There is a school of thought that you can take even more liberties with your batting, that India has a fairly good batting line-up today, a much better one than, say, five years ago.
I really don't know how to put it across, because I can never make everyone happy. If I play a big shot and get out, some people will say what's the need to do that when there are so many strokeplayers around, can't he just try to play 50 overs? I feel I should play the way I think I should play and not according to how XYZ feels. There might be a day when we need 100 runs in the first 15, and I will bat differently.

Do you feel it's a no-win situation for you: no matter how you play you will still end up disappointing some people?
It's very easy to say that you should go out and play your natural game, but sometimes you end up taking plenty of risks, and if you get out doing that, people start talking one way. And when you try to do what the team has planned, they think differently. So it is difficult for any player to keep outsiders happy. We have to think about what the team has planned. As long as I know I am doing the right thing, I don't need to worry about what people are saying. People keep saying, "Ah, he is not playing the same number of shots as before," but if you look at the strike-rate, you'll see I'm scoring at the same pace, just scoring in a different way. As you spend more and more time in the team, your role changes. It cannot be what it was 15 years ago or seven years ago. I don't think there is any player in the world who has played in the same gear throughout his career.

One thing can be said about you. The geometry of your game has changed perceptibly.
If I kept playing the same way throughout my career, it would mean the opposition have not been using their brains. The opposition works on your game and comes up with certain plans. The bowlers think, OK, this is how he likes to play and these are the shots he plays, and I will block these shots and make him play somewhere else. Or give him a run and bowl more at the other guy. If they decide to bowl to you on off stump with seven fielders on the off side it is not necessary to still play flamboyant cover-drives. So sometimes you shuffle across and play on the leg. You have to adapt, you have to do what is necessary. I hope people get sharp enough to understand that there were times when

bowlers attacked you and you counter-attacked. Cricket is often about not doing what your opponents want you to do. You have to be smart.

But your game has noticeably become more leg-oriented, even in one-day cricket where fielders are more evenly distributed.
Sometimes it's intentional, sometimes it's not. Let's say that the body and mind are not going to be working in the same direction all the time. Sometimes your body doesn't move in the same direction as your mind. You want to go there but you just can't because it's a body, not a machine. Sometimes you know you should leave that ball but you just can't. That innings in Sydney I played like that [predominantly on the leg side] intentionally. But there may have been other occasions when I have not done it intentionally – it just happened.

You used to play a lot straighter, towards mid-off and mid-on.
As I was saying earlier, the opposition studies you too. If you see now, the field placements are different. I don't want to hit where there are fielders, I want to play somewhere I can score runs, so I have to look for different shots.

There were three strokes which used to be your trademark shots in one-day cricket. The pull to balls just short of a good length, for which it was impossible to set a field in the early overs, the lofted drive over the bowler's head, and the cover-drive on the up that you played standing on your toes. We don't see much of those shots these days.
That may be because my role is being played by someone else. When Virender Sehwag is going bang-bang, there is no need for me to do all that. The plan is that out of the top three batters someone should try to stay till the end. That's the team plan and I am going with that.

You brought out a few of those shots during the World Cup. That pulled six off Andrew Caddick had your stamp all over it.
Throughout that tournament I was batting at a faster rate than Sehwag. I was prepared to take more risks at that time and I was the one who was playing the role of unsettling the bowlers. Ultimately, it's not about what I do or what Sehwag does, what matters is that the team puts up a good total.

For years you played a dominating game. Now you're playing a game of conservation because you see that as your role. But do you sometimes miss the Sachin of old, the thrill of cutting loose, seeing the fear in the eye of the bowler?
Not really. It's not that I have intentionally cramped my style of play. I have never said no, I will not play any shots. Yes, there are times you bat

to the needs of the situation. Also, it is a part of growing. You don't do at the age of 35 what you did at 16. The thinking changes. There are days I go all out. In many matches in the World Cup I batted like that. Or in that match in Hyderabad against New Zealand [in 2003, when Tendulkar and Sehwag put on 182 in 30 overs], I remember telling Veeru, "*Aaj toh tera role mein khel raha hoon, aur mera role tu kar raha hai.*" [Today I'm playing your role, and you're playing mine.]

And then in that World Cup match against Pakistan, you launched into Shoaib.
Let me tell you something. It wasn't pre-planned. In fact the plan was to bat out the first ten overs without losing a wicket. We just wanted to play out the new ball. But as it happened a few balls came our way and we connected. So we said, it's working well, let's go for it. You've got to be prepared to change your plans and you should be able to do that.

I particularly remember the assault against Glenn McGrath in the ICC Knockout at Nairobi.
That *was* planned. The ball was seaming around and after I played the first over I said to myself, if you don't do anything he is going to bowl all his eight, nine overs at the same spot and it will be no good for us. You have to try to do something to unsettle him. I went after him and it worked. I got a quick 40-odd.

There's another thing that has perhaps changed with age. The old Tendulkar was always keen to establish his supremacy, particularly when it came to big-reputation bowlers. The way you asserted yourself against Shane Warne in 1998 is legendary. But the Tendulkar of today takes a measured approach, he doesn't mind grafting.
I have always tried to bat according to the situation. In Australia I got out a couple of times trying to play big shots. Then I said, who am I trying to prove wrong? I had to contribute towards the team cause, so I said I'm going change my game. Eventually what do you want? You want India to score 600, so it doesn't matter how I play if we can put 600-plus on the board.

It has perhaps come to a stage where bowlers have little to lose in bowling at you, whereas it's a no-win situation for you. If a new bowler comes up and gets hammered for four fours, it will create no ripple, but you remain the wicket to take. In the Asia Cup there was an award for your wicket.
Yes, I read that, and obviously I didn't want to get out. But you can't let these things clutter your mind while batting; you can't change the way

you bat because of things like this. The worst thing about facing a bowler from teams like these is that you don't know what he does, how he swings it or what angles he bowls. But if you start thinking about these things it will affect your batting. The best way to bat is to shut everything out. It's not easy, but it's the ideal situation.

That's called being in the zone, isn't it?
Probably six out of ten times we can manage to do that. Sometimes you think, oh, the bowler will do this and I have to do that. Other times you go in with a blank mind; you get into that zone where you are not thinking of anything else. All you can see is the ball and nothing else. You see the ball you play and then it really doesn't matter if there are people moving around in front of the screen or whatever. Otherwise, even a small hanky disturbs you.

When did this happen for you last?
In Sydney, in Rawalpindi.

Didn't you go into the Sydney Test with a predetermined mindset?
Yes, it was different kind of a zone. In my mind, I was pretty sure what I wanted to do, so I literally programmed my body. I created a shell around myself and said, I'm not going to go out of this shell. I am not going to go into fourth gear, I am going to drive in third gear all the time whether I'm batting on 170 or 17.

Does watching Sehwag bat remind you of yourself?
Yes, it does. I used to think like that. In fact I used to be worse. But with time you change.

Does it also have anything to do with the body slowing down?
As you grow older, obviously the body is going to change physically and your thinking obviously changes. You have to keep fighting that. The body will slow down, the question is about how much time it takes and how you adjust to the change.

Have you started feeling the changes?
I have pushed myself all the time. At least at this moment, my body feels all right.

Ramakant Achrekar, your first coach, recently said that you should seriously consider using a lighter bat.
I don't think I can play with a really light bat. I have tried using one before and it just doesn't help my bat swing. But that said, I am using a relatively lighter bat now. It's about 2lb 11oz now, down from 3lb 2oz.

I have been using it for the last two years. I can't start using an extremely light bat. If it has to happen, it will happen gradually.

How does it feel to undergo so much public scrutiny? Everything you do or say is analysed, commented upon. Do you feel a sense of siege?
You get used to it. But that could be one of the reasons why I keep my guard. I don't open out easily. That's my nature anyway. I still don't think I am comfortable with the limelight. You know, I still feel embarrassed with television cameras around me. I am used to it now, but I am not 100 per cent comfortable. I am still shy by nature, and I would rather walk quietly to my room and just sit and relax.

After being India's most celebrated public figure for so long, there is still so little that is known about you. The flip side of it is that people say you don't take a stand on issues.
I have taken stands before, but often whatever I say gets misinterpreted and meanings are attached to it. I don't want to go into specifics now, but I felt this is going to happen, so why get into it?

But your voice carries such a lot of weight. By speaking out, you could make a difference.
If you know that whatever you say will become a controversy, why get into it unnecessarily? And I feel, OK, there are people who are managing those issues, and my job, at least for the time being, is to play cricket, so let me focus on that.

Recently you expressed your disappointment over missing out on a double-century, and it became a big controversy.
What happened in Pakistan was that the moment I entered the press conference, the first question was asked: are you surprised and disappointed? I said, yes, I am disappointed. I'd have been lying if I had said no. I am entitled to feel disappointed. I was 194 not out and it was the second day. But that didn't mean I was going to carry the disappointment into the game. What happened happened, and I put it behind me. Where is the controversy when Rahul and I both had a chat and cleared up the whole misunderstanding? The whole drama was created by the press; there was nothing going on between the players.

You're just 31, but you've already made 20,000 international runs and 65 hundreds. There is almost non-stop cricket these days with so many one-day tournaments. How do you keep yourself mentally fresh? Does your mind ever feel jaded?
I want to keep playing with the same attitude like I have always done. I am not going to think about how many years I have got left, but just

go out and enjoy it. You can't think of how many more runs you are going to get.

Is something like a second-best-ever career average a goal?
I don't even know what the second-best average is. I don't think if I average 64 people are going to call me a great player and if I average 57 people will call me a lesser player. You are not focusing on these things. Whatever years are left to me, I am going to push myself harder because the time I have is never going to come back again. There is plenty of time to do other things. I want us to win a World Cup. That will be a real icing on the cake.

Would you like another shot at the captaincy?
I gave it up. I am not thinking about that.

Javagal Srinath recently wrote something about your captaincy. He said you could bowl leg-spin, swing the ball, and of course bat like Tendulkar, and you expected the same standards from everyone.
All I expected was 100 per cent effort. I said, I will not say anything to you if you fail. But if you fail to give 100 per cent, I'll see to it that you are made to realise that. If after giving 100 per cent, you fail five times in a row, that's fine. But if you have not tried, if you have taken things lightly, then I am not the guy you should come to. I didn't expect anything more than that. I didn't ask anyone to bowl like Malcolm Marshall or bat like Vivian Richards. Every individual has his own talent and limitations and is expected to perform accordingly. Hundred per cent commitment is not too much to expect, is it?

If you were to do the job again, is there anything you would do differently?
The day I gave in my resignation, I have never thought of it after that. I felt we were not all heading in the right direction and it was affecting me as person. I couldn't switch off at all. Even ten days after a match, I would still be thinking about why this happened and why that happened, and it started affecting me as a person. Not as a player as some people pointed out because I scored over 1,000 runs in both forms of the game that last year. Also, I felt there was lack of support from every direction.

From within the team too?
No, not the team, but from outside. I felt that if everyone had spent their energy in the right direction, we could have moved ahead.

You were particularly unhappy with the selectors.
Yes. I was not happy with the selectors at all. It just didn't work out. They had different ideas, I had different ideas. The only thing is, I had to go in there and play with their ideas.

One of those ideas was getting V. V. S. Laxman to open.
Exactly. I mean, it all happened literally in the middle of a meeting. Till then he had been a middle-order batsman, and suddenly he was an opener.

But why didn't you speak up against it? Why didn't you stand up and say, I will take none of this?
I always felt that, you know, everyone will change and they will make the effort to do something for Indian cricket. Captaining India was obviously a great honour for me, but it wasn't the ultimate thing for me. The ultimate thing was to play cricket for India and at that time, when I was removed from the captaincy, I said in my statement that you can stop me from leading India, but no one can stop me from playing cricket. Playing cricket is the ultimate thing in my life. I want to play for India.

You were quite hurt when you were removed from the captaincy.
Obviously. I felt that if you made somebody captain then he should be given a fair run, with the kind of support required. Things have changed a lot since then.

So you captained the team at the wrong time, in the wrong atmosphere?
Well, I don't have any regrets now. So long as I know that I tried my best, it really doesn't matter. You know, I would not sit back after 20 years and think that I didn't try my best. The guys who had different ideas, they would definitely think that they didn't do their best. I am pretty sure that I did whatever I thought was best for Indian cricket.

The team have gone in the right direction since then, under Sourav Ganguly.
I am a firm believer that it's not about captaincy, but about how the team plays, how the individuals perform. If you are going to score 700 runs in Australia, you are going to be on top, but if you score only 220, obviously it will be a different story.

But there's something different about this team.
Simply, there are plenty of match-winners in this team. There are enough players who can win a match single-handedly.

Rahul Dravid is one player who has really come on as a wonderful match-winner, in Test cricket particularly. What's the biggest change you have noticed in his batting?

I think he has become more positive. I remember having discussions with him and I used to tell him, your concentration level is going to last for a certain number of hours and within those hours you should be batting on 100-plus and not on 70 or 60. When you know that you are settled, then you should shift into the next gear, and then again maybe if someone is bowling well you can come down a little. I think he has been doing that quite well and he has been playing more shots. I also think that wicketkeeping has helped. When you're keeping you are watching the ball all the time, and you are watching the game from where the action is taking place. I feel that angle helps.

You used to field in the slips but not any more.

I had a lot of finger injuries, and still have plenty of problems and struggle with my fingers. I have very small hands and my fingers have never been strong. That's why I moved away from the slips.

Coming to the series that everyone is talking about, what's it about Australia that brings out the best in you? You've got seven hundreds against them.

It is just a coincidence. I try to do my best against all teams. I have always enjoyed being there, it's a fabulous place to play cricket.

Your first series there was special. It made the world sit up and take notice. Did you find playing cricket in Australia any different?

I was perhaps too young to realise all that. I felt I should just go and do what I could and not really worry about what they are trying to do. I remember that all I was keen about was hitting boundaries. That tour certainly made a huge difference to my career. Perth was considered one of the most difficult tracks to bat on and scoring a hundred there gave me a lot of self-belief.

This will perhaps be the biggest season for India in recent times. Australia, South Africa and then Pakistan.

It's huge for us. The last series against Australia at home was mind-blowing. The best I have played in. Both the Test series and the one-day series were decided in the last half-hour.

Do you think if India manage to beat Australia and South Africa, they can claim to be the No. 2 team in the world?

That will be a great step forward. But I think we still need to go and win some series abroad. Only then can we be counted as one of the top teams in the world.

INTERVIEWING SACHIN

Rohit Brijnath, *Wisden Asia Cricket*, September 2002

In early February of 1989, I flew from Calcutta to Bombay to interview a boy – an encounter that would effectively alter my life. Cricket had yet to explode across the nation, money was tight at *Sportsworld* (salaries barely paid the bar bill), and teenagers who hadn't yet played for India came to the office and pleaded for a paragraph – you did not go to them. But this kid, even then he demanded your attention.

Of course, it was a disaster. Sachin Tendulkar was 15, squeaky, uncomfortable, and in the end politely asked, "OK, can I get back to the cricket?" For the first and only time, I agreed, with alacrity. Corpses have told better tales. The only story worth remembering was that he spoke cricket in his sleep, and surely still does: "Sourav, run, for God's sakes, run."

A decade and more later, the prodigy had turned master; everything had changed, and nothing. For the choirboy, interviews still resembled an appointment with a thumbscrew. Always there was this sense of a private man discomforted by this most public of lives. His art, he felt, was a sufficient explanation of who he was.

He was never going to be loquacious like Ganguly; still, to be fair, he would occasionally lift his veil (not on his personal life but on his cricket), and let you glimpse the mechanics of his genius…

But it wouldn't have mattered if he had spoken in Japanese monosyllables, Tendulkar was still the biggest story we had. He was an inspiration for an entire generation of Indian sportswriters… He was something we had never had before: genius close-up, and he challenged our imagination.

Of course, he changed my life. If there wasn't a Tendulkar, *India Today* would never have spent lakhs allowing me to sunbathe in South Africa and pub-crawl through England. Magazines hired palmists, or was it a crystal ball-gazer (this is true), to read his mind; when his back gave him trouble, *Wisden* was replaced with *Grey's Anatomy*, and we silenced Saturday-night parties with lectures on his sacroiliac muscles.

And he? He seemed resigned, almost irritated, by this celebrity, asking me once, "I don't want a public discussion on it. Why is everyone so interested in my back?" How did one explain that, let alone his future, ours depended on it?

He could seem alarmingly ordinary, resembling almost some reluctant hero, averse to attracting attention to himself...

But, of course, he was anything but ordinary. One afternoon in Sri Lanka, we played table tennis, a rare convivial moment. Except, he would not lose. The better I played, the better he did, game after game refusing to submit: for an instant, a microcosm of what occurs on the field where we would never be, it was a taste of his flaring competitiveness.

During interviews he rarely made bold statements, or used his untouchable status to bully the board (he should have done both), or vented his displeasure at a team-mate's performance (often you had to read between the lines, or put off your tape recorder, to be better educated).

He handled pressure with a quiet dignity, but there was, you sensed occasionally, beyond his powerful ambition, a certain frustration with the constant expectation that pursued him.

Mostly though, if he complained, it was in private... So his answers were very carefully calibrated, caution replacing spontaneity. He had an acute awareness of the impact of his words, which once said could not be retrieved.

Which is why he called one evening, the only time he did, to ask what headline I was using for the previous day's interview. Then captain, he had mentioned that India needed a foreign coach (for him, quite an admission), but one working in tandem with an Indian coach. It was the obvious headline, but he (perhaps disinclined to embarrass then coach Madan Lal, or even to vaguely spark a controversy) said, no, please don't, leave it in the copy, but use something else. I reminded him of my freedom to choose headlines; he laughingly reminded me of the access he constantly granted. Principle lost...

Access to him, considering his status, was not difficult. He did not agree to every interview or acquiesce to every demand for a quote. But he did not rail, or snarl. His craft may be arrogant, but off the field he packed it in his suitcase... If you wanted to speak to him, you called him...

April–May, 1998, Sharjah, when he scored two centuries against Australia, is a powerful memory for various reasons. *India Today* had planned a major story on him and, after the tournament, I was to fly back to Bombay and do the interview there. Except, after his first electric century on Wednesday night, my editors called, demanding the story on Thursday night. Impossible, we hadn't even spoken. Friday, the day of the final, was his birthday, and on Thursday, the rest day, his manager, the late Mark Mascarenhas, threw a typically lavish party... Tendulkar was in an ebullient mood; distracted too...

Yet when I explained the situation to him, he did not offer the obvious excuse. Instead, amid the clamour, he found a table in the middle of the party. I grabbed a napkin and Ayaz Memon, then of *Mid-Day*, opened his notebook, and Tendulkar gave us ten minutes. It was an unforgettable act of generosity.

He was still the choirboy, still a tad uncomfortable, still polite and professional, but he gave me a quote that stood at the top of my story. "I don't think anything is impossible. Of course, I'm not always right."

He returned to the party, we to our typewriters. One more tale of Sachin to tell.

Chapter 9

Thank You and Goodnight

I
t may have lacked the shock value of Don Bradman's last-innings duck, but neither was there a farewell century. Seventy-four was hardly to be sniffed at, but it did not provide any neat symmetry for a man who, in a career spanning four decades, dealt in numbers, runs and records, and also in dreams, hopes and aspirations.

There was a quantitative element to Tendulkar's success, in its runs and riches, that appealed to all post-socialist, neo-capitalist Indians. More importantly, his success involved a qualitative element too: quite simply, he made his fans angry when he failed, and happy when he succeeded. There was no better barometer of the national mood. For cricket-lovers around the world, Tendulkar's feats were beauteous and significant in themselves: his perfect balance at the crease, his technical acumen, his shot-making, his hand-eye co-ordination, his ability to spot the length of the ball so early he knew exactly what to do next. But for Indian cricket-lovers, there was the context of nationhood and identity. For Indians, his career is a monument in its own right: it has made Indians as proud as they are of the Taj Mahal.

He was the obsessive-perfectionist, single-minded practitioner who made cricket his life, at the cost of all else, and yet never seemed to lose perspective of his place in the world. All of this perhaps explains why Tendulkar's departure culminated in reams of impassioned outpourings from sportswriters and fans, who took to quoting W. H. Auden's Funeral Blues. The idea of Tendulkar being "My North, my South, my East and West" is one that will provoke a wry grin from bowlers who must have felt as if they were being hit to all parts of the compass.

It also may explain why the Wankhede wore a funereal air on November 16, 2013, the third and final day of the Second Test against West Indies, and Tendulkar's last as an international cricketer. A 63-year-old woman, never a great fan or Tendulkar-worshipper, was crying openly as she watched him make his farewell speech; it was the first and only Test match she had watched in the flesh. This is what Sachin did: he allowed a nation of people, often emotionally repressed, to channel their feelings. Sachin made it all right for grown-ups to cry, and for teenagers to dream.

NO. 4 HAS LEFT THE BUILDING

Dileep Premachandran,
The Nightwatchman, Winter 2013

As Sachin Tendulkar walked back to the pavilion, he paused a couple of times to raise his bat in the direction of the various stands. By then, the eerie silence that greeted his dismissal had made way for the sort of tear-stained ovation that most of us had never seen. Thousands in the stands, dozens in the press box, many more in the swanky corporate hospitality areas… everyone was on their feet, with handclaps, cheers, chants and sobs marking the end of an era.

As he glanced one final time at the stand that bears his name, I summoned up another image. The teenager in Perth. Not the boy on the burning deck who made the brilliant 114 that prompted Merv Hughes to tell Allan Border, "This little prick's going to get more runs than you, AB," but the bowler who sent down six balls in a Tri-Series game against West Indies two months earlier.

India had managed just 126 on a surface that provided extravagant seam movement in addition to being lightning-fast. Curtly Ambrose, Malcolm Marshall, Patrick Patterson and Anderson Cummins had been nearly unplayable. Ravi Shastri top-scored with 33, but laboured 110 balls for those runs.

Tendulkar, who had made just one with the bat, was thrown the ball in the 41st over of the West Indian reply. Cummins and Patterson, the final pair, were at the crease, with six needed for victory. Bowling off a few paces, he got the ball to hoop in as though he was a slow-medium version of Imran Khan. The penultimate ball of the over moved too much through the air, though, and Patterson was able to squirt it through midwicket for three runs that tied the scores.

Tendulkar, just 18 at the time, was unfazed. He went back to his mark, shuffled in and pitched one a foot outside off stump. The inward movement drew Cummins into the stroke, and the thick outside edge was brilliantly held by Mohammad Azharuddin, diving to his left at second slip. In the pandemonium that followed, the kid seemed the calmest person on the field. Nearly a century earlier, Rudyard Kipling – no fan of "flannelled fools" – had written: "If you can keep your head when all about you are losing theirs…" No words were more apt for Tendulkar.

Back then, he was the boy wonder, the one from whom Gavaskar-like runs and Richards-like dominance were expected. He had yet to become a quasi-deity. The burden of expectation was already there, but it hadn't become an Atlas-like load. Irrepressible exuberance hadn't yet made way for inscrutability. He was just "our kid", albeit the one we all wanted to be.

How does anyone deal with such hero-worship, with being in the pantheon of millions of believers? It's hard to think of anyone in modern sport who has inspired such adulation. Diego Maradona came close in his glory years, when his most fervent fans simply referred to him as D10S, a combination of the number on the back of his shirt and the Spanish word for the Almighty.

But even as they idolised him, Argentines were well aware of the dark side, which manifested itself both on and off the field. "He is someone many people want to emulate, a controversial figure, loved, hated, who stirs great upheaval, especially in Argentina," said Jorge Valdano, who played alongside him on the 1986 World Cup-winning team. "Maradona has no peers inside the pitch, but he has turned his life into a show, and is now living a personal ordeal that should not be imitated."

Tendulkar, incredibly, wore the India colours for nearly a quarter-century without his keeper-of-the-flame image being tarnished. There was the odd hullaballoo – allegations of ball-tampering in South Africa in 2001, noises from the Australian camp about changed testimony during the Harbhajan Singh racism hearing – but for the most part team-mates and opponents alike cited him as the beau ideal for what a cricketer should be.

There was also little to cherish in Maradona's winter. His international career ended with a positive drugs test during the World Cup in the United States in 1994. When he returned to La Bombonera and his beloved Boca Juniors a year later, he was a wan imitation of the player that gave defenders vertigo. Addicted to cocaine, and with a paunchy figure that seemed more suited for a deckchair than playmaking, he was yesterday's hero. When he asked to be taken off at half-time in his final game, against bitter rivals River Plate, the man who replaced him helped transform a 0–1 deficit into a 2–1 win. In the years that followed, Juan Roman Riquelme would become a Boca idol second only to El Diego.

It was Riquelme I thought of once Tendulkar had vanished into the pavilion. The man who marked his guard, Virat Kohli, is temperamentally as far removed from Tendulkar as the laidback Riquelme was from Maradona. And when he laced the first ball he faced through cover for four, it was a sign that Indian cricket would not look back. The generation that Tendulkar inspired was ready.

There had been plenty to savour in his twilight years. Between 2008 and 2011, at the heart of a team that would take the No. 1 ranking in Test cricket and win the World Cup, he played with the freedom and authority that had been on view during the late 1990s, when he could scarcely do any wrong.

In 2010, as India consolidated top-dog status in Test cricket, he scored 1,562 runs with seven hundreds. He started the following year with a fabulous 146 at Newlands, a mano-a-mano tussle with Dale Steyn that was as good as anything cricket has seen. Those that watched it would never have imagined that it would be his 51st and last Test century.

Tours of England and Australia saw only glimpses of the old mastery. By the time the next home season came round, the decline appeared irreversible. New Zealand's young bowling attack kept breaching his defence, and though there were a couple of innings of substance against England and Australia, there were few signs of the batsman that Kevin Pietersen had called Superman after an unbeaten 103 carried India past a target of 387 at Chennai in December 2008.

The countdown to 100 international centuries – a media-manufactured apples-and-oranges landmark – had become the longest circus the sport had ever seen, and it clearly disturbed the equilibrium of even Tendulkar, the man whose serenity when on "his" turf had been his greatest quality. His critics spoke of selfishness and an obsession with records, while his team-mates grew weary of the endless questions about the significance of No. 100.

The last two years were not golden ones – he averaged 32.34 in 23 Tests after that Cape Town epic – but declining form didn't mean that Tendulkar became a parody of himself as Maradona had. There was no shooting at journalists from a balcony with an air-gun, no foul-mouthed rants at fellow players. Just the quiet retreat.

As for his peers, the respect and hero-worship remained. When Shakib Al Hasan, who was two when Tendulkar made his debut, wrote a newspaper column after hearing of his retirement, he started it thus: "I should have sought the permission of Sachin before attempting to write on him. He is the God of cricket and how can I be expected to write about the God?"

Not The Greatest, not Cricketer in Excelsis. But God. No pressure.

The Eden Gardens in Kolkata has never done moderation. As far as venues go, it's cricket's girl with the curl. When they're good, the crowd can be incredible, a raucous knowledgeable twelfth man capable of introducing doubt into the minds of even the toughest opposition. On their bad days, when they turn on the home team and light bonfires in the stands, they can be an embarrassment, a seething mass of humanity utterly lacking perspective.

Perspective was in very short supply during Tendulkar's 199th Test. It was as though administrators and fans in the stands were in a competition for who would come up with the corniest tributes. The music album with Tendulkar paeans came close, but was comfortably trumped by the Cricket Association of Bengal's plan to have a low-flying aircraft disgorge 199 kilograms of rose petals over the Eden Gardens on the fifth and final day of the game. Fortunately, West Indies were so inept that the Test was over in three.

On the eve of the match, Tendulkar had been asked to pose for pictures next to a wax model of him created by a local artist. It wasn't exactly Madame Tussauds, but he didn't complain, talking to the artist and signing autographs, even as his focus was a hundred yards away, on the 22-yard strip that he called his temple.

With West Indies not able to combat reverse swing or spin, Kolkata would get to see just one Tendulkar innings. Twice, he flicked Shane Shillingford through midwicket, as he once had Shane Warne in his heyday. But when Nigel Llong upheld a leg-before appeal off the 24th ball he faced, the crowd's energy gave way to listlessness.

Some things didn't change. A home-maker living in the suburbs still cooked his favourite seafood dishes, and sent them to his hotel. He bowled with the effervescence of old, trapping Shillingford in front, and was never less than polite with the legion of well-wishers who wanted a piece of him in a city that wears its sentimentality on its sleeve.

The atmosphere was no less charged in Mumbai, with fans incensed by the lack of tickets made available. But for 3,500 tickets that went up for sale online – predictably, the website crashed many times, with upwards of 20m people trying their luck – everything else in the 32,000-capacity stadium was set aside for the clubs, gymkhanas and sponsors.

The organisers had also acceded to Tendulkar's request for 500 tickets. His family, which usually stayed away for fear of disrupting his focus, planned to attend, as did his coach, Ramakant Achrekar. His mother, Rajni, had never been to a stadium to watch him play any level of cricket. To ensure that she could watch his 664th and last international appearance for India, Tendulkar had requested the association for ramps to facilitate wheelchair access.

In the days leading up to the game, his usually reticent relatives had opened up. Ajit Tendulkar, his older brother, spoke at length at an event. A long-haired version of Sachin – the resemblance is uncanny – Ajit had been both mentor and chief sounding board. And whereas the Maradona story featured its fair share of leeches and those that sought to cash in on his fame, Tendulkar was blessed when it came to family and managers. Right from his mother, who sold insurance and who commuted two hours or more every day for four years to see him when he lived with his uncle and aunt near Shivaji Park, to the cousins who did whatever they could to make sure his eyes stayed on the ball, Tendulkar has cherished a support system that allowed him to just go out and play.

There were good men and women elsewhere too. Dwarkanath Sanzgiri, a Marathi journalist, covered his first Ranji Trophy game. "I noted down every stroke," he told me. "You just knew this boy would go places." Unlike the buffoons of bluster on television and the keyboard warriors that take up so much of the current Indian media space, Sanzgiri – "Pappu" to his friends – is old school, a man steeped in the game's traditions and techniques. I once sat next to him in the press box as he predicted how a Chinaman bowler would set up and dismiss a diffident left-hand batsman. It happened exactly as he had described.

The day Tendulkar came out to bat, to the sort of roar that some of us may never hear again, I could spot tears in Pappu's eyes. At stumps, by which time he had eased to 38, we spoke excitedly about the freedom with which he had played, and the signature strokes that had been dusted off and exhibited one final time. "This is how a champion should go out," he said. I nodded.

That was the recurring theme the following day, even after he had cut Narsingh Deonarine to slip to be out for 74. Once the faithful had serenaded him off – the chant of "Sach-in, Sach-in" was Indian cricket's "You'll Never Walk Alone" for a quarter-century – they enthused about the way he had played, especially the straight-drives off Tino Best and Shannon Gabriel.

The next morning, at 11.47 a.m., it was all over, as a Mohammed Shami yorker flattened middle stump. Tendulkar rushed in from fine leg and grabbed one of the stumps as a souvenir before his team-mates lined up on either side of the pitch and asked him to lead them off. He looked down at the turf as he did so, wiping away a tear or two before shaking hands with the West Indies team and support staff on the boundary.

The speech he gave later, with references to his father ("Every time I raised my bat, it was for him"), his wife ("The best partnership of my life") and the fans ("The Sachin-Sachin chant will reverberate in my ears till the day I stop breathing") reduced most in the stands to sobbing wrecks. In the press box, grey-haired eminences who had watched his first Test all those years earlier, closed their laptops and wept. Tendulkar, who was then chaired around the ground on his team-mates' shoulders, appeared to be the calmest person on the ground.

Or at least he was till he broke away from the posse before disappearing from view for ever. With every ticket-holder still watching red-eyed from the stands, he walked to the pitch. Some might think it just a strip of clay, dust, grass and roots. Others have no qualms about urinating on it. For Tendulkar, these rectangles of turf were canvases for his greatest work. They were also his houses of the holy.

He bent down and touched the pitch reverently with both hands, before the same fingertips touched his forehead – a Hindu gesture that can best be equated with the sign of the cross. This time, you could see the tears streaming down his face as he walked away. A stadium cried with him. Not just for what it had lost, but for what it would never see again.

A couple of days before the match had begun, Suresh Raina had spoken of how easily Tendulkar, everyone's hero, managed to be one of the boys in the dressing-room. Apparently, he drew the line only when it came to music. Not for him *bhangra* or Sean Paul. Before he walked out to bat, he would insist on some Kishore Kumar. The Bengali singer, something of a maverick in his day, died more than 26 years ago. After much coercion, Raina, who has a reputation as the team's "voice", agreed to sing the first couple of lines of Tendulkar's favourite song. "*Lehron ki tarah yaadein* [Memories like waves]," it begins.

When it comes to Tendulkar, most that love Indian cricket will find the memories as immense as Hawaii's Big Pipe. From boy wonder to lone warrior, to "God" and then cherished memory… it was quite a journey. Highs and lows, twists and turns, false dawns and halcyon years. Those that put him on a pedestal, to the discomfiture of the atheists among us, seldom lost their faith.

I have a friend who compared the emotions he felt around the final Test to those he had experienced when his father passed away. He broke down several times as he tried to explain it to me. It's probably no exaggeration to say that there are thousands of others like him, whose cricket-watching lives were inextricably linked to the exploits of their Peter Pan.

I didn't cry that afternoon as Tendulkar said goodbye. For quite a few of us, it probably won't sink in till India lose their second wicket at the Wanderers in December. Then, instead of that familiar anticipatory buzz, we will feel just emptiness. No. 4 has left the building, and he isn't coming back. He's taken the best days of our lives with him.

THE END IS NIGH

Nagraj Gollapudi, *Wisden* 2014

This was not so much a series as a pilgrimage – and all in honour of one man.

In fact, the series was not even supposed to be happening: according to the schedule, West Indies had not been due to arrive in India until October 2014. That they were asked to advance their travels by 12 months was primarily because the BCCI wanted to give Sachin Tendulkar a fond farewell in his 200th Test.

The preamble was far from smooth. The Indian selectors had been growing restless and, keeping in mind future overseas assignments, were desperate to test out new batsmen. Not-so-young pretenders such as Rohit Sharma and Ajinkya Rahane had been kicking their heels for too long. But, as usual, all eyes were on Tendulkar. In the 21 Tests after January 2011, when he had last scored a century, his average had been 31. He still could muster fifties every now and then, but his reflexes were in terminal decline, and bowlers were breaching his defences. News leaked out that chairman of selectors Sandeep Patil had told BCCI president N. Srinivasan that Tendulkar's time was up; Patil called the reports "nonsense". But Tendulkar understood it was over. He conveyed that message to the BCCI, and two Tests against West Indies were quickly put in place. So the expectation – enticing to many – that Tendulkar's career would end at the turn of the year in South Africa, against the world's No. 1 Test side, was scotched. To South Africa's understandable annoyance, the BCCI promptly halved India's tour there, in part to find room for Tendulkar's home jamboree.

And so the circus moved from Lahli in northern India, venue of Tendulkar's final Ranji Trophy appearance, to Kolkata in the east, before arriving on the west coast in Mumbai, his home city. His reputation had been constructed using bricks of purity. He was a man who would grow to become best batsman, captain, senior statesman, mentor and inspiration. Thousands of devotees turned up at the three venues to pay homage.

He did not disappoint them. In the dusty village of Lahli, on a ground surrounded by rice and cane fields, Tendulkar came out to bat for Mumbai in a tricky run-chase against Haryana. On a green pitch, in swinging conditions, against nagging medium-pacers, he slowed the pace of the game, steadily transferring the advantage towards Mumbai. He finished undefeated on 79. That innings boded well for the Tests.

However, Tendulkar was sawn off in Kolkata by a doubtful lbw decision. It was his only innings of the game, which was over by the third evening – catching the local authorities off guard. The Bengal chief minister had to cancel all her appointments and rush to the ground to felicitate Tendulkar. There were plans for 199kg of rose petals to be showered across the stadium's expanse to symbolise his 199th Test, and for 65,000 Tendulkar face-masks to be distributed among the crowd – but time ran out. The Cricket Association of Bengal had invited Brian Lara, his one equal as a batsman in the 1990s, to be part of the celebrations. But Lara was reportedly stranded in mid-air when the match finished.

Mistakes were made, too. M. S. Dhoni pointed out that Tendulkar's first name has been misspelt as "Sachine" above his portrait – painted by the Bengali artist Jogen Chowdhury – which hung from the High Court End. On the first day, the electronic scoreboard referred to his wife as "Mr Anjali Tendulkar" for nearly half an hour before the error was corrected. The men responsible were given a fearsome rebuke by a CAB official.

In Mumbai, Tendulkar finally regained his footing. He walked out after two wickets fell in an over to Shane Shillingford's off-breaks, returned unbeaten on 38 at the end of the first day, and next morning briefly dazzled a full house, crossing 50 with an exquisite straight-drive, one of his signature strokes. Such fluency and command led all to assume that a valedictory hundred was a given. The stands were swelling as the countdown began. But just after the first drinks break, Tendulkar tried to cut Narsingh Deonarine's off-spin, and Darren Sammy clung on at slip. A momentary hush wrapped around the ground like a cold blanket. For one last time India's show-stopper walked back, head bowed, eyes full of tears.

West Indies had arrived in reasonable nick, having won their last three Test series 2–0, admittedly against New Zealand, Bangladesh and Zimbabwe. But they had not played a Test since March, and they had little more planned than a team-building exercise in Miami ahead of their tour of New Zealand when they got the call from their impoverished board. Suddenly, they were upping sticks for India. Compelled to play cheerleaders at Tendulkar's carnival, West Indies merrily donned the pom-poms – rather too merrily, for some tastes.

They could not keep either Test alive even for three days, occupying just 234.3 overs across four innings, and mustering two individual half-centuries. Their batsmen averaged 18 (their fourth-lowest in a series) and their bowlers 48. Shillingford was the only player to hold his own, and joined Charlie "Terror" Turner, Tom Richardson and Alec Bedser as bowlers to have taken five successive five-wicket hauls in Tests. But so easily did West Indies collapse that he bowled in only two innings. Their former captain Clive Lloyd declared: "They are drunk on Twenty20 cricket."

Yet the most profound moment of all followed Tendulkar's final dismissal. After observing a mournful silence, then a standing ovation, the crowd did not flood out of the ground – as had been the custom in India whenever his wicket fell. Instead, they stayed to appreciate the calmness of Cheteshwar Pujara, the daring of Virat Kohli, the wristiness of Sharma and the pace of Shami. Deep down, Tendulkar would have been proud: it was he who had taught the youngsters to dream big. The India of the 1990s, which had relied on him, was a chapter from the previous millennium. All these young men, most of them toddlers when he first wore the India cap, had grown into match-winners. On the eve of the series, Dhoni said he and his troops would do their bit, which implicitly suggested Tendulkar would have to do his bit too. Both parties honoured their word.

THE FINAL TEST   Nagraj Gollapudi, *Wisden* 2014

India v West Indies

Second Test, at Mumbai, November 14–16, 2013

West Indies 182 (P. P. Ojha 5-40) and **187** (P. P. Ojha 5-49);

India 495 (C. A. Pujara 113, R. G. Sharma 111*).

India won by an innings and 126 runs.

Tendulkar: 74

It was never going to be a tearless farewell. As soon as Tendulkar walked out to bat in his 200th Test – a world record – with 20 overs of the first day remaining, anxiety set in. His every move was watched, noted, and interpreted as his innings spilled over into the second day. It was the story of his career – and it was about to come to an end.

Pujara, who batted with Tendulkar throughout his two and a half hours in the middle, later told of how distracted he became by the extreme reaction of the near-full house, and of his admiration at how composed his partner remained. Pujara and Tendulkar had come in after the fall of openers Shikhar Dhawan and Murali Vijay within three balls, both offering catches off Shillingford. And although Pujara walked out at No. 3, it was Tendulkar who faced a ball first – after he had threaded his way through a guard of honour formed by Pujara, the West Indians and, a touch controversially perhaps, the two umpires. Early in Tendulkar's innings, it wasn't entirely clear whether the crowd wanted him to be on or off strike, such was the nervous tension every time the bowler ran in. Luckily for them, Tendulkar did not appear to succumb to any emotion until he walked back unbeaten on 38 at the close, and allowed himself a wave of the bat to the crowd and his loved ones.

The second day marked precisely 24 years since Tendulkar's Test debut at Karachi. Hearts were in mouths when, on 48, he tried to upper-cut Best, but missed by some distance. He once said he never batted while harbouring negative thoughts. And so, next ball, he hit that straight-drive: the inimitable punch played with minimal movement or flourish.

As he passed 70, anxiety levels started to spike once more. Two years ago, against the same opponents on the same ground, he had walked back in disbelief as he fell six runs short of what would have been his 100th international hundred. Sammy, the man who had caught him superbly back then, was standing at slip now. The players had taken drinks after the first hour. The ground was filling up fast. There was a lot of movement in the stands. Tendulkar tried to cut hard and fine against the off-spinner Deonarine, and Sammy picked up a smart catch with both hands in front of his face. It took a few seconds for the crowd to react. Then they stood as one and gave a rousing ovation.

The rest of the match – before and after Tendulkar – followed the same pattern as Kolkata. In their first innings, West Indies' impetuosity bordered on criminal. The wicket of Darren Bravo, who had flailed against Bhuvneshwar Kumar but come through it, sparked a collapse of nine for 96 to the spinners. The Indians used these pliant opponents to enhance their Test records.

Soon after Tendulkar's dismissal, Pujara had a lucky escape on 76, when third umpire Vineet Kulkarni somehow ruled that Kieran Powell had not got his fingers under a catch at short leg; Pujara took advantage to press on to his fifth hundred in 15 Tests. Sharma, meanwhile, was busy transforming his reputation, and joined a small group (Lawrence Rowe, Alvin Kallicharran, Sourav Ganguly and Yasir Hameed) to score centuries in their first two Test innings.

On a pitch taking turn and bounce, West Indies remained hapless against the spinners, and lost the match before lunch on the third day. Shivnarine Chanderpaul, who through all the Tendulkar idolatry had become the first West Indian to play 150 Tests, was cast in the familiar role of firefighter – and eventually overwhelmed by the flames. One last bauble eluded Tendulkar: Dhoni brought him on to bowl at eight wickets down in the hope that he could finish off the match. Denesh Ramdin and Shillingford survived Tendulkar's 12 balls, but barely much longer. At only 210.2 overs, it was India's second-shortest completed home Test in terms of balls bowled, following their 2004-05 victory against Australia, also on this ground. But the story was already over.

A TEST – OR A PAGEANT?   Lawrence Booth, *Wisden* 2014

As Sachin Tendulkar walked out to bat shortly after 3.30 p.m. on the opening day of the Second Test, he was greeted by a guard of honour and, somewhere out there, a billion salutes. One of the Wankhede's giant screens helpfully advised: "Don't even blink!!"

Mumbai likes a superfluous instruction (signs above the city's roads forbid horn honking). After all, spectators did not seem inclined to rise from their seats in disgust and ask for their money back. And so no one blinked, which may explain why many appeared to have tears in their eyes. After 24 years of imagined intimacy with cricket's least knowable star, this was it.

The mood was hard to reconcile with Test cricket. The best of the genre encompasses grudgingly relinquished ebb and hard-fought flow, plus the unspoken conviction that all 22 players would rather be nowhere else. Yet the basic premise of cricket as a team game felt under threat. The scoreboard told you it was India v West Indies. Everything else told you it was a pageant.

Conflicting emotions filled the sticky air. The crowd wanted to see Tendulkar, but they knew one ball would be enough – and West Indies, already bundled out for 182, were unlikely to make India bat again. There was nothing for it but to follow a well-worn template. They went berserk.

Tendulkar's first run was – Homer nodding – a leg-side smear off Shane Shillingford. Soon, he cut a long-hop for four, then eased four more past mid-off. Shannon Gabriel was driven through extra cover. When Marlon Samuels was glanced to fine leg, Tendulkar's mother, Rajni, appeared on a giant screen, staring down impassively – or was it nervously? – as if from Mount Olympus. This was her first Test match. Who, frankly, was going to dare claim her son's wicket?

Tendulkar reached stumps on 38, and stumbled on the pavilion steps as he made his way up to the dressing-room – a touching moment of humanity. Next morning, the crowds gathered. "I consider myself the most fortunate person in the world because I have seen God in a new avatar," declared a text message on the tireless screen. "I will tell this for life. I was here today," read a banner. Another lamented: "Cricket is retiring with this match."

As for the *mis*match, few cared. This was a full-scale celebration now, with Tino Best ramping up his role as court jester, apparently having promised his son the birthday present of Tendulkar's wicket. When it came – though not to Best – it was as if the parents had arrived home and spoiled their teenage son's party by switching on the lights. Narsingh Deonarine was the pooper, finding turn and bounce as Tendulkar steered an off-break to slip.

There are reckoned to be no fairytale endings, and "c Sammy b Deonarine" seemed to confirm as much; India did not bat again. But Tendulkar did address the crowd once the match was over. Again, no one blinked. The occasion may have been manufactured. The emotions were gratifyingly real.

THE PROSPECT OF HIS ABSENCE   Supriya Nair, *Wisden India Extra*, November 2013

The children were always there in Shivaji Park – young, grim, working metronomically on swinging back, crouching, blocking and adjusting their stances against the oncoming efforts of their coaches and small colleagues and coaches. Like caricatures of genteel expectations of cricketing stoicism, they spoke little, and mostly in scowls. They looked ready, as Wendy says of the Lost Boys in Peter Pan, to die like English gentlemen. From time to time, as the water from the sprinklers evaporated in the heat, a fine, sifting red dust would begin to rise in drifts from the earth.

When I worked in Dadar, I walked around Shivaji Park sometimes to watch these dustbowl tableaux, a few dozen of which are always going on simultaneously, and wondered what it would take to make these boys happy. Was their single-minded pursuit of cricket a symptom of their childhood, or a denial of it? Would they remember these days fondly if they ever made the Test team of one of the world's most competitive sides? Would they pause long enough to crack a smile if an IPL contract dropped softly on their ducked, sweating heads? Or was this the bloody root of Bombay cricket's notorious *khadoosi* — not the smiling grit that seems to implant itself in so many graduates of, say the Australian domestic system, but the jealous rapacity of the 40-time Ranji Trophy victor?

I thought these things with a certain remoteness. You think of cricket idly, and with an ironic distance, when you have expatriated from the country of sheer joy and cringing terror where you dwelt when you were a child, feeling your heart swell as it fought its way, delivery by delivery, over by over, to an uncertain fate in match after match. That is what Sachin Tendulkar recalls for men and women who grew up – regardless of how old they were – watching him, and that, perhaps, is the overwhelming regret of his impending retirement. He will no longer be there to enchant us back into childhood.

Perhaps few other cricketers have earned the moral and emotional earnestness which Tendulkar evoked, even as a teenaged prodigy. There have been, at all times, at least ten other men on the field with him, ready to absorb the burden of those thundercloud emotions, but few others for whom they were held so closely in trust. Apart from a brief moment at age four or five when I was overwhelmed by the certainty that I would marry Imran Khan one day, I have never known cricket without knowing that kinship with Tendulkar. I remember him and Vinod Kambli, almost from the beginning, a sort of composite, aspirational alter-ego – the best, the boldest, the most dextrous we could hope to be. Something was irretrievably lost to Indian cricket as their paths began to diverge, but Tendulkar alone proved more than capable of sustaining the most optimistic fantasy anyone has ever experienced in Indian sport. We thought he carried us with him when he played. Buoyed as he was at the crease by the shouts and cheers of millions, there was no difference between us and him; and because of him, there were no differences among any of us.

An apparent lack of poetic ambiguity in Tendulkar's game makes it difficult for amateurs to deconstruct the synthesis of flair and discipline. His was a comprehensive, bullying sort of domination. More so than with his other, more specialist colleagues, the emotions responded to his presence before the intellect did. When the brain caught up, his quantifiable successes made a wonderful, if unimaginative refuge for his fans. Even on the days his body failed and bowlers showed up his usually uncanny vision, there was something about him which could not be gainsaid. Through the despondent years of his captaincy, when the lights faded over alien stadia and his insubstantial tenor voice piped up to acknowledge that his India had made mistakes, there was no doubt that, with him at least, failure was temporary. Over time, that unanswerable thing became clearer and clearer. It was a transparent, relentless hunger; the desire to "bat and bat and bat", as Gideon Haigh wrote. As he fed it, he fed us, too.

It seems strange that he was loved so much in spite of such an unlikeable quality. But hunger is the one aspect of genius which can be cultivated, acquired and nurtured and practised. And so, now that I think about it, the dutifulness of the boys in Shivaji Park, playing in shifts from seven in the morning to seven at night, makes perfect sense, because if all that misery can set you, even one among thousands, to grinding that mill, with your blood in the wheat, then it has put something in motion for all time.

Tendulkar was young for a very long time – wasn't it Allan Border who, after Sharjah, said, "Yes, but imagine what he'll be like when he's 28"? But he was ageing, too, for a great many years. We have said many impatient things about athletes who do that before our eyes, but they are actually a vital resource. I have a smug theory that female fans are vastly better equipped to absorb the shock of seeing their male sports idols grow old, since our gender circumvents the arrogance of identifying too closely with them. But to propound it I must forget that Sachin disproved this, too. Watching a Test match for the first time in months in 2008, I sat transfixed by his 154 at the SCG against Australia, an innings that epitomised the spareness of the older Tendulkar, sinews and cockles exposed by his injuries. He bared his head slowly on achieving the century, the manner of a man receiving a blessing, and tears pricked my eyes as it dawned on me: so that's going to happen, too.

When you love and place your faith in sport and in a sports team, even the air around you can make your skin burn on a match day. I don't think I am the only person who, uncomfortable with the depraved political economy that governs cricket, unwilling to participate in its rituals of macho patriotism, said a provisional goodbye to the country where cricket can do that to you. By 2011, when India won the World Cup, I did not even wish to be repatriated. Tendulkar was, in the most immediate ways, marginal to that victory. But then, he had long answered the question of what he could do for his people. What remains from that night at the Wankhede – the stadium where his own crowd once booed him off the field, and where he will have his last bow – are the voices of his younger team-mates. Of Virat Kohli saying, he carried us for years, now we'll carry him; and of Suresh Raina, before the semi-final, saying in words what Tendulkar silently promised to those who watched him every day for two decades: I am there. So he has been. So, after him, will remain the country that erupted in fireworks around him that night; an imaginary homeland, hovering slightly above the ground, like the cloud of red dust that rises from a cricket field on an evaporatingly hot day.

"'SACHIN, SACHIN' WILL REVERBERATE IN MY EARS"

Excerpts from Sachin Tendulkar's farewell speech on the final day of his international career:

All my friends, settle down, let me talk, I will get more and more emotional. My life – between 22 yards for 24 years – it is hard to believe that that wonderful journey has come to an end. But I would like to take this opportunity to thank people who have played an important role in my life… It's getting a little bit difficult to talk, but I will manage.

The most important person in my life, and I have missed him a lot since 1999 when he passed away, was my father. Without his guidance, I don't think I would have been standing here in front of you. He gave me freedom at the age of 11, and told me, "Chase your dreams, but make sure you do not find short cuts. The path might be difficult, but don't give up." And I have followed his instructions. Above all, he told me to be a nice human being, which I will continue to try, and try my best. Every time I have done something special, showed my bat, it was for my father.

My mother… I don't know how she dealt with such a naughty child like me. I was not easy to manage. For a mother, the most important thing is that her child remains safe and healthy and fit. She has taken care of me for the past 24 years that I have played for India… Her prayers and blessings have given me the strength to go out and perform. So a big thank you to my mother for all the sacrifices.

In my schooldays, for four years, I stayed with my uncle and aunt because my school was quite far from my home, and they treated me like their son. After a hard day's play, I would be half-asleep, and my aunt would be feeding me food so I could go again and play the next day. I can't forget these moments. I am like their son and I am glad it has continued to be the same way.

My eldest brother Nitin and his family have always encouraged me… The first cricket bat of my life was presented to me by my sister. It was a Kashmir willow bat. But that is where the journey began…

Ajit, my brother, now what do I talk about him? I don't know…
We have lived this dream together. He was the one who sacrificed
his career for my cricket. He spotted the spark in me. And it all
started from the age of 11 when he took me to [Ramakant]
Achrekar Sir, my coach, and from there on my life changed. You
will find this hard to believe but even last night he called up to
discuss my dismissal knowing that there was a remote chance of
batting again… Maybe when I'm not playing cricket we will still
be discussing technique… We have had arguments and
disagreements, but when I look back at all these things in my
life, I would have been a lesser cricketer…

The most beautiful thing happened to me in 1990 when I met
my wife Anjali. Being a doctor, there was a wonderful career in
front of her. When we decided to have a family, Anjali took the
initiative to step back and say that: "You continue with your
cricket and I will take the responsibility of the family." Without
that I don't think I would have been able to play cricket freely
and without stress. Thanks for bearing with all my fuss and all
my frustrations… and always staying by my side through all
the ups and downs. You are the best partnership I've had in
my life.

Then the two precious diamonds of my life, Sara and Arjun.
They have already grown up. My daughter is 16, my son is 14.
Time has flown by. I wanted to spend so much time with them
on special occasions like their birthdays, their annual days, their
sports days, going on holidays, whatever. I have missed out on
all those things. Thanks for your understanding. Both of you
have been so, so special to me you cannot imagine… I have not
spent enough time with both of you, but the next 16 years or
even beyond that, everything is for you…

In the past 24 years that I have played for India, I have made new
friends, and before that I have had friends from my childhood…
When I was injured, I would wake up in the morning because I
couldn't sleep and thought that my career was over because of
injuries, that is when my friends have woken up at three o'clock
in the morning to drive with me and make me believe that my
career was not over. Life would be incomplete without all those
friends. Thanks for being there for me.

My cricket career started when I was 11... when Ajit took me to Achrekar Sir. I was extremely delighted to see him up in the stands. Normally he sits in front of the television and he watches all the games that I play... On a lighter note, in the last 29 years, Sir has never ever said "Well played" to me, because he thought I would get complacent and I would stop working hard. Maybe he can push his luck and wish me now well done on my career, because there are no more matches, Sir, in my life...

The journey has been special. The last 24 years I have played with many senior cricketers, and even before that there were many senior cricketers I watched on television. They inspired me to play cricket, and to play the right way...

Rahul, Laxman, Sourav and Anil... and my team-mates right here in front me. You are like my family away from home. I have had some wonderful times with you. It is going to be difficult to not be part of the dressing-room...

When M. S. Dhoni presented me the 200th Test match cap on day one morning, I had a brief message for the team... all of us are so, so fortunate and proud to be part of the Indian cricket team and serving the nation... I believe we have been the lucky ones to be chosen by the Almighty to serve this sport. Each generation gets this opportunity to take care of this sport and serve it to the best of our ability. I have full faith in you to continue to serve the nation in the right spirit and to the best of your ability, to bring all the laurels to the country. All the very best...

I want to thank all the people here who have flown in from various parts of the world, and have supported me endlessly, whether I scored a nought or a hundred-plus. Your support was so dear to me and meant a lot to me... I want to thank you from the bottom of my heart, and also say that time has flown by rather quickly, but the memories you have left with me will always be with me forever and ever, especially "Sachin, Sachin" which will reverberate in my ears till I stop breathing. Thank you very much. If I have missed out on saying something, I hope you understand.

Goodbye.

Sachin Tendulkar's final Test contained all the best bits of Indian cricket – and all its excesses. The nation was on red alert, the hero made a few runs, and the emotion was as thick as the Mumbai air. On the second morning, as he progressed to 74, the Wankhede was in a trance. Don Bradman had once spotted something of himself in Tendulkar's batting. Now, it was as if Tendulkar was righting one of sport's great wrongs – Bradman's farewell duck in 1948 – all by himself.

But it was hard to ignore the whiff of reality TV, with the West Indians the wide-eyed arrivals at the Big Brother house, and the in-your-face ads for skin-fairness cream conveying a sinister superficiality. The result of the game seemed neither here nor there.

Tendulkar's 200th Test should actually have been in Cape Town, but politics and money put paid to that: the BCCI wanted to bloody the nose of Cricket South Africa's chief executive Haroon Lorgat, and there were broadcasters to sate. Besides, Tino Best and Darren Sammy were less likely than Dale Steyn and Morne Morkel to embarrass an ageing superstar. Most conveniently, perhaps, the setting allowed Tendulkar's mother to watch him play for the first time. This was touching, but not a policy found in most textbooks on sporting governance.

The hysteria and the machinations detracted from a cracking human story – of an obsessive driven by a passion, yet grounded by the love of parents wary of letting their son be defined by hundreds or ducks. A survey carried out late last year by the Australian Cricketers' Association claimed that a quarter of those who had quit or retired since 2005 went on to suffer "depression or feelings of helplessness". In particular, the ACA flagged up the link between identity and sporting achievement. Ramesh and Rajni Tendulkar had recognised the dangers many years earlier.

Most cricketers decide they have had enough of the goldfish bowl after a decade or so. Tendulkar played Test matches in front of the most demanding fans in the world for 24 years. If further proof was required of just how astonishing this was, it came at Perth in December, when for a few moments one Cook and one Clarke added up to exactly one Tendulkar: 200 Test caps, 15,921 runs and 51 hundreds.

Sport's pleasure resides in meaning so much to so many, while being essentially meaningless itself. Think about this for too long and you'll get a headache. But Tendulkar came closer than anyone to making sense of it.

SACHIN TENDULKAR, WORLD CELEBRITY

How the media loved him

The following are taken from Sachin Tendulkar's many mentions in *Wisden*'s Chronicle section. It is safe to assume this is another appearance record.

Wisden 2001

The Russian chess grandmaster Peter Svidler has been nicknamed "Tendulkar" because he became a cricket fan after being introduced to the game by Nigel Short. (*Daily Telegraph*)

Wisden 2002

Tom Gueterbock approached the wisden.com website to help publicise the sale of his £495,000 home in Battersea, south London, which he thought might particularly appeal to Indian cricket fans. The address was 10 Dulka Road. (*Daily Telegraph*)

Wisden 2003

The Sachin Tendulkar lookalike, Balvirchand, who had already co-starred with Tendulkar in an advert for Visa cards, has been chosen to play him in the movie *Kaisi Mohabbat*, in which the heroine fulfils her dream by meeting the great man. (*Gujarat Samachar, Ahmedabad*)

Wisden 2004

Parthiv Patel's uncle, Jagat Patel, has sworn to marry only after the wicketkeeper is performing consistently for India's Test XI, a tactic once tried, successfully, by Sachin Tendulkar's brother, Ajit. (*Rajasthan Patrika, Ahmedabad*)

Wisden 2005

The Indian government waived customs duty and the requirements for a roadworthiness certificate so Sachin Tendulkar could import a £90,000 Ferrari Modena 360. Bharat Petroleum also blended special fuel so the car could run on Indian roads; the 97-octane petrol the car requires is not sold in India. (*Indian Express*)

Sachin Tendulkar is now on the Indian curriculum: children in schools in and around Delhi will study the life and times of the nation's idol. New textbooks for those in the 10–12 age group include an interview with Tendulkar, where he talks about his own childhood and what it takes to be a successful cricketer. Krishna Kumar, an education official, said that the move to include a first-person account of Tendulkar's life was part of an effort to make education "a more pleasurable experience". (*Cricinfo*)

Indian captain Sourav Ganguly's new Kolkata restaurant – Sourav's, The Food Pavilion – was opened by his team-mate and fellow restaurateur Sachin Tendulkar, who owns two similar establishments in Mumbai. Sourav's is described as "Kolkata's first four-storeyed multiplex restaurant". Ganguly had earlier reportedly been alarmed that Tendulkar was planning to beat him to it by opening a branch in Kolkata. (*Sify.com/Press Trust of India*)

Rahul Dravid has been voted sexiest Indian sports personality in the 2004 Durex global sex survey. Yuvraj Singh was second with Sachin Tendulkar third. (*Free Press Journal, Mumbai*)

Wisden 2006
The Indian government has reversed a ruling that barred Sachin Tendulkar from displaying the national flag on his helmet. The cabinet said it will amend the Prevention of Insults to National Honour Act, and will allow the flag to be used on sporting uniforms – but not below the belt or on underwear. (*Mid-Day, Mumbai*)

Wisden 2007
Sachin Tendulkar is India's highest earner, according to a new survey, making 1,163 rupees (£13.39) every minute, compared to 361 rupees for film star Amitabh Bachchan and 57 paise (0.6p) for the prime minister, Manmohan Singh. (*The Asian Age*)

Wisden 2008
Sachin Tendulkar is to appear in comic books as the Master-Blaster, a superhero. (*The Asian Age*)

Wisden 2011
A new variety of mango, developed by a horticulturist in Uttar Pradesh, has been named "Sachin" in honour of Sachin Tendulkar. However, the grower claimed he would not be selling the fruit. "Our Sachin is a world hero and he is priceless," said Hajj Kalimullah. "My attempt will be to send all the mangoes on this tree to Sachin so he can enjoy them with his friends." (*Asian Tribune*)

Sachin Tendulkar was made an honorary Group Captain in the Indian Air Force, complete with uniform and epaulettes, at a ceremony in New Delhi. (*Times of India*)

Wisden 2012

An Indian tax tribunal upheld an appeal from Sachin Tendulkar that he should be classed as an actor for his modelling work. This enabled him to claim tax deductions. "As a model, the assessee brings to his work a degree of imagination, creativity and skill to arrange elements in a manner that would affect human senses and emotions and to have an aesthetic value," the tribunal ruled. (*Press Trust of India*)

The municipality of Brihanmumbai have given Sachin Tendulkar a final warning after spending 11 years trying to get him to attend a civic felicitation. "We have sent several reminders to Sachin, but he hasn't replied," said a spokesman. "We will now send him a final letter." (*The Asian Age*)

Wisden 2013

Australian Test players were irritated when their prime minister, Julia Gillard, told an official reception for the Indian team that her country's cricket fans were "looking forward to what may be a very special hundred made in Australia" – meaning Sachin Tendulkar's 100th international century. Michael Clarke said his team hoped the century would come somewhere else. His team-mate Mike Hussey called the prime minister's comment "strange". (*Sky News*)

The Mumbai Cricket Association intends to shower Tendulkar with a hundred gold coins for reaching 100 international centuries. (*Press Trust of India*)

Ratilal Parmar, 56, whose hobby is collecting banknotes that have special associations with Sachin Tendulkar, has acquired a new prize: a ten-rupee note numbered 240412, the date of Tendulkar's 39th birthday. Parmar wants to present his hero with the notes connected with his milestones, especially 160312, the date of the 100th international hundred. He estimates he has spent a million rupees building his collection, sometimes by pleading with bank clerks for help. (*ESPNcricinfo*)

British prime minister David Cameron told how he had found his wife Samantha playing French cricket with a bat signed for him by Sachin Tendulkar in the grounds of Chequers and had to warn her: "No, darling, put it down; this is probably the most valuable possession I have." He donated the bat for an auction at Lord's raising £3,400 for the Rwanda Cricket Stadium Foundation. (*Daily Telegraph*)

Sachin Tendulkar has been sworn in as a member of the Indian upper house, the Rajya Sabha. "It has been my dream to be remembered as someone who worked for all sports instead of just cricket statistics," he said after taking the oath. However, he warned that, as an active player, he would continue to focus on his own game. Tendulkar was chosen as one of the 12 members of the parliament the president is allowed to nominate, although some critics claimed that a sportsman did not fulfil the criterion of "special knowledge or practical experience in… literature, science, art and social service" specified for selection under the constitution. (*The Hindu*)

Australian prime minister Julia Gillard made Sachin Tendulkar an honorary member of the Order of Australia on a visit to India, but the award came under fire for not meeting the rule that such awards for non-Australians should reflect "extraordinary service to Australia or humanity at large". Independent MP Rob Oakeshott said: "I love Sachin, I love cricket, but I just have a problem with soft diplomacy. It's about the integrity of the honours list." (*Sydney Morning Herald*)

Wisden 2014
Sachin Tendulkar's waxwork at the new Madame Tussauds museum in Sydney has been given the wrong shirt. It was dressed in an Indian shirt for the World Twenty20, in which Tendulkar never appeared. (*Mid-Day, Mumbai*)

From *Wisden* 2014

BATMAN *AND* SUPERMAN   Suresh Menon, *Wisden India*, 2014

The fallacy of proximity is not unique to sport, but it tends to skew judgments all the same. With players of different eras, the one who played earlier is usually seen as superior – this reputation having grown with repetition. For those who think history is bunk, the most recent hero is the one that matters. At his best, Sachin Tendulkar had only one contemporary who was rated his equal – Brian Lara. By the time he played his 200th and final Test in Mumbai, there were those who would place him above even Don Bradman.

It is likely that in the years to come Tendulkar will be seen as a better player with every stroke he does not play. Distance lends enchantment, and past players tend to get the better press. Yet the figures alone are staggering. Besides the Tests, there were 463 one-day internationals too. Also 100 international centuries, 15,921 Test runs, 18,426 ODI runs including the first double-century in the format, and a grand total of 34,357 international runs. Of the four players who had longer international careers than Tendulkar's 24 years, Frank Woolley played the most Tests, 64.

The Tendulkar Era was the golden era of Indian cricket, when the country went to No. 1 in Tests and won the World Cup. It was the era in which India won more Tests (78) than they lost (60). Before Tendulkar, in comparison, the results were 43 won to 89 lost.

Bradman played 52 international matches over 20 years, at an average of 2.6 matches per year. Tendulkar's combined total of 664 international matches in 24 years meant he played an average of 27.6 matches annually. While Bradman played on ten grounds in two countries, Tendulkar played on 105 grounds in 16 countries. As C. L. R. James said in another context, "You need not build on these figures a monument, but you cannot ignore them."

Taken all in all, then, Tendulkar was probably the finest all-round batsman the game has seen and, given the pressure of expectation that even Bradman and the Jamaican George Headley didn't always experience, or the range of injuries he had to overcome, there is a good case for moving Tendulkar from the pages of *Wisden* into a standard dictionary. Few cricketers have become adjectives, but "Tendulkarine" bids to take its place alongside "Bradmanesque".

It was never about statistics alone. When a grateful nation gave Tendulkar its highest civilian award, the Bharat Ratna, it was acknowledgment that the player had evolved from a prodigy good enough to play Tests at 16 to a symbol of everything Indian. While "Bradmanesque" is usually limited to a description of cricket and averages, "Tendulkarine" would include such qualities as hope and aspiration and sportsmanship and integrity.

On his last day of international cricket – in the same week as he had made his debut 24 years earlier – Tendulkar bowed out with a speech that captured his essential simplicity and gratitude for all that cricket gave him. It was emotional, and had a nation in tears. To be admired is wonderful, but to be loved too and acknowledged as an important element in the maturing of a nation and its people is historic. Millions wept along with Tendulkar as he caused his country to come to a standstill one last time as a player.

In a nation with an average age in the twenties, Tendulkar had been the Great Constant. For over two decades, Tendulkar was our version of Dorian Gray, keeping us youthful and in some permanent world where everybody was in his twenties. We didn't grow old because he didn't grow old. Those in their twenties when he made his debut are in their fifties now, yet they can invoke their youth without effort thanks to Tendulkar. Important dates in their lives are bookmarked by his centuries, at Perth and Sydney and Old Trafford and Chennai. Governments have changed, economic policies have evolved, the Berlin Wall has fallen, the Soviet Union no longer exists, apartheid has been dismantled, Rahul Dravid has retired. Through it all, Tendulkar has gone about the business of making runs with single-minded focus.

In his elegy to Sigmund Freud, the poet W. H. Auden wrote:

> To us he is no more a person now
> But a whole climate of opinion
> Under whom we conduct our different lives.

He might have been talking of Tendulkar.

Long before his final innings, Tendulkar had ceased being a person for his fans – he was merely a figure of television, indistinguishable from characters such as Batman and Superman. The illusion was strengthened by the number of occasions he arrived when the team was in trouble and took them to safety.

In one-day cricket, Tendulkar's place at the top is assured. He played more games, made more runs and scored more centuries (49) than anybody else. Of the top ten batsmen – those with over 10,000 runs – only Jacques Kallis has the marginally better average, only Sanath Jayasuriya the better strike-rate, and only Ricky Ponting held more catches. Statistics do not lie: Tendulkar was indeed the best of the lot, the first choice in a game for Earth versus Mars.

India won more than half the matches Tendulkar played in, his importance underlined by his average of 56.63 (career average: 44.83) and strike-rate of 90.31 (career: 86.23) in those games. He is no longer the only man to have made a double-century in the format – but he was the first to suggest that possibility.

He played 69 matches before living up to the expectations generated by the mauling he gave Abdul Qadir in Peshawar in an unofficial match. He opened the batting in Auckland, made 82 off 49 balls. The first century came later, after ten more matches, but it had begun in Peshawar. Half his unbeaten 53 (from 18 balls) came in one over from Qadir. He was 16 then, a boy among men, but there was a light in his eyes and steel in his wrists as he even mis-hit for six. It changed the face of one-day cricket, for India found the man who could play the new game the old way, or innovate if that was the need.

It seems only yesterday he was making 143 in Sharjah at more than a run a ball, against an Australian attack that was actually grateful for the sandstorm that held up play. It is a decade since he taught Shoaib Akhtar to be more respectful by not only hitting him over third man for a six but following that up with a cover-drive of such delicacy that we knew beauty and the beast co-existed in the little man from Mumbai.

It was never easy to be Sachin Tendulkar. The spotlight that first turned towards him at the age of 15 when he made his debut in the Ranji Trophy with a century never really left him. For a private man, he lived much of his life in public. His successes were a nation's validation, his failures cause for national mourning; his injuries were discussed more than political upheavals, his various body parts – ankle, knees, shoulder, back, any part that malfunctioned – were analysed with the attention usually reserved for legal documents.

Above all, his ambitions were not his own. A nation emerging into economic nirvanahood in the 1990s saw him as the symbol of change: he was young, successful, and had the curious mix of humility and genius much favoured by the middle classes. He was always somebody everyone could be proud of, someone we could bring home to mother. It was a point made by Bishan Bedi, manager on his first tour of England. "Mothers all over England swooned over him," he said.

When he made 10,000 runs, his fans wanted 15; when he made 35 centuries to go past the world record, they wanted him to make it 40, 45, 50. Incredibly, for a while, his record-breaking raced ahead of popular ambition. All this came with the bonus of a sterling character. We don't expect our novelists or movie-makers or actors or politicians or economists to be paragons of virtue. But cricketers, especially the "great" ones, have to be, or they lose their audience. Sachin was naturally well-behaved. In a decade when his colleagues were hauled up for various misdemeanours, he stood like a rock – the one others tested their own incorruptibility on.

It must have been difficult to carry such responsibility – that of being the moral compass as well as the leading run-scorer. But Sachin did it lightly.

In the end, the comparisons do not matter. Like few sportsmen, Tendulkar was both aspiration and fulfilment, both a creature of his times and the signpost to the future. When he finally won a World Cup medal at his sixth attempt, he had no more worlds to conquer. Yet his motivation was strong, his focus undimmed. When, by his own admission, his 40-year-old body told him the time had come he simply quit. His final innings, a classy 74, recalled his salad days.

"In my heart I will always play for India, and pray for India," he said. A nation approved. It was enough to know that he would continue to bat for India.

Appendix

Statistics

MOST TEST RUNS

	Span	Mat	Inns	NO	Runs	HS	Ave	100	50
S. R. Tendulkar (India)	1989/90-2013/14	200	329	33	15921	248*	53.78	51	68
R. T. Ponting (Aus)	1995/96-2012/13	168	287	29	13378	257	51.85	41	62
J. H. Kallis (SA/ICC)	1995/96-2013/14	166	280	40	13289	224	55.37	45	58
R. Dravid (India/ICC)	1996-2011/12	164	286	32	13288	270	52.31	36	63
K. C. Sangakkara (SL)	2000-2015	134	233	17	12400	319	57.40	38	52

MOST ODI RUNS

	Span	Mat	Inns	NO	Runs	HS	Ave	100	50
S. R. Tendulkar (India)	1989/90-2011/12	463	452	41	18426	200*	44.83	49	96
K. C. Sangakkara (SL/Asia/ICC)	2000-2014/15	404	380	41	14234	169	41.98	25	93
R. T. Ponting (Aus/ICC)	1994/95-2011/12	375	365	39	13704	164	42.03	30	82
S. T. Jayasuriya (SL/Asia)	1989/90-2011	445	433	18	13430	189	32.36	28	68
D. P. M. D. Jayawardene (SL/Asia)	1997/98-2014/15	448	418	39	12650	144	33.37	19	77

MOST INTERNATIONAL RUNS

	Span	Mat	Inns	NO	Runs	HS	Ave	100	50
S. R. Tendulkar (India)	1989/90-2013/14	664	782	74	34357	248*	48.52	100	164
K. C. Sangakkara (SL/Asia/ICC)	2000-2015	593	664	67	27966	319	46.84	63	153
R. T. Ponting (Aus/ICC)	1994/95-2012/13	560	668	70	27483	257	45.95	71	146
D. P. M. D. Jayawardene (SL/Asia)	1997-2014/15	652	725	62	25957	374	39.15	54	136
J. H. Kallis (SA/Afr/ICC)	1995/96-2014	519	617	97	25534	224	49.10	62	149

LONGEST INTERNATIONAL CAREERS

	First match	*Last match*	*Span*	*Tests*
W. Rhodes (Eng)	1 Jun 1899	12 Apr 1930	30y 315d	58
D. B. Close (Eng)	23 Jul 1949	13 Jul 1976	26y 356d	22
F. E. Woolley (Eng)	9 Aug 1909	22 Aug 1934	25y 13d	64
G. A. Headley (WI)	11 Jan 1930	21 Jan 1954	24y 10d	22
S. R. Tendulkar (India)	15 Nov 1989	16 Nov 2013	24y 1d	200

Tendulkar's Individual Records

TEST DOUBLE-CENTURIES

248*	v Bangladesh	Dhaka	2004/05
241*	v Australia	Sydney	2003/04
217	v New Zealand	Ahmedabad	1999/00
214	v Australia	Bangalore	2010/11
203	v Sri Lanka	Colombo (SSC)	2010
201*	v Zimbabwe	Nagpur	2000/01

HIGHEST ODI SCORES

200*	v South Africa	Gwalior	2009/10
186*	v New Zealand	Hyderabad	1999/00
175	v Australia	Hyderabad	2009/10
163*	v New Zealand	Christchurch	2008/09
152	v Namibia	Pietermaritzburg	2002/03

TEST RUNS BY CALENDAR YEAR

	Mat	*Inns*	*NO*	*Runs*	*HS*	*Ave*	*100*	*50*
1989	4	6	0	215	59	35.83	0	2
1990	7	10	1	373	119*	41.44	1	2
1991	2	4	0	78	40	19.50	0	0
1992	7	11	1	419	148*	41.90	3	0
1993	8	9	2	640	165	91.42	2	5
1994	7	11	1	700	179	70.00	2	3
1995	3	4	2	58	52*	29.00	0	1
1996	8	15	0	623	177	41.53	2	2
1997	12	17	1	1000	169	62.50	4	3
1998	5	9	1	647	177	80.87	3	1
1999	10	19	3	1088	217	68.00	5	4
2000	6	10	1	575	201*	63.88	2	1
2001	10	18	2	1003	155	62.68	3	6
2002	16	26	1	1392	193	55.68	4	5
2003	5	9	0	153	55	17.00	0	1

2004	10	15	5	915	248*	91.50	3	2
2005	6	10	0	444	109	44.40	1	3
2006	8	12	1	267	63	24.27	0	1
2007	9	16	2	776	122*	55.42	2	6
2008	13	25	3	1063	154*	48.31	4	3
2009	6	9	1	541	160	67.62	2	3
2010	14	23	3	1562	214	78.10	7	5
2011	9	17	1	756	146	47.25	1	5
2012	9	15	0	357	80	23.80	0	2
2013	6	9	1	276	81	34.50	0	2
TOTAL	200	329	33	15921	248*	53.78	51	68

ODI Runs By Calendar Year

	Mat	Inns	NO	Runs	HS	Ave	100	50
1989	1	1	0	0	0	0.00	0	0
1990	11	10	0	239	53	23.90	0	1
1991	14	14	2	417	62	34.75	0	4
1992	21	20	2	704	84	39.11	0	6
1993	18	17	4	319	82*	24.53	0	1
1994	25	25	2	1089	115	47.34	3	9
1995	12	12	1	444	112*	40.36	1	1
1996	32	32	2	1611	137	53.70	6	9
1997	39	36	3	1011	117	30.63	2	5
1998	34	33	4	1894	143	65.31	9	7
1999	22	22	2	843	186*	42.15	3	1
2000	34	34	0	1328	146	39.05	3	6
2001	17	16	3	904	146	69.53	4	3
2002	20	19	5	741	113	52.92	2	3
2003	21	21	1	1141	152	57.05	3	8
2004	21	21	1	812	141	40.60	1	5
2005	16	16	1	412	123	27.46	1	2
2006	16	16	2	628	141*	44.85	2	3
2007	33	32	2	1425	100*	47.50	1	13
2008	12	12	1	460	117*	41.81	1	3
2009	21	20	2	972	175	54.00	3	3
2010	2	2	1	204	200*	204.00	1	0
2011	11	11	0	513	120	46.63	2	2
2012	10	10	0	315	114	31.50	1	1
TOTAL	463	452	41	18426	200*	44.83	49	96

Runs In World Cups

	Mat	Inns	NO	Runs	HS	Ave	100	50
1991/92	8	7	1	283	84	47.16	0	3
1995/96	7	7	1	523	137	87.16	2	3
1999	7	7	1	253	140*	42.16	1	0
2002/03	11	11	0	673	152	61.18	1	6
2006/07	3	3	1	64	57*	32.00	0	1
2010/11	9	9	0	482	120	53.55	2	2
TOTAL	45	44	4	2278	152	56.95	6	15

TEST RUNS HOME AND AWAY

	Mat	Inns	NO	Runs	HS	Ave	100	50
Home	94	153	16	7216	217	52.67	22	32
Away	106	176	17	8705	248*	54.74	29	36

TEST RUNS IN EACH COUNTRY

	Mat	Inns	NO	Runs	HS	Ave	100	50
Australia	20	38	4	1809	241*	53.20	6	7
Bangladesh	7	9	3	820	248*	136.66	5	0
England	17	30	1	1575	193	54.31	4	8
India	94	153	16	7216	217	52.67	22	32
New Zealand	11	18	1	842	160	49.52	2	5
Pakistan	10	13	1	483	194*	40.25	1	2
South Africa	15	28	3	1161	169	46.44	5	3
Sri Lanka	12	19	2	1155	203	67.94	5	4
West Indies	10	14	1	620	117	47.69	1	5
Zimbabwe	4	7	1	240	74	40.00	0	2

ODI RUNS HOME AND AWAY

	Mat	Inns	NO	Runs	HS	Ave	100	50
Home	164	160	15	6976	200*	48.11	20	38
Away	147	146	10	5065	163*	37.24	12	24
Neutral	152	146	16	6385	152	49.11	17	34

ODI RUNS IN EACH COUNTRY

	Mat	Inns	NO	Runs	HS	Ave	100	50
Australia	47	46	3	1491	117*	34.67	1	10
Bangladesh	16	16	0	827	141	51.68	2	5
Canada	12	11	2	313	89*	34.77	0	3
England	26	26	2	1051	140*	43.79	3	4
India	164	160	15	6976	200*	48.11	20	38
Ireland	4	4	0	204	99	51.00	0	2
Kenya	4	4	0	171	69	42.75	0	1
Malaysia	4	4	1	222	141*	74.00	1	1
New Zealand	22	22	1	821	163*	39.09	1	5
Pakistan	13	13	0	480	141	36.92	2	1
Singapore	5	5	0	253	100	50.60	1	1
South Africa	40	38	0	1453	152	38.23	4	6
Sri Lanka	44	41	5	1531	138	42.52	5	6
United Arab Emirates	42	42	5	1778	143	48.05	7	7
West Indies	9	9	3	282	65*	47.00	0	3
Zimbabwe	11	11	4	573	127*	81.85	2	3

TEST RUNS FOR EACH CAREER 1000

	Inns	Date reached
1000	28	27 Nov 1992
2000	44	20 Mar 1994
3000	67	8 Dec 1996
4000	86	4 Dec 1997
5000	103	19 Feb 1999
6000	120	2 Mar 2000
7000	136	3 Nov 2001
8000	154	21 May 2002
9000	179	2 Jan 2004
10000	195	16 Mar 2005
11000	223	28 Jul 2007
12000	247	17 Oct 2008
13000	266	17 Jan 2010
14000	279	10 Oct 2010
15000	300	8 Nov 2011

ODI RUNS FOR EACH CAREER 1000

	Inns	Date reached
1000	34	7 Mar 1992
2000	70	13 Apr 1994
3000	93	9 Apr 1995
4000	112	17 Apr 1996
5000	138	12 Feb 1997
6000	170	14 Jan 1998
7000	189	7 Jul 1998
8000	210	8 Jun 1999
9000	235	19 Mar 2000
10000	259	31 Mar 2001
11000	276	28 Jan 2002
12000	300	1 Mar 2003
13000	321	16 Mar 2004
14000	350	6 Feb 2006
15000	377	29 Jun 2007
16000	399	5 Feb 2008
17000	424	5 Nov 2009
18000	440	24 Mar 2011

DISMISSALS IN TESTS

caught	169
lbw	63
bowled	54
run out	9
stumped	1

TEST RUNS BY CAPTAINCY

	Mat	Inns	NO	Runs	HS	Ave	100	50
Captain	25	43	3	2054	217	51.35	7	7
Not Captain	175	286	30	13867	248*	54.16	44	61

ODI RUNS BY CAPTAINCY

	Mat	Inns	NO	Runs	HS	Ave	100	50
Captain	73	70	5	2454	186*	37.75	6	12
Not Captain	390	382	36	15972	200*	46.16	43	84

TEST RUNS BY RESULT

	Mat	Inns	NO	Runs	HS	Ave	100	50
Won	72	113	17	5946	248*	61.93	20	24
Lost	56	112	2	4088	177	37.16	11	18
Drawn	72	104	14	5887	241*	65.41	20	26

ODI RUNS BY RESULT

	Mat	Inns	NO	Runs	HS	Ave	100	50
Won	234	231	34	11157	200*	56.63	33	59
Lost	200	200	2	6585	175	33.25	14	35
Tied	5	5	0	166	120	33.20	1	0
No Result	24	16	5	518	105*	47.09	1	2

TEST RUNS BY MATCH INNINGS

	Inns	NO	Runs	HS	Ave	100	50
1st	91	6	5608	241*	65.97	20	20
2nd	106	3	5692	248*	55.26	18	26
3rd	72	8	2996	176	46.81	10	15
4th	60	16	1625	136	36.93	3	7

CAREER BOWLING AND FIELDING

	Balls	Mdns	Runs	Wkts	BB	Ave	Econ	SR	Ct
Tests	4240	83	2492	46	3-10	54.17	3.52	92.1	115
ODIs	8054	24	6850	154	5-32	44.48	5.10	52.2	140

TEST BEST BOWLING

5-1-10-3	v South Africa	Mumbai	1999/00
11-3-31-3	v Australia	Kolkata	2000/01
6-2-7-2	v New Zealand	Wellington	1998/99
4-2-10-2	v Australia	Adelaide	1991/92
7-0-30-2	v New Zealand	Hamilton	1998/99

ODI BEST BOWLING

10-1-32-5	v Australia	Kochi	1997/98
10-1-50-5	v Pakistan	Kochi	2004/05
10-1-34-4	v West Indies	Sharjah	1991/92
9.1-0-38-4	v Australia	Dhaka	1998/99
9-2-54-4	v Bangladesh	Dhaka	2004/05
10-0-56-4	v South Africa	Faridabad	1999/00

BOWLERS TO DISMISS TENDULKAR MOST OFTEN IN TESTS

9 times	J. M. Anderson (Eng)
8 times	M. Muralitharan (SL)
6 times	J. N. Gillespie (Aus), G. D. McGrath (Aus)
5 times	W. J. Cronje (SA), A. A. Donald (SA), D. L. Vettori (NZ), B. Lee (Aus)

BOWLERS FOR WHOM TENDULKAR WAS THE FIRST INTERNATIONAL WICKET

Those marked # were in a Test match, all others were in an ODI:
C. R. Matthews, H. H. Streak, D. J. Callaghan, Sultan Zarawani, B. S. Browne, M. L. Nkala, Azhar Mahmood, T. B. M. de Leede, Mohammad Rafique, Manzoor Akhtar, C. J. Drum, S. B. Styris, Mushfiqur Rahman, Asim Saeed, R. K. Whelan, M. A. Ealham #, N. C. Johnson #, M. S. Panesar #, P. M. Siddle #, P. R. George #

Also, Tendulkar was the first ODI wicket for D. J. Nash **and the first Test wicket for** W. J. Cronje, U. Ranchod, R. S. Kalpage, J. D. P. Oram, C. L. White and A. J. McKay

The statistics are up to date to September 1, 2015

Acknowledgments

A number of people generously committed their knowledge, time and expertise to make *Tendulkar in Wisden* possible. Thanks, firstly, to Charlotte Atyeo for entrusting me with the task of condensing one of cricket's greatest careers into a 248-page book. At Bloomsbury, my thanks also go to Holly Jarrald and the design team; and, at Wisden, to Chris Lane and Hugh Chevallier for their invaluable assistance and advice, and to Steven Lynch and Charles Barr for their eagle-eyed copy-editing and proof-reading.

I'm grateful to all the writers who agreed to have their work reprinted, especially Sambit Bal and Suresh Menon, who were more than happy to share material from publications they edit. Neil Robinson and Robert Curphey generously helped me with access to the Marylebone Cricket Club archives at Lord's.

My love for the sport is all thanks to my dad, Ajit, who fed me with many rich moments from India's cricket history, and with whom I have shared some of the most wonderful childhood and adolescent memories, pacing anxiously about our living-room, dancing to the tune of India's occasional successes, and shrinking in despair when it seemed like the world was falling apart. Cricket was our love, language, sustenance and entertainment.

This relationship with cricket would have been infinitely poorer without Sachin Tendulkar. My heartfelt thanks to him for providing some of the happiest moments to the highlights reel of my life for nearly three decades: the memories of his magic and the emotions evoked by his accomplishments – and failures – will stay with me for ever.

Thanks, too, to my mum, Harsha, for her unfailing support. The deadline for this manuscript coincided with our moving house: she had to tolerate piles of dusty boxes during her annual visit to London, when I seemed to spend most of my time with my head buried in a laptop. She helped us unpack, made sure I was well fed, and kept up a steady supply of tea, coffee and my favourite snacks as I focused on getting the manuscript together.

Most of all, I'd like to thank my husband, Lawrence, for his love, encouragement, advice and support through every stage of this process. Not only did he put up with papers and proofs taking over our dining table, front room (and our life, it seemed at times), he was also available throughout – across time zones, and in the midst of daily-deadline madness – as my sounding board. Not to mention it was rather handy to have a resident cricket expert, copy editor and proofreader. Above all, I'm grateful for his calm perspective on just about everything. I can't thank him enough for who he is.

Anjali Doshi
November 2015

Index